Who Should Read This Book?

"**R**ead" may be the wrong word. "Engage" would be better, because this is not so much a book as it is a classic text, and Jewish classics are not read so much as they are engaged. Included here is a classic text of Jewish prayer, spanning 2,000 years of Jewish experience with the world and with God; and nine thoughtful commentaries on that text, each one reaching back in a different way, again through 2,000 years of time. The question ought to be "Who should engage this book in personal dialogue?"

If you like to pray, or find prayer services baffling: Whether you are Orthodox, Conservative, Reconstructionist, or Reform, you will find that *My People's Prayer Book* tells you what you need to know to pray.

- The Hebrew text here is the most authentic one we have, and the variations among the Jewish movements are described and explained. They are all treated as equally authentic.
- The translation is honest, altogether unique, and outfitted with notes comparing it to others' translations.
- Of special interest is a full description of the Halakhah (the "how to") of prayer and the philosophy behind it.

If you are a spiritual seeker or Jewishly curious: If you have wondered what Judaism is all about, the prayer book is the place to begin. It is the one and only book that Jews read each and every day. The commentaries explain how the prayers were born, and synopsize insights of founding Rabbis, medieval authorities, Chasidic masters, and modern theologians. The layout replicates the look of Jewish classics: a text surrounded by many marginal commentaries allowing you to skip back and forth across centuries of insight.

If you are a teacher or a student: This is a perfect book for adult studies, or for youth groups, teenagers, and camps. Any single page provides comparative insight from the length and breadth of Jewish tradition, about the texts that have mattered most in the daily life of the Jewish people.

If you are a scholar: Though written in friendly prose, this book is composed by scholars: professors of Bible, Rabbinics, Medieval Studies, Liturgy, Theology, Linguistics, Jewish Law, Mysticism, and Modern Jewish Thought. No other work summarizes current wisdom on Jewish prayer, drawn from so many disciplines.

If you are not Jewish: You need not be Jewish to understand this book. It provides access for everyone to the Jewish wisdom tradition. It chronicles the ongoing Jewish-Christian dialogue, and the roots of Christian prayer in Christianity's Jewish origins.

My People's Prayer Book

TRADITIONAL PRAYERS, MODERN COMMENTARIES

Vol. 2 — The *Amidah*

EDITED BY RABBI LAWRENCE A. HOFFMAN

COMMENTATORS

MARC BRETTLER   ELLIOT N. DORFF

DAVID ELLENSON   MARCIA FALK

JUDITH HAUPTMAN   JOEL M. HOFFMAN

LAWRENCE A. HOFFMAN   LAWRENCE KUSHNER

DANIEL LANDES   NEHEMIA POLEN

Jewish Lights Publishing
Woodstock, Vermont

My People's Prayer Book: Traditional Prayers, Modern Commentaries
Vol. 2 — The *Amidah*
©1998 by Lawrence A. Hoffman

Library of Congress Cataloging-in-Publication Data
My people's prayer book : traditional prayers, modern commentaries /
edited and with introductions by Lawrence A. Hoffman.
p.   cm.
Includes the traditional text of the siddur, English translation, and
commentaries.
Contents: vol. 2. The Amidah.
ISBN 1-879045-80-X (hc)
1. Siddur. 2. Siddurim — Texts. 3. Judaism — Liturgy — Texts.
I. Hoffman, Lawrence A., 1942–   . II. Siddur. English & Hebrew.
BM674.39.M96   1997
296.4'5 — dc21   97-26836
                                    CIP

First edition

10 9 8 7 6 5 4 3 2

Manufactured in the United States of America
Jacket design: Glenn Suokko
Text design: Reuben Kantor

Published by Jewish Lights Publishing
A Division of LongHill Partners, Inc.
Sunset Farm Offices, Route 4, P.O. Box 237
Woodstock, Vermont 05091
Tel: (802) 457-4000   Fax: (802) 457-4004
www.jewishlights.com

Contents

COMMENTATORS

MARC BRETTLER	*Our Biblical Heritage*
ELLIOT N. DORFF	*Theological Reflections*
DAVID ELLENSON	*How the Modern Prayer Book Evolved*
MARICA FALK	*Feminist Theology*
JUDITH HAUPTMAN	*Talmudic Traditions*
JOEL M. HOFFMAN	*What the Prayers Really Say*
LAWRENCE A. HOFFMAN	*Origins of the Liturgy*
LAWRENCE KUSHNER AND NEHEMIA POLEN	*Chasidic and Mystical Perspectives*
DANIEL LANDES	*The Halakhah of Prayer*

About My People's Prayer Book

My People's Prayer Book is designed to look like a traditional Jewish book. Ever since the dawn of modern printing, Jews have arranged their books so that instead of reading in a linear fashion from the first line of the first page to the last line of the last one, readers were encouraged to linger on a single page and to consult commentaries across the gamut of Jewish thought, all at one and the same time. Every page thus contained a cross-cut of the totality of Jewish tradition.

That intellectual leap across many minds and through the centuries was accomplished by printing a text in the middle of the page and surrounding it with commentaries. Readers could scan the first line or two of the various commentaries and then choose to continue the ones that interested them most, by turning the page — more or less the way newspaper readers get a sense of everything happening on a single day by glancing at all the headlines on page one and then following select stories as they are continued on separate pages further on.

Each new rubric (or liturgical section) is, therefore, introduced in traditional style: the Hebrew prayer with translation in the middle of the page, and the beginning lines of all the commentaries in the margins. Commentaries are continued on the next page or a few pages later (the page number is provided). Readers may dwell for a while on all the comments, deciding which ones to pursue at any given sitting. They may want to compare comments, reading first one and then another. Or having decided, after a while, that a particular commentator is of special interest, they may instinctively search out the opening lines of that commentator's work, as they appear in each introductory page, and then read them through to arrive at a summary understanding of what that particular person has to say.

Prayer As Petition

The Philosophic Basis for Halakhic Prayer

Daniel Landes

Halakhah speaks a language of obligation and form. Applied to prayer (*t'fillah*), the concerns of obligation include the questions of *who* should pray and *what* are the circumstances that compel it. The concerns of form are *when* prayer is uttered, *where* one should pray, and *how* it should be said. Surprisingly, Halakhah seems to not really address the question of *why* prayer is necessary, but to assume instead that it is sufficient to command this religious requirement.

Defenders of Halakhah often say that this is quite enough. According to their reasoning, Halakhah provides sufficient context within which to ask all questions of meaning, including the ones regarding the rationale behind prayer. Therefore, if one obeys the Halakhah by praying the required liturgy three times a day, and if one commits the time and attention to it that the Law demands, the meaning behind prayer will become clear. It will either spring up from the Siddur (prayer book) itself or make itself manifest in other ways, usually of a pronounced spiritual nature, such as mysticism. Alternatively, one might attach another religious practice to *t'fillah,* such as prior Torah study or meditation, that somehow unlocks the deeper experience of prayer. Simply put, according to this defense, the Halakhah is absolutely *necessary* for the Jewish institution of prayer and for the individual who prays but is itself actually *insufficient* to achieve a profound *t'fillah* experience.

This "defense" of the Halakhah actually sells it short. It pictures the Halakhah's manifold rulings regarding prayer as a series of obstacles that need to be overcome. No wonder that many who wish to pray and are impatient with requirements in general attempt to bypass the Halakhah. This is a pity, for Halakhah contains within itself the key that unlocks the deeper meanings and dynamics of prayer. Halakhah rivals and is more profound than even the archly spiritual sources of Judaism such as mysticism, with which it often conflicts.

HALAKHIC VERSUS SPIRITUAL PRAYER

A paradigmatic example of the collision between halakhic and mystical understandings of prayer finds its focus in the first recorded communal prayer. "The king of Egypt died and the children of Israel sighed by reason of the bondage, and they cried out and their plea rose up to God by reason of the bondage. And God heard their groaning and God remembered his covenant with Abraham, with Isaac and with Jacob" (Exod. 2:23–24). A plain reading of the text demonstrates a cause and effect — the redemption of the people beginning with God's remembering his covenant is the result of the entreaty of the people. If they had not prayed, they would not have been redeemed. Prayer thus becomes the activating cause for the central event in Jewish history — the Exodus. But what was the nature of the prayer? Here "spirituality" and Halakhah differ.

The Zohar (Exod. 20a, the primary document for Jewish mysticism) heaps lavish praise on the spontaneous prayer that arises directly from the human heart and claims, therefore, that the *t'fillah* of Exodus was effective because it was the outpouring of the individual soul: "Rabbi Judah said: Of all the three expressions for prayer used in the Exodus narrative, crying out (*tsa'akah*) is the greatest of all because it is entirely a matter of the heart . . . this crying comes nearer to the Holy One blessed be He than imploring and praying in words (He is using a play on words: The verse uses the word *za'akah* ["to cry"], which R. Judah reads as *tsa'akah* ["to cry out"]). Rabbi Berachiah said: When people pray and weep and cry so intensely that they are unable to find words to express their sorrow, theirs is the perfect prayer, for it is in their heart, and this will never return to them empty" (From the Zohar, Exod. 20a. The Zohar is the primary document for Kabbalah; it is composed in midrashic form, and associated with the second-century Tanna, Simeon bar Yochai).

Mystical prayer thus is typified by a concentration upon three elements. First, the ideal prayer is genuine weeping that arises because words not only cannot be expressed but seem to be of little or no value. Consequently, prayer is, in the end, a matter of the heart. Finally, prayer is essentially a personal enterprise; one can only really cry for oneself. "Spiritual" prayer is therefore inarticulate, internal, and individual.

Halakhic prayer differs radically. The halakhic view can be found reflected in a midrash on the Exodus account: "The children of Israel groaned and cried out to the Lord, and He heard their cries, as it says, 'The children of Israel sighed because of the bondage, and they cried out, and their plea rose to God.' Immediately the ministering angels recited, 'Blessed are You, Ado-nai, who hears prayer'" (From *Torah Sh'lemah,* Exod., p. 183. *Torah Sh'lemah* is a modern compendium of early Rabbinic commentary).

This fanciful angelic echoing of the Israelites' prayer reflects halakhic sensitivities. "Blessed are You, Ado-nai, who hears prayer" is the concluding line (the *chatimah*) to the sixteenth benediction of the *Amidah* (see p. 146). By having the angels recite a central line from the *Amidah* that will only be invented epochs later, the author of the midrash has the angels confirm the need for a halakhically fixed prayer: that is, a set liturgy beyond spontaneous "crying out," such as the Zohar would have it. For

Maimonides, the establishment of a fixed prayer by the Men of the Great Assembly meant an end to gibberish (*shibush*) to which most people are prone ("Laws of Prayer," 1:4). Moreover, such prayer must be recited out loud ("The words must be pronounced with one's lips" ["Laws of Prayer," 5:9]) — which is to say, this prayer is a conversation; it assumes a responsive listener. Finally, both prayers — of the Israelites and the angels — reflect the halakhic preference and definition of prayer as group activity. That is why the Halakhah obliges us to find a *minyan* with which to pray, even if we might conceivably achieve deeper intent (*kavvanah*) alone at home (From *Iggrot Moshe* [Moshe Feinstein (1895–1986), Russia and New York], O. Ch., 3:7). For similar reasons, leaving the *minyan,* if we are one of the ten people necessary for the *minyan* to exist, is considered a sin, to which is applied the phrase, "Those who leave the Lord" (From *Rema* [Moses Isserles (1530–1572), Cracow, Poland], O. Ch. 55). Likewise, the third benediction, and central piece of the *Amidah,* the *K'dushah,* is forbidden to be said without a *minyan,* for "I shall be sanctified within the community of Israel" (Lev. 22:32; cf. *Meg.* 23b. See, however, the Ran [Rabbenu Nissim ben Reuben Gerondi (1310–1375), Spain] on *Meg.* 23b, who rules in accordance with the Yerushalmi that if the service started the *Amidah* with a minyan and several left to reduce the number to under ten, the service nevertheless continues, including evidently even Kedushah). The "spiritual" interpretation, such as we saw in the Zohar, views true prayer as inarticulate, internal, and individual. The Halakhah mandates it as *t'fillah:* articulate, conversational, and communal.

There is a fourth difference, which perhaps goes deeper yet in explaining the uniqueness of halakhic prayer as opposed to spiritual prayer. Halakhic prayer is petitionary in its very essence, and human beings are, by nature, conversationalists who rightly make petitions.

As an illustration of this fourth characteristic of halakhic prayer, consider more closely the specific blessing that the angels in the midrash are pictured as reciting: "Blessed are You, Adonai, who hears prayer" (*shomei'a t'fillah*). But that is not the only kind of blessing there is. As Maimonides stipulates, blessings have three general usages:

Just as we recite blessings for enjoyment that we derive from the world, so we should also recite blessings for each *mitzvah* before we fulfill it. Similarly, the sages instituted many blessings as expressions of praise and thanks to God and as a means of petition ("Laws of Blessings" 1:3).

The three major forms of blessings, therefore, are (1) *hana'ah:* blessings recited upon "enjoying" a pleasure of this world; (2) *mitzvah:* blessings said alongside the performance of a *mitzvah;* and (3) *t'fillah:* blessings that constitute a normal part of fixed prayer. This last form (*t'fillah*) contains a subset of three: *shevach* ("praise"), *hodayah* ("thanksgiving"), and *bakashah* ("petition"). In our fixed liturgy of the *Amidah,* the order is *shevach* (the first three blessings), *bakashah* (the middle thirteen), and then *hodayah* (the final three).

It is clear that the angelic choir speaking for the Israelites in Egypt is not uttering a blessing of enjoyment or of *mitzvah.* It is obviously a blessing of *t'fillah,* more specifically, of *bakashah,* "petition." It is crucial to note that the blessing selected by them, "who hears prayer" (*shome'a t'fillah*) is not just any petition, but the final, summary, and paradigmatic blessing of request. Indeed, in the special form of the *Amidah* that the Talmud provides for emergencies, all the other blessings contained within it are abridged to the point where they are referred to in merely a word or phrase, without the critical ending line (the *chatimah*) that begins, "Blessed are You, Ado-nai, who. . . ." Not so the blessing, "who hears prayer"; the emergency *Amidah* ends by citing it in full: "Blessed are You, Ado-nai, who hears prayer." Moreover, petition (*bakashah*) occupies a central place in the *Amidah*. To begin with, its sheer length (thirteen of the nineteen blessings) is indicative of its importance; then too, the Halakhah rules that if one prays the weekday *Amidah* (which contains the petitions) on Shabbat (when petitions are normally omitted, out of fear of disturbing the serenity of the day) one has fulfilled the *mitzvah* of t'fillah anyway. The *Or Sameach* (a classic commentary on Maimonides' *Mishneh Torah* by R. Meir Simcha of Dvinsk, Russia [1843–1926]) quotes earlier rabbinic comments to demonstrate that by petitioning the proper way, a worshiper imitates Moses', David's, and Solomon's etiquette, for they too bracketed their petitions (*bakashah*) by proper adorations of God, namely, *shevach* ("praise") before and *hodayah* ("thanksgiving") after. In the case of the Hebrew slaves in Egypt, therefore, we find a simple minimalist prayer being recited by the angels; it must be the bare minimum, the very essence of the conversation that human beings need to have with God. And it is *bakashah*. For petition is the essence of prayer. It is the expressed need of the Israelites that effects God's response of deliverance.

Rabbi Joseph B. Soloveitchik points out that *bakashah* (and, therefore, Jewish prayer in its very essence) is extremely *this-worldly* and democratic. Jewish prayer does not evoke a perfected life that needs no help or improvement. Jews are sensitized by Halakhah to become constantly aware of their need for God's assistance. We are to formulate that need in our thoughts and to pray for it in stipulated ways each day.

Bakashah is thus the prime requirement and definition of halakhic prayer. Indeed, even on Shabbat and holidays, when *technically* we do not ask for things, Jewish law mandates some reference to our petitionary needs. Halakhic prayer is the polar opposite of spiritual prayer, which finds *bakashah* embarrassing. The tendency in philosophic apologies for prayer is often to emphasize *t'fillah* as "self-judgment" (an etymological explanation of the word *t'fillah,* which is probably forced in any event) or to explain it away as an expression of apt humility in the face of our acknowledgment of our human finitude. The real issue, however, is the queasiness that is felt by contemporary, rational prayer-writers and commentators when it comes to admitting that God might actually deliver a response to our requests. Among spiritualists of a mystical bent, the emphasis seems to be to "get beyond" mundane requests — it is the all too human that makes this group queasy — in order to achieve a true cleaving to the Infinite.

Indeed, the classical mystics go a step further: they deny that we human beings are even the initiators of prayer. The Kabbalah identifies human affairs with the all-pervasive and imminent presence of the Divine, so that what we take to be mere human affairs can equally be identified as the inner workings of the all-embracing aspects of God (known as the *s'firot*). For the Zohar, therefore, it is *God,* not Israel, who can be interpreted as having offered the paradigmatic cry in Egypt. Chasidic lore continues this trend, as, for instance, in the interpretation of the Mei Hashilo'ach, R. Mordecai Joseph of Ishbetz (nineteenth century), who says that God stirred the Israelites to utter their cry. But this Chasidic strain goes even farther: it advocates a mystic quietism that sees God as initiating not just petition but *all* true prayer. Further, the influential school of the Maggid of Mezeritch (a disciple of the Baal Shem Tov, or Besht, the founder of Chasidism) himself dismisses all petitionary prayer for oneself, because he thinks that prayer is worthy only when it is "for the *Sh'khinah"* (God's mystical presence). Such prayer in its higher contemplative state leads to even the search for "extinction of personality" (known as *bittul hayesh*) as the worshiper wishes to lose all sense of being an individuated self, so as to find mystical union with God (Rivka Shatz Uffenheimer, *Hasidism as Mysticism* [Princeton, NJ, 1993]).

Through its insistence on genuine human *bakashah,* however, halakhic prayer affirms the truly dialogic quality of *t'fillah.* It affirms human beings in all our neediness and the capacity of God to hear our petitions and to act upon them. The Halakhah sees prayer as communication between two (not necessarily equal) partners: a finite human being whose finitude does not prevent him from beseeching God, and a God whose absoluteness is penetrable. The nature of this dialogue is a radical affirmation of the claim that both partners have on each other.

There is even an element in the angelic recitation of *shome'a t'fillah* ("who hears prayers") on Israel's behalf that partakes of the blessing that is said upon performing a *mitzvah.* Halakhah is rooted in reality; it deplores "a blessing said in vain" (a *b'rakhah l'vatalah*). We may not implore God to do the impossible, for example — the prime example in the Mishnah is asking God to spare our home from a fire that we know has already occurred, so that nothing can be done about it. The blessing of the angels therefore presupposes God's ability to listen; we may even say that it actually compels God at least to listen to His people's prayer. For if He were not even to listen, the angel's recitation would be a blessing in vain. God, therefore, must (Halakhah insists) listen. This view goes unquestioned by our authorities; it is considered normative in every generation, as even Maimonides asserts: "The prayer of the community (*tsibbur*)," he says, "is always heard" ("Laws of Prayer" 8:1).

INDIVIDUAL VERSUS COMMUNITY PRAYER

Halakhic prayer is, therefore, an articulate conversation between the community of Israel and God. It is actually a dialogue that affirms the power and needs of both participants, their relationship to each other, and their ability to communicate and to act. Two questions remain: Does halakhic prayer speak also to the individual, not just the community? And, given the fact that all authorities agree that the form of halakhic prayer derives from rabbinic enactment, why is the Halakhah that the Rabbis determined so exacting as to the details of how one should pray?

To respond to these questions, we need to turn to a famous talmudic argument concerning the origin of the primary prayer of all: the *Amidah*.

Rabbi Jose ben Rabbi Chanina says: "The *T'fillot* [meaning here the three daily *Amidah* services] were instituted by the Patriarchs. Rabbi Joshua ben Levi says: The *T'fillot* were instituted to parallel the daily sacrifices" (*Ber.* 26b).

The Rabbis were deeply concerned with this issue of origin. Intellectually, they knew that the *Amidah* had been instituted in real historical time, by their predecessors. But they had also experienced the destruction of the Temple, and they knew that the demise of the *avodah* there (the sacrificial service) had made the liturgy outside the Temple — especially the *Sh'ma* and Its Blessings and the *Amidah* — the sole remaining and, therefore, the dominant form of worship.

The Talmud thus cites arguments for both sides. R. Jose ben Hanina relies on proof from Genesis: Abraham, Isaac, and Jacob are depicted doing relatively innocuous activities morning, afternoon, and night, which are, however, identified by verbal forms known elsewhere as indicating prayer. Thus "Abraham rose up early in the morning to the place where he had stood" (Gen. 19:27); since in another context, "standing" implies prayer, it can be said that Abraham instituted the morning *Amidah* (*Shacharit*). "Isaac went out to meditate in the field at eventide" (Gen. 24:63); since "meditation" is also prayer, Isaac is credited with establishing the first afternoon *Amidah* (*Minchah*). "Jacob came upon a spot" (Gen. 28:11); "came upon" too can denote prayer, so Jacob is said to have instituted the *Amidah* for evenings (*Ma'ariv*).

R. Joshua ben Levi's position — that the *Amidah* parallels the daily sacrifices — is supported by extensive rabbinic discussions on the proper timing of the *Amidah,* which parallel the times that the sacrifices were to be offered. The two positions seem evenly matched, except for the case of the *Musaf Amidah* (the additional *Amidah* for Shabbat and holidays), which has no patriarchal precedent, but correlates perfectly with the existence of a *Musaf* sacrifice. But the Talmud provides R. Jose ben Chanina with a response even to this seemingly insurmountable hurdle: "The patriarchs instituted the *T'fillot* [plural of *T'fillah,* again meaning the *Amidah* prayer in particular], but the Rabbis found support for them in the [institution of the] sacrifices." This talmudic conclusion is accepted thereafter by all subsequent rabbinic authorities.

According to this accepted resolution, the institution of the *Amidah* can be looked at from two supportive perspectives: patriarchal and sacrificial. The significance of the patriarchs lies not just in the assumption that they instituted them but in the further view that they also gave them their essential nature. Consider closely the proof texts: Abraham prays the morning prayer from a cliff, where he arose early in the morning so as to witness down below the destruction of Sodom and Gomorrah, two cities that he strove in vain to save. The reference to Isaac occurs only after his binding and near sacrifice by his father and the subsequent death of his mother. Never again speaking to his father, and unable to know that his future mate, Rebekah, is soon to appear, he wanders in a field as the sun is about to set. And Jacob "comes across a place" only after gaining both the birthright and the blessing, but then having to flee the land he is to inherit so as to escape from his jealous and murderous brother, Esau. All three patriarchal moments of prayer reflect their deepest personal crises: Abraham's failure to save Sodom, Isaac's loneliness created by his estrangement from his father and the death of his mother, Jacob's terror as he falls to the ground in exhaustion.

Halakhah thus recognizes, no less than the Zohar, that prayer *begins* in a cry, a personal *tsa'akah.* But it provides a prepared liturgy as an institutionalized vehicle for articulating that cry. That is why the main characteristic of the *Amidah* is the *bakashah,* which includes an entire array of petitions that invariably touch closely upon personal issues such as health and a livelihood, as well as communal, national, and universal needs. The way of halakhic prayer is double: it *expresses* the needs that people carry within them, in an elegant and concise language that is available to all; and it *evokes* from people the awareness of the crises they face. By confronting the daily *Amidah,* the Jew must confront his and her life and turn that life to God. Halakhic prayer prepares each Jew to replicate the path of the *avot* by turning to God with personal petitions.

But then we must also consider the *sacrificial* aspect of prayer — its parallel to the *avodah,* the divine service of the Temple. This is the aspect of rendering up to God one's prayers, making the *Amidah* an actual offering. By analogy, consider a ballet. A ballet has many elements — plot, music, timing, movement, lighting, and so on — that all must cohere to create the right effect. The *avodah* too attempted to display a perfection of human effort: it called for a precise choreography of movement by the officiants and a certain grace and beauty that would inspire awe in the heart of the community who watched it or who heard of it indirectly from someone else who had been there. The *Amidah* is an *avodah* in its own right: it is directed to God by people who cannot sacrifice but who know they are a kingdom of priests.

One senses that the talmudic resolution of the two opinions is a uniting of opposites rather than a synthesis. I believe that to be equally true of halakhic prayer, as it is lived. The two elements — expression of personal crisis and formal sacrificial service — exist in a dialectical tension. At times one element is predominant. There will also be situations in which a worshiper responds more readily to one aspect over the other. That is what Maimonides, echoing the Rabbis, means when he defines *t'fillah* as *avodah she'balev,* literally, "the [sacrificial] service that is within the heart" (Laws of Prayer 1:1).

To pray halakhically is to enjoy the opportunity to experience both aspects intensely and deeply. This is accomplished through the alternation of the private, silent *Amidah* and the subsequent recitation by the prayer leader. The repetition originated to serve the needs of the uneducated who could not pray on their own. With greater education, however, and with the widespread availability of the Siddur, the urgency of this need waned. The repetition has therefore been halakhically reinterpreted. Current halakhists distinguish between the two types of prayer: *t'fillah b'tsibbur* and *t'fillat hatsibbur,* "prayer *within* the community" and "prayer *of* the community."

First, we have the private *Amidah.* This is *t'fillah b'tsibbur,* "prayer *within* the community." It is a silent devotion performed within the context of community, but worshipers pray out of their own personal needs. They share the same liturgy but direct their hearts to God in their own distinctive ways. Second, we find the repetition by the prayer leader, who prays out loud with at least nine other obligated people attentively present. This is *t'fillat hatsibbur,* "prayer *of* the community." It is equivalent to *korban hatsibbur,* "a sacrifice of the community." Early authorities relate that even the *am she-basadot,* "the people in distant fields" who cannot attend the service, fulfill their obligation by this prayer, for it is a prayer of the community in which they are included" (R. Moshe Shternbuch, *Mo'adim Uz'manim Hashalem* [Jerusalem, 5724 (1974)]).

Where people know how to pray, both forms of prayers are invested with great attention and intention. During the *t'fillah b'tsibbur* ("prayer *within* the community"), time is provided for each individual to turn to God with her or his own special cry. And then, when that quiet and outwardly still period is over, the *t'fillat hatsibbur* ("prayer *of* the community") commences with great song and response. Our teacher, the *Rov* (Rabbi Joseph B. Soloveitchik) taught us often that the term for prayer leader is *sh'liach tsibbur,* "the agent of the community," and agency has a precise halakhic definition: *Sh'liach adam ke'moto,* "the agent of a person is like that person" in all legal matters. That is, one's appointed agent can conduct all business and legal transactions for the one who does the appointing, in all matters for which the appointment was intended. All agreements intended at the time of appointment are subsequently binding in full upon the appointee. With regard to purpose, the *Rov* notes that the *sh'liach tsibbur* is the community's agent to God. The agent has become the community, and the community, as it listens and responds to his prayer, becomes one with him. That is why one must respond to all the blessings and never interrupt the repetition. Indeed, precisely because we are one community, the *Rov* would stand, throughout the repetition, in the same upright position as the *sh'liach tsibbur.* His students continue that tradition.

Halakhic prayer demands much from us. We are to articulate the expression and evocation of our deepest needs and fears: our cry. We do so because we believe that such needs and fears are valid, stemming, as they do, from our deepest essence. We also affirm, in this dialogue with God, that God can and will act within our lives and in this world. These prayers are offered in two guises: as our individual and private call to God, and as part of an inclusive and public communal offering of divine *avodah* ("service"). Halakhic prayer certainly demands much from us; but do we not demand even more from God?

Introduction to the Liturgy

What to Look for in the Service

Lawrence A. Hoffman

Liturgy can seem confusing, more like a shapeless mass of verbiage than a carefully constructed whole; a jumble of noise, not a symphony; a blotch of random colors, hardly a masterpiece of art. But prayer *is* an art form, and like the other arts, the first step to appreciation is to recognize the pattern at work within it.

There are three daily services: morning *(Shacharit)*, afternoon *(Min-chah)*, and evening *(Ma'ariv* or *Arvit)*. For the sake of convenience, the latter two are usually recited in tandem, one just before dark, and the other immediately after the sun sets. All three follow the same basic structure, but the morning service is the most complete. It is composed of seven consecutive units that build upon each other to create a definitive pattern. Though the words of each unit remained fluid for centuries, the structural integrity of the service has remained sacrosanct since the beginning.

Services are made of prayers, but not all prayers are alike. Some are biblical quotations, ranging in size from a single line to entire chapters, usually psalms. There are rabbinic citations also, chunks of Mishnah or Talmud that serve as a sort of Torah study within the service. Medieval poetry occurs here too, familiar things like *Adon Olam* or older staples (called *piyyutim;* sing., *piyyut)* marked less by rhyme and rhythm than by clever word plays and alphabetic acrostics. And there are long passages of prose, the work again of medieval spiritual masters, but couched in standard rabbinic style without regard for poetic rules.

Most of all, however, the Siddur is filled with blessings, a uniquely rabbinic vehicle for addressing God, and the primary liturgical expression of Jewish spirituality.

Blessings (known also as benedictions, or, in Hebrew, *b'rakhot;* sing., *b'rakhah)* are so familiar that Jewish worshipers take them for granted. We are mostly aware of "short blessings," the one-line formulas that are customarily recited before eating, for instance, or prior to performing a commandment. But there are "long blessings" too, generally whole paragraphs or even sets of paragraphs on a given theme. These are best thought of as small theological essays on such topics as deliverance, the sanctity of time, the rebuilding of Jerusalem, and the like. They sometimes start with the words *Barukh atah Adonai . . .* ("Blessed are You, Adonai . . ."), and then they are easily spotted. But more frequently, they begin with no particular verbal formula and are hard to identify until their last line, which invariably does say, *Barukh atah Adonai . . .* ("Blessed are You, Adonai . . .") followed by a short synopsis of the blessing's theme (". . . who sanctifies the Sabbath," ". . . who hears prayer," ". . . who redeems Israel," and so forth). This final summarizing sentence is called a *chatimah*, meaning a "seal," like the seal made from a signet ring that seals an envelope.

The bulk of the service as it was laid down in antiquity consists of strings of blessings, one after the other, or of biblical quotations bracketed by blessings that introduce and conclude them. By the tenth century, the creation of blessings largely ceased, and eventually, Jewish law actually opposed the coining of new ones, on the grounds that post-talmudic Judaism was spiritually unworthy emulating the literary work of the giants of the Jewish past. Not all Jews agree with that assessment today, but the traditional liturgy that forms our text here contains no blessings later than the tenth century.

The word we use to refer to all the literary units in the prayer book, without regard to whether they are blessings, psalms, poems, or something else, is *rubric*. A rubric is any discrete building block of the service, sometimes a single prayer (this blessing rather than that, or this quotation, but not that poem) and sometimes a whole set of prayers that stands out in contradistinction to other sets: the *Amidah*, for instance, the topic of this volume, is a large rubric, composed of nineteen discrete blessings strung together one after the other and divided into three sections, on the larger themes of praise, petition, and thanksgiving. Relative to the *Amidah* as a whole, however, we can consider each of the blessings as a rubric in itself.

The *Amidah* is the second of three large rubrics that constitute the core of the synagogue service. The first one (and the subject of Volume One in this series) is the *Sh'ma* and Its Blessings, which represents what Jews believe, and is recited twice daily: morning *(Shacharit)* and evening *(Ma'ariv)*. Since it is also the official beginning of congregational prayer, the *Sh'ma* and Its Blessings is introduced by an official call to prayer, called the *Bar'khu* (literally an invitation to "praise" God).

The *Amidah*		
Praise	Petition	Thanksgiving
3 Blessings of Praise	16 Blessings of Request	3 Blessings of Thanksgiving
Nineteen blessings in all: each one is a small "rubric" within the large "rubric" of the *Amidah* as a whole.		

The *Amidah* (which is the subject of this volume) follows. It is known also as the *T'fillah* or *Sh'moneh Esreh*. It is a little harder to characterize than the *Sh'ma* because its nature changes, depending on the occasion on which it is recited. On weekdays, however (though not on Shabbat and holidays), it is largely petitionary, so it can be thought of as representing what Jews pray for. Another way to look at it is to say that the *Sh'ma* and Its Blessings is a Jewish conversation *about* God; the *Amidah* is a Jewish conversation *with* God. The *Amidah* is part of every service: morning *(Shacharit)*, afternoon *(Minchah)*, and evening *(Ma'ariv)*.

The third major rubric (and the topic of a later volume) is the public reading of Torah. The *Sh'ma* and Its Blessings and the *Amidah* are recited every day; Torah is read on Monday and Thursday (market days in antiquity, when crowds were likely to gather), and on Shabbat and holidays. The Torah reading is a recapitulation of revelation as at Mount Sinai, an attempt to discover the will of God through sacred scripture.

We should picture these three units building upon each other in a crescendo-like manner, as follows:

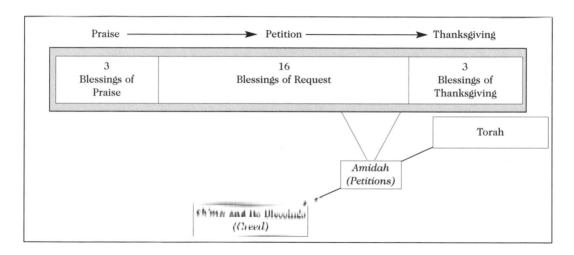

It is, however, hard for individuals who are normally distracted by everyday concerns to constitute a community given over wholeheartedly to prayer. Already in the second century, therefore, we hear of some Rabbis who assembled prior to the actual Call to Prayer in order to sing psalms of praise known as a *Hallel;* and even before that — at home, not the synagogue — it was customary to begin the day immediately upon awakening by reciting a series of daily blessings along with some study texts. By the ninth century, if not earlier, these two units too had become mandatory, and the home ritual for awakening had moved to the synagogue, which is where we have it today. The warm-up section of psalms is called *P'sukei D'zimrah* — meaning "Verses of Song" — and the prior recital of daily blessings and study texts is called *Birkhot Hashachar* — "Morning Blessings." Since they now precede the main body of the service, gradually building up to it, the larger diagram can be charted like this:

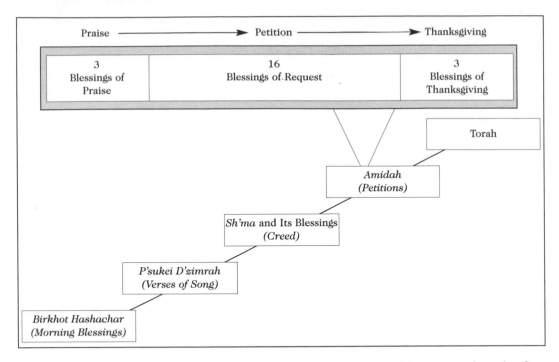

Two other expansions of this basic structure probably occurred in the first two centuries C.E., although our evidence for their being that early is less certain.

First, a Conclusion was added. It featured a final prayer called the *Kaddish,* which as yet had nothing to do with mourning, but merely followed the Torah reading, and therefore closed the service, by looking ahead to the coming of God's ultimate reign of justice. Eventually, other prayers were added to the Conclusion, including the *Alenu,* which had originally been composed as an introduction to the blowing of the shofar on Rosh Hashanah but was moved here in the Middle Ages.

Second, the Rabbis, who were keenly aware of the limits to human mortality, advised all Jews to come to terms daily with their frailty and ethical imperfection. To do so, they provided an opportunity for a silent confession following the *Amidah,* but before the Torah reading. In time, this evolved into silent prayer in general, an opportunity for individuals to assemble their most private thoughts before God; and later still, some time in the Middle Ages, it expanded on average weekdays into an entire set of supplicatory prayers called the *Tachanun.*

The daily service was thus passed down to us with shape and design. Beginning with daily blessings that celebrate the new day and emphasize the study of sacred texts *(Birkhot Hashachar),* it continues with songs and psalms *(P'sukei D'zimrah)* designed to create a sense of community. There then follows the core of the liturgy: an official call to prayer (our *Bar'khu),* the recital of Jewish belief (the *Sh'ma* and Its Blessings) and communal petitions (the *Amidah).* Individuals then pause to speak privately to God in silent prayer (later expanded into the *Tachanun),* and then, on select days, they read from Torah. The whole concludes with a final *Kaddish,* to which other prayers, most notably the *Alenu,* were added later.

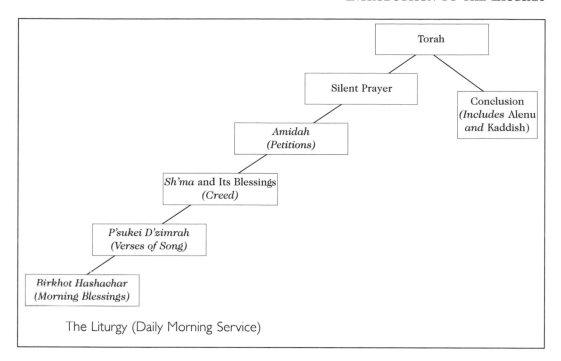

The Liturgy (Daily Morning Service)

On Shabbat and holidays, this basic structure expands to admit special material relevant to the day in question and contracts to omit prayers that are inappropriate for the occasion. On Shabbat, for instance, the petitions of the *Amidah* are excluded, since Shabbat — a time of perfect peace — makes petitioning unnecessary. But (1) an entire service is added, a service called *Musaf* (literally, "Addition"), to correspond to the extra sacrifice that once characterized Shabbat worship in the Temple. Similarly, (2) a prophetic reading called the *Haftarah* follows the Torah reading, and (3) extra psalms and readings for the Sabbath are inserted here and there. The same is true for holidays when, in addition, (4) numerous *piyyutim* are recited, especially for the High Holy Days, when the sheer size of the liturgy seems to get out of hand. But even there, the basic structure remains intact, so that those who know its intrinsic shape can get beyond what looks like random verbiage to find the genius behind the liturgy's design.

THE *AMIDAH*: THE JEWISH CONVERSATION WITH GOD

The *Amidah* is usually thought of as the petitionary part of Jewish worship; and indeed, it is that, but it is also more. On Shabbat and holidays, for instance (as we saw), the middle petitionary section is removed altogether and replaced by a single blessing that celebrates the sanctity of the day in question. If the essence of the *Amidah* were only its petitions, we would not say it at all on sacred occasions. But we do; we just change it somewhat to reflect the nature of the day on which we are gathering. While ordinary days prompt thoughts of what we wish we had to make our lives fuller and more fulfilling, sacred times evoke different thoughts within us.

When we say that the *Amidah* is petitionary, therefore, we really mean to affirm the natural inclination of human beings to turn to God for ultimate matters such as wisdom, forgiveness, healing, justice, and hope — the larger issues without which life would seem meaningless. Since Shabbat and holidays are presumed on their own to provide assurance of such transcendent meaning, the nature of the Jewish conversation with God changes then. But human life is mostly pursued between the sacred heights that punctuate the calendar. It is our day-to-day existence that we probably find most challenging. For those days, then, Judaism provides a conversation with God where we are encouraged to think beyond the present and imagine life at its best — which is to say, we dare to ask what seems impossible: that the God of all the cosmos should stop to listen to us.

Far from being a dogmatic religion, Judaism has encouraged diverse views of the divine. Jewish thought is, therefore, rich in suggestions on the many ways to conceptualize a God who listens. The Rabbis of old seem largely to have pictured God as a parent, ready and able to grant our requests. Philosophic views of the Middle Ages were less likely to see God that way. Modern thinkers offer a vast spectrum of opinion. Some reaffirm the rabbinic perspective and insist that God listens to us the way our parents do, lovingly prepared to hear our pleas, but, in addition, all-knowing and all-powerful. Others see God as a natural force for good in the universe, the equivalent (in the moral order) of the force of gravity (in the physical universe). Still others insist that God is known the way we know another person, even though God is not, in essence, such a person at all; or that God is all-knowing and all-good, but not all-powerful, so that God (like a parent) hears our pleas, and even welcomes them, but may not be able to grant them all. If God could do whatever we want, there could be no universal laws of nature and no free will allowing human beings to be distinctively what we are. The price of having dependable laws of nature and our precious human freedom to act as our conscience demands is God's willing abandonment of the role of "superparent" able to intervene in human affairs at a moment's notice.

In the end, we cannot know for sure just what or who God is; our minds are too finite to grasp the infinite. We do, however, believe that whatever God may be, God is not so impersonally distant from us that we have no access to the divine. How, then, do we plot the way to God? Other faiths answer that question in their own distinctive ways. It is hard to characterize any religion as doing just one thing; they all practice many acts of devotion. But each one has its own quintessential act of worship, without which we can hardly imagine it being what it is. Quakers gather silently to await the call of the Holy Spirit; Pentecostals speak in tongues; Buddhists meditate; Roman Catholics take communion. Jews find God through conversation, framed in blessing format.

The late Henry Slonimsky, once a dean at the Hebrew Union College–Jewish Institute of Religion in New York, put it brilliantly:

> Prayer is the expression of our needs and aspirations, addressed to a great source of help — to the Friend whom we suppose to exist behind the phenomena. . . . What are those needs? First and foremost, health and food and life itself, without which there is nothing; then, on a higher plane, the need for forgiveness of sin and wrongdoing; and finally that all the great and good causes of the human heart shall be brought to victory, that the poor and oppressed shall be comforted, and wrong righted, and justice done and goodness prevail.

What we cannot abide is the thought that the "great and good causes of the human heart" might have no chance of being brought "to victory." The *Amidah* implicitly affirms that we are not alone in our concern for these monumental passions that insist on a day with "wrong righted, justice done, and goodness prevailing." It is our conversation about what matters most in the grand scheme of things, of which we are only a speck in time; and the very fact that it is that conversation implies that we are not an unimportant speck, but a cosmically significant one, like the tiniest of cells, without which an entire organism would never come to be, or a single musical note, without which the entire world of song would fall silent. The *Amidah* is petitionary in the grand sense of its affirming our right to aspire to a higher plane and our right to believe that our aspirations are not futile.

We saw above that the daily *Amidah* is divided into three parts: a set of three blessings on the theme of praise; then sixteen blessings devoted to petition; and finally, three blessings expressing gratitude. That, at least, is the way the Rabbis describe the prayer. The matter is far more complex than that, however. Precisely because the *Amidah* is so central to the way Jews meet with God, it has attracted more attention from traditional commentators and modern scholars than any other rubric in our liturgy. The evolution of what Jews have said about the *Amidah* is fascinating enough to deserve a chapter of its own. What follows, then, is the intriguing tale of how the *Amidah* began. I call it "A Jewish Detective Story."

How the Amidah *Began*

A Jewish Detective Story

Lawrence A. Hoffman

Everything about the *Amidah* is intriguing. We do not know for sure when Jews started saying it or even why. Most puzzling of all is how it came to consist of nineteen benedictions, since the *Amidah* is also named the *Sh'moneh Esreh* — that is, "the Eighteen [not nineteen!] Benedictions." Couldn't the Rabbis count? As we shall see, the Talmud itself noted the numerical discrepancy, thereby inaugurating a 2,000-year-old tradition of ferreting out which one of the nineteen is the elusive "extra" benediction that, somehow, must have slipped in surreptitiously.

People who think scholarly arguments are boring have never consulted the age-old debate over the history of the *Amidah*. It was the Rabbis' favorite prayer, after all, known originally as *Hat'fillah,* that is, *"The* Prayer." Literally thousands of learned Jews have spent their lives reading and rereading those few classical texts that purport to explain how it came about, and since the dawn of modern times, nearly every scholar, student, or sage in Jewish life has had to wrestle with the question of the *Amidah's* origins — really and truly, a Jewish detective story.

The first step toward solving it is to look at the two accounts carried by rabbinic literature itself, our first two clues regarding how this prayer of prayers arose.

OUR FIRST CLUE: PROPHETS, ELDERS, AND MEN OF THE GREAT ASSEMBLY

A second-century midrash holds that "the early prophets instituted the practice of the daily recital of the Eighteen Benedictions" (Sifre to Deut. 343). The Babylonian Talmud says, similarly, "A hundred and twenty elders, including many prophets, instituted the Eighteen Benedictions" (Meg. 17b). And the Palestinian Talmud concurs: "One hundred and twenty men, including about eighty elders and thirty prophets, instituted the daily *Amidah*" (Ber. 2:4. The text is corrupt. As it stands, it reads, "One hundred and twenty elders including eighty and some prophets instituted the daily *Amidah."* My translation is an emendation suggested by the great talmudist Louis Ginzberg). But who are these people? When did they live?

The prophets are easy to identify. The first prophets in Jewish history are court personalities like Elijah who appear before Israel's kings in the tenth and ninth centuries B.C.E. to champion divine causes. They work miracles to prove the existence of Israel's God, and they serve the poor and despised in the land, sometimes even bringing children who die of disease back to life. By the eighth century, however, a new kind of prophet appears — not wonder-workers like Elijah and Elisha but literary prophets like Amos and Isaiah. They still serve as God's messengers to the mighty, and they still represent the downtrodden, but they leave behind written testimonies of how they were called by God, usually against their will, and they predict the end of Israel's sovereignty, a punishment for its sins. More prophets of this sort (for instance, Ezekiel) write from Israel's exile in Babylon (from 587 to 538 B.C.E.), and others still (like Malachi and Obadiah) represent God's word after Israel returns to its land.

The elders are harder to identify. The most famous reference to them is a passage from Pirkei Avot, a chapter in the first Jewish law code, the Mishnah (dated 200 C.E.). "Moses received the Torah at Sinai and handed it down to Joshua. Joshua to the elders, and the elders to the prophets; and the prophets handed it down to the Men of the Great Assembly" (Avot 1:1). Apparently a group of people called the Elders are assumed to have lived even before the prophets.

But if so, we know nothing about them; and in any event, the Bible seems completely oblivious to anything remotely like an *Amidah*. The only kind of public worship known to the prophets or to the society in which they lived is the sacrificial cult. The only kind of prayer they know is private prayer, the spontaneous outpouring of the human heart to God. There are no synagogues and no fixed times when biblical men or women assemble to pray.

Since the passage from the Mishnah also cites the Men of the Great Assembly, it has been suggested that it is they who actually developed the *Amidah,* especially since the Talmud elsewhere says, "the Men of the Great Assembly *[Anshei k'nesset hag'dolah]* instituted blessings for Israel" (Ber. 33a). *K'nesset,* however, can also imply a synagogue (which we call *bet k'nesset* in Hebrew), so some writers refer to the group as "the Men of the Great Synagogue" and assume that its members cared especially for the liturgy. But the Hebrew *k'nesset,* and the Greek *synagoge* (="synagogue") really mean "assembly." The synagogue (or *bet k'nesset)* arose as a place where people assembled for any number of reasons, but not to pray. Its prayer function was added much later, perhaps as late as the second century C.E., which is after the time when the *Amidah* began. The *Anshei k'nesset hag'dolah* were therefore "Men of the Great Assembly," not "Men of the Great Synagogue," if, by synagogue, we mean anything like the institution that we know by that name today.

However we translate their title, looking to the Men of the Great Assembly (or Synagogue) for the origins of the *Amidah* does not help us very much, since we do not know who they were in any event. Tradition assumes that the Great Assembly was the governing body in the Land of Israel following the rule of Ezra and Nehemiah, about 450 B.C.E., but it is equally likely that the Men of the Great Assembly never really existed at all. The Great Assembly was probably a hypothetical construct of later Rabbis who recognized that their own history as a rabbinic class went back, at the most, to the second century B.C.E. Knowing virtually nothing of Jewish history from roughly 450 to 150 B.C.E., but anxious to fill the void somehow, they posited a group of authorities called the Men of the Great Assembly.

Even today, with all our manuscripts, libraries, and sophisticated scholarship, the historical gap between the return from the Babylonian exile and the rise of the Rabbis is something of a black hole. We can certainly understand how the Rabbis too had to guess at the likeliest shape of the murky era that preceded them. When they say, therefore, that the *Amidah* goes back to prophets or elders, they mean only that the origins of the *Amidah* are old.

They were not altogether wrong. Our first set of clues returns us to an era beyond easy memory, albeit not necessarily as far back as the actual prophets and elders of the Bible. There must have been a period when the *Amidah* was just beginning but was still so poorly developed that no one paid enough attention to it to record it. We can call it the era of a "proto-*Amidah*," a time when what would eventually become a full-fledged *Amidah* was just being born. It did not necessarily have eighteen or nineteen blessings yet. Neither the number of the blessings nor their topics had been fixed. Jews were just starting to conceive of the idea of a formal public prayer service, such as we have today. The notion was just occurring that Jews might gather as a covenanted community and give God the words of their lips rather than the smoke of burnt sacrifices. That simple idea, which we take for granted today, was a spiritual revolution. An *Amidah* had been conceived, if not yet born, and the exact date of its conception is unknown to us. The number of blessings and their topics would not be fixed until the days of Rabban Gamaliel II.

A Second Clue: Rabban Gamaliel II

In addition to its recollection that some unknown prophets and elders initiated the *Amidah,* rabbinic tradition also credits Rabban Gamaliel II with its organization. Gamaliel was the Patriarch (or chief Rabbi) at the end of the first century C.E. The Mishnah recalls him as ruling, "Every day, one should say eighteen benedictions." The Talmud then adds the following account: "Our Rabbis taught: Shimon Hapakuli ['Simon the flax merchant'] arranged the eighteen benedictions in order before Rabban Gamaliel in Yavneh. Rabban Gamaliel said to the sages, 'Can any among you frame a blessing regarding the heretics?' Shmuel Hakatan ['Samuel the Younger'] arose and framed it" (Ber. 29a).

Rabban Gamaliel is well known to us as the most influential Rabbi in the period following the Roman destruction of the Temple. The war against Rome had been fought by a coalition of Jewish parties whom we can conveniently lump together under the general designation "militants." The Rabbis were part of the war effort, though I think it likely that they joined it hesitantly, as a fifth column, hoping to scuttle it before the mighty Roman army utterly destroyed both Jews and Judaism. When the war ended, Rome established the Rabbis in Yavneh (still a city on the Mediterranean coastline, not far from today's downtown Tel Aviv). Some historians think of Yavneh as a sort of camp where the Romans exiled its former prisoners of war; others see it as an intellectual center where a wide variety of activists and thinkers assembled — something like the New York circles for Jewish émigrés from the Nazis in the 1940s. Others believe the Rabbis were sent there as agents of the Roman authorities, precisely because they had opposed the war in the first place and could be counted on as the Romans' best bet to rebuild a loyal Jewish populace in the war's aftermath. Whatever the case, rabbinic Judaism as we know it was largely shaped in Yavneh.

These Rabbis were not yet an organized class, however — nothing like a union or a professional body like doctors, lawyers, teachers, or even rabbis in our time. What made them "Rabbis" was their shared assumptions regarding God's revelation to the Jewish People and the manner in which Judaism was to be practiced. At the core of their belief was the conviction that, at Mount Sinai, God had provided not only a written Torah but an oral commentary also and that this twin revelation had been carried down through the ages to their own day. They took as their calling the obligation to study God's written and oral message to the Jewish People and to spell out the consequences for how Jews should behave. They agreed, therefore, on a general philosophy as well as on certain derivative principles, like the nature of the Jewish calendar, the priority of studying Torah, and the elementary requirements of leading a Jewish life (like fasting on Yom Kippur, avoiding Shabbat work, and honoring Jewish values). But they differed on details, and they had no professional organization — no committees, no congresses or conventions, no executive body — for harmonizing differences of opinion or hammering out compromises among them.

So too, the Rabbis all studied Torah, kept kosher, demarcated Shabbat from weekdays, fasted on Yom Kippur, and met for public prayer. But they had no way of reaching consensus on the details that constituted such behavior. In the early years, two rival schools of thought had coalesced around two leaders known as Hillel and Shammai, with the Hillelites dominating. By the first century C.E., certain Rabbis, mostly Hillelites, emerged as more influential than others, and one of them, Yochanan ben Zakkai, became a first among equals in Yavneh. Many Jews today know the talmudic account of how Yochanan ben Zakkai was smuggled out of Jerusalem in a coffin during the Roman siege. In all probability, however, if he was smuggled out at all, it was not because the Romans were fooled by the ruse — is it likely that they would refuse to let one man out but would permit six coffin-bearers to go free? It was probably the militants within the city from whom Yochanan escaped, in order to pursue the terms of surrender that would eventuate in rabbinic rule from Yavneh. When the war ended, Yochanan led the rabbinic party to its new-found home and headquarters, where he served as the chief Rabbi until his death a decade or so thereafter. Those who followed him were eventually known as the *Nasi* (literally, "the Prince," but translated generally as "Patriarch"), and while the others of his party were called "Rabbi," meaning "My Teacher," Yochanan is known to us as "Rabban," meaning "Our Teacher."

But the rabbinic party did not take quickly to an autocratic ruler among them; without a single academy, *yeshivah,* or agreed-upon final court of appeal, its members remained divided on almost every issue. Within the broad set of categories that all Rabbis took for granted, each Rabbi attracted his own set of followers and promulgated his own opinion. The Patriarch who followed Yochanan dedicated himself to achieving unity among his colleagues by standardizing practice among them, declaring some views right and others wrong. That man was Gamaliel II, who exercised greater authority than Yochanan had, partly because, unlike Yochanan, he was an actual descendent of Hillel. He is remembered as wielding heavy-handed power to unify the disparate Rabbis, even going so far as to "stack the court" by adding members to the Sanhedrin to ensure its support of his initiatives. His codification of the *Amidah* was part of his larger agenda of standardizing rabbinic practice in general.

The Talmud was not finally edited until the sixth or seventh century, by which time both tales of the *Amidah*'s origins had already been recorded: first, that it went back to prophets and elders; and second, that Rabban Gamaliel organized it. The Talmud had inherited the two accounts as sacred memories that could not easily be jettisoned, so its editor tried to harmonize them by imagining that after the elders and prophets composed the Eighteen Benedictions, "they were forgotten and Gamaliel reformulated them anew" (Meg. 18a). That seems highly unlikely to modern scholars, who suggest other answers. The most likely possibility is that until the time of Gamaliel, some communities recited an *Amidah* and others did not; those who did, said blessings on different themes, and the number of blessings in any given place varied widely. This proto-*Amidah* period came to an end when Gamaliel ordained that from now on everyone would have to say eighteen blessings daily. Gamaliel set the number and the topics of the blessings. Other Rabbis fought Gamaliel's innovation, but in vain. By the end of the second century, when the Mishnah was compiled, the daily service contained an *Amidah* just as Gamaliel had ordered.

The problem remains, however, that the prayer known as the Eighteen Benedictions has nineteen parts. Even the Talmud wonders out loud about the discrepancy in number: "Eighteen benedictions? But there are nineteen benedictions!" it exclaims (Ber. 28b). It is in that context that it cites the story of Rabban Gamaliel in the first place, namely, that Simon the flax merchant arranged the eighteen benedictions in order before Rabban Gamaliel and that Rabban Gamaliel had Samuel the Younger write a benediction against the heretics. The Talmud concludes, therefore, that one of the blessings, the one against heretics (#12 in our *Amidah),* is the extra blessing. After Simon's initial editorial labor, Gamaliel must have recognized that his composition was lacking a benediction against heresy. He therefore charged Samuel with the task of formulating it, but by that time the name "Eighteen Benedictions" had already been established. Even after the number had grown by one, the old name stuck.

This talmudic answer lasted for 1,800 years before it was proved false. A new clue would first have to be unearthed, and that clue was not discovered until the remarkable find known as the Genizah fragments. But before getting there, we need to look at the great age of Jewish scholarship, which would eventually crack the puzzle. A series of brilliant investigators arose mostly in Germany during the nineteenth century. I think of them as a set of Jewish sleuths bent on uncovering the secrets of the Jewish past. When they began, we knew almost nothing about Jewish literature, history, and thought. When the great age of Jewish scholarship ended, Jewish culture had been catalogued, its history unfolded, and its greatest thinkers chronicled.

HOW IT ALL UNRAVELED: THE AGE OF JEWISH SLEUTHS

As a scholar myself, I often marvel at the advice people give me when I try to explain to others what I do: "Don't be too scholarly," they say — meaning, "Don't be boring." But real scholarship is anything but boring. It is more akin to a Sherlock Holmes narrative, a case of reconstructing what happened once upon a time by following up clues that have been left behind in the sands of time.

Modern Jewish sleuthdom began with Leopold Zunz (1794–1886), a genius not far removed from Holmes in time and capacity, although there was this major difference: Holmes was pure fiction; Zunz really lived. He had been raised in a thoroughly traditional environment, mastering talmudic literature by the time he was a teenager. But he had the good fortune of living through the Napoleonic revolution, when Jews were freed from their ghettos and offered the opportunity to attend college. Zunz thereby discovered the methods of modern textual criticism, which he applied to traditional Jewish sources. Almost single-handedly, he catalogued post-biblical Jewish literature into the categories that we now take for granted, and basing himself on the thousands of manuscripts that he managed to find, he wrote histories of everything from midrash to poetry.

His political agenda included demonstrating the worth of Jewish culture to a generation of Jews and non-Jews who lived in the post-Napoleonic era, when the atmosphere was becoming more and more reactionary. Napoleon had emerged from the Age of Reason, an emphatic celebration of universal human values epitomized by the motto of the French Revolution, "Liberty, Equality, Fraternity." But the Romantic Era that followed rolled back the positive evaluation of humanity as a whole and replaced it with nationalistic fervor and the romanticization of the past. Zunz found himself surrounded by German scholars who were intent on recovering the glories of Teutonic culture, particularly the genius of German poetry. He therefore set himself the task of uncovering the splendor of the Jewish literary heritage, so as to display the Jewish case for being taken seriously as a culture with thinkers, poets, and writers who rivaled even those of Germany. Jewish poetry, however, tends to be liturgical; it had been composed as early as the fifth century in the form of *piyyutim,* insertions for the Sabbath and holiday prayer service. In order to get at the poetry, he had to turn first to Jewish liturgy, which no one had yet studied in any great detail — especially the *Amidah,* the prayer for which most of the holiday poetry had been created.

The nineteenth century was in love with theories of evolution wed to a romantic yearning for a return to the purity of primitive origins. Gauguin traveled to Tahiti; anthropologists studied Australian Aborigines, art historians sought out the pure forms of early Greece, and cultural critics looked for pristine instances of national genius in antiquity. Zunz, therefore, embarked on a scholarly quest for the origin of the *Amidah.* By applying literary criticism to the prayer as he had inherited it, he would remove the medieval accretions and uncover the original text, which would surely reveal rabbinic genius at its best.

Zunz began by labeling the nineteen benedictions according to their topics, following the talmudic understanding of what each blessing was about. Then he divided them into the three categories by which Jewish tradition had labeled them: three initial benedictions of praise, thirteen "middle" benedictions of petition, and three final blessings of thanksgiving, as follows:

A. Praise:
   1. For God's covenant with our ancestors
   2. For God's power
   3. For God's holiness

B. Petition:
   4. For wisdom
   5. For repentance
   6. For forgiveness
   7. For deliverance
   8. For healing
   9. For "years" (agricultural fertility in the Land of Israel)
   10. For the gathering of the exiles
   11. For a restoration of just judges
   12. For punishment of heretics
   13. For reward of the righteous
   14. For the rebuilding of Jerusalem
   15. For the coming of the messiah
   16. For God to hear prayer

C. Thanksgiving:
   17. For worship
   18. For gratitude
   19. For peace

Good detectives know better than to accept on blind faith whatever their informants tell them. So Zunz questioned the validity of the entire traditional scheme of "Praise, Petition, Thanksgiving." The seventeenth blessing, for instance, though technically in the section of "Thanksgiving," not "Petition," is nonetheless petitionary: it asks God to "return the sacrifice to the Holy of Holies," and the nineteenth, similarly, pleads, "Grant us peace." Zunz knew also that on Shabbat and holidays, instead of saying nineteen blessings, we say only seven: the first three and the last three blessings remain, while the middle blessings (the "petitions," technically) are replaced by a single central blessing that proclaims the sanctity of the Sabbath day. Traditionally, the change is explained by the desire to avoid petitioning on sacred occasions, which are presumed to be so perfect that what we normally lack cannot even be felt, let alone expressed in prayer. But if two of the three blessings in the final triad are really petitionary, that traditional explanation is suspect. Why then, Zunz wondered, are the middle blessings *really* dispensable on holy days, whereas the first and last three are not?

Perhaps, Zunz theorized, the first and last three blessings are more ancient than the middle thirteen. While the Rabbis could easily omit the relatively recent middle blessings on Shabbat, they were unable to skip over the first and last three because people knew them too well; they would miss them if they were removed. He therefore dated the introductory and concluding benedictions earlier than the others.

His suspicions seemed confirmed by another curious fact: a rabbinic discussion from the second century cites titles for the first and last three blessings, but not for the middle ones, which are referred to instead just by their opening few words. Zunz reasoned that things develop titles only after many years of conversation about them. The middle blessings had no titles because they were more recent. The other blessings did have titles because they were so old.

The original *Amidah* must therefore have been the first and last three blessings which eventually became incorrectly known as "Praise" and "Thanksgiving," even though they were really as petitionary as the middle thirteen.

But maybe the middle thirteen also could be put on a time line and dated in relative terms to each other. Again like a master detective, Zunz listed his evidence: the thirteen middle blessings that had hitherto been lumped together as all the same ("petitions"), but which Zunz wanted to differentiate from each other.

4. For wisdom
5. For repentance
6. For forgiveness
7. For deliverance
8. For healing
9. For "years" (agricultural fertility in the Land of Israel
10. For the gathering of the exiles
11. For justice (the restoration of just judges
12. For punishment of heretics
13. For reward of the righteous
14. For the rebuilding of Jerusalem
15. For the coming of the messiah
16. For God to hear prayer

As he stared at his list he discerned a subtle difference among the blessings that composed it. Some of the entries seemed *personal* in nature; others dealt with the destiny of the entire People of Israel — in Zunz's nineteenth-century vocabulary, they were *national* in sentiment. Determining which is which is to some extent a matter of subjective judgment, but one reasonable way of sorting them out looks like this:

4. For wisdom: personal
5. For repentance: personal
6. For forgiveness: personal
7. For deliverance: national
8. For healing: personal
9. For "years" (agricultural fertility in the Land of Israel): national
10. For the gathering of the exiles: national
11. For justice (the restoration of just judges): national
12. For punishment of heretics: national
13. For reward of the righteous: national
14. For the rebuilding of Jerusalem: national
15. For the coming of the messiah: national
16. For God to hear prayer: personal

If our paradigmatic modern detective, Sherlock Holmes, was a British Victorian, his scholarly Jewish parallel, Leopold Zunz, was a German romantic. What comes first in human evolution: petitions for national renewal or cries that explode from the very core of the human condition? Clearly, Zunz voted for the latter, making the original *Amidah* the first and last three blessings plus the "natural" outcries of the human heart, the personal petitions in the middle section. The national petitions, he thought, had evolved one at a time, as political responses to conditions in the Roman empire.

Zunz thus drew a time line, on which he arrayed his findings.

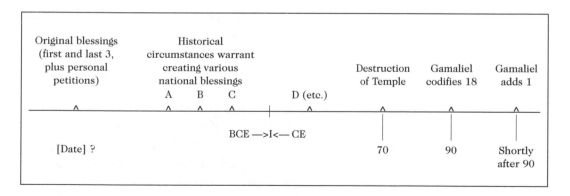

The "original" version of the *Amidah* (at the extreme left) could not be dated exactly; Zunz could say only that it was early, after the Bible but prior to the Rabbis, so that the era of the so-called Men of the Great Assembly might not be far off the mark. The maelstrom of events that marked Roman conquest had then prompted a series of national additions (marked A, B, C, D, etc.). When, for instance, the Jewish Sanhedrin had been dismissed, a petition to restore Jewish judges (#11) had been added; the Roman destruction of Jerusalem had prompted the blessing for the rebuilding of Jerusalem (#14); and so forth. By the time of Rabban Gamaliel, the number of blessings had reached eighteen. Gamaliel codified what he had, demanding it of every Jew from then on. Some time later, however, he realized that he was lacking a blessing against heresy, so he had Samuel the Younger add that one, just as the Talmud says, making the total nineteen.

Most of the scholars who followed Zunz agreed with him, except in details. They dated this blessing or that one somewhat differently, depending on the historical event that they thought most likely to have prompted it, but they accepted the general scheme that Zunz had devised: an original core of blessings some time after the end of the biblical era; the addition of national petitions in response to Roman occupation; and a final canonization by Gamaliel, first as eighteen benedictions, and then with an extra nineteenth, to fight the heretics (by which most people had in mind the rise of Christianity).

A Third Clue: The Genizah Fragments

What is the greatest archeological find of all time? The ruins of Pompeii, maybe, an entire Roman city covered over by volcanic ash, its inhabitants and their daily pursuits frozen in time for us to resurrect. Or, perhaps, one of the many human fossils uncovered in east Africa, allowing us to reconstruct the origins of human consciousness. Jewish history too has its archeological high points: the dig at Jericho, for instance, or the first and famous shaft sunk deep into the past at the site of the Temple, allowing us to imagine what it had been like when crowds of pilgrims came to offer sacrifices some 2,000 years ago. Sometimes history gets rewritten because upstart historians are smart enough to rearrange what their teachers took for granted. More often, however, the students are just luckier than their masters: they live later and have at their disposal evidence that no one had before.

Zunz had to catalogue the Jewish literary heritage from manuscript evidence that was rarely more than a few centuries old. Most of his reconstruction was guesswork — good guesswork, as it turned out, but guesswork nonetheless, since he rarely had access to really ancient material, written before the year 1000, for instance, and preserved for modern use ever since. That situation changed dramatically in 1896, just ten years after Zunz died. Two Christians visited Cairo that year and bought some medieval Hebrew documents from a street vendor. On their return to England, they showed their acquisition to Solomon Schechter, then a Reader of Rabbinics at Cambridge University. Schechter recognized the documents as a Hebrew version of a famous ancient work known as *The Wisdom of Ben Sirah*. The original Hebrew had been lost, but the book itself had been translated and canonized as part of the Christian Bible (Catholics still have it, although Protestants do not). It dawned on Schechter that he was probably looking at the only surviving manuscript of the original Hebrew book!

As soon as he could, Schechter hurried off to Cairo himself and was shown into an attic of the old Ezra Synagogue, where, before his eyes, was the largest cache of Jewish manuscripts of all time: the soon-to-be-famous Cairo Genizah. A genizah is a room where documents are stored rather than being thrown away; it comes from the Hebrew word *ganaz,* meaning to "file away" or "secrete." This genizah was massive and old, some of its contents going back all the way to the eighth century. It contained all sorts of things: personal letters, business contracts, wills, sacred books, collections of synagogue poetry *(piyyutim),* and handwritten prayer books from before the Crusades. By the time he was finished, Schechter had packed up 100,000 pages, which he carried back to Cambridge, and other scholars who followed removed thousands of pages in addition, so that collections of Genizah fragments were lodged in libraries all over the world. The most famous to this day is still in Cambridge, however, where Schechter began the awesome task of storing, studying, and publishing what Zunz could only have guessed at. His first publication was a version of the *Amidah* from which Palestinian Jews had prayed, before the Crusaders destroyed Palestinian Jewish culture in 1096. To everyone's surprise, this copy of the *Amidah* had only eighteen benedictions!

Schechter's publication of the old *Amidah* text appeared in 1898 and was avidly read by scholars all around the world, including a gifted twenty-four-year-old graduate student named Ismar Elbogen.

Elbogen is remembered today as the world's greatest student of Jewish liturgy, which he studied equally as a scholar and a Jew. Committed to the view that Judaism had survived because its continual evolution had prevented it from fossilizing into irrelevance, he dedicated himself to charting its development in the past and then directing its further evolution as the ever spiritual lifeblood of the Jewish People. More than an ivory-tower scholar, Elbogen worked at the very center of the affairs that shook the Jewish world in the middle years of this century. From across the Atlantic, he wrote biweekly letters to Rabbi Stephen Wise, advising him on how to hire a faculty for his new rabbinic seminary, the Jewish Institute of Religion in New York (it would later merge with Cincinnati's Hebrew Union College). Back in Germany, where he lived, he directed the premier institution of higher Jewish learning, Berlin's famous Lehranstalt. Early on, in 1922, he put his learning to practical use by serving as Hebrew editor for a prayer book that he hoped would unify German liberal Jews the way the *Union Prayer Book* had helped to standardize Reform Jewish practice in North America.

Later, Elbogen watched Hitler come to power. Few people realize that it was he who pled the cause of German Jewish scholars to Julian Morgenstern, the president of the Hebrew Union College, as a result of which, Morgenstern agreed to rescue such well-known personalities as Eric Werner (the founder of Jewish musicology) and Abraham Joshua Heschel. Like Leo Baeck (a faculty member in Elbogen's Lehranstalt), Elbogen too refused to emigrate until the bitter end, when he thought he could be of no further use to Germany's Jews anymore. By then, the United States had virtually closed its borders to Jews, and Elbogen managed to be saved only because the Hebrew Union College of Cincinnati, Steven Wise's Jewish Institute of Religion in New York, the Jewish Theological Seminary of America, and Philadelphia's Dropsie College *all* guaranteed employment to this outstanding scholar and leader who had worked so tirelessly for his People. He died in 1943 and was buried with great honor out of the Jewish Theological Seminary in New York.

In 1896, however, the tortuous path that awaited German Jews could hardly have been imagined. Elbogen was then merely an aspiring scholar with a special interest in prayer. He had read the work of Leopold Zunz, of course — every scholar had — and he had reached his own conclusions about dating the various prayers in the liturgy, including those to which Zunz had paid little attention. In 1913, his studies would culminate in *Jewish Liturgy, Historically Considered,* undoubtedly the most comprehensive and influential volume on the subject ever written. But back in 1896, he was just beginning.

This was where Elbogen's detective work benefited in ways that Zunz's could not. Elbogen got lucky: the Genizah fragments lying before him demonstrated without doubt that Zunz and the Talmud had the problem of the extra blessing all wrong. All he had to do was compare the Palestinian fragment in his hands with the *Amidah* text that Jews have now. If the blessing on heretics (#12) had been added later (as Zunz and the Talmud thought), it ought to be the one that was missing from the ancient fragment with only eighteen blessings. But it wasn't. Not only was it present; it reflected an older wording from a time before medieval censors had gotten hold of it. Among the groups being singled out for God's wrath were *notsrim,* that is, "Nazareans," Jewish converts to Christianity in the first century. On the other hand, Blessing 15 (on Jerusalem) and Blessing 16 (on the coming of the messiah) were combined as one blessing with a common synoptic line (the *chatimah,* which summarizes a blessing's intent): "Blessed are You . . . God of David who builds Jerusalem."

So Elbogen returned to Zunz's paradigmatic solution and tinkered with it. As Elbogen saw it, Zunz had been basically correct. There had been an early and basic *Amidah* many years before Gamaliel, to which new blessings had been added in response to historical events. But when Gamaliel collected the blessings as they had evolved to his day, he must have found only seventeen, not eighteen. He then added the blessing on heretics (#12), making the grand total eighteen, not nineteen as the Talmud and Zunz had reasoned. No wonder Gamaliel had called it the *Sh'moneh Esreh,* "the Eighteen Benedictions." That was what it was, until the single blessing on Jerusalem and the messiah (#15) was *later* divided into two (#14–15, now). The division of one blessing into two had occurred only in Babylonia, possibly as early as the third century, and for reasons that we can only guess at. The result, however, was that from then on, Babylonian Jews had nineteen blessings, whereas Palestinians retained only eighteen. No wonder, several centuries later, when the Babylonian Talmud was codified, its editor had expressed surprise at the number of blessings he said each day, guessing, wrongly, that the blessing on heretics was the additional one. The Palestinian Talmud lacked that whole discussion, since in Palestine, the prayer called the *Sh'moneh Esreh* remained exactly what its name implied, and as late as the tenth century, Genizah fragments showed Palestinian congregations still saying their ancient eighteen-blessing form of the *Amidah,* just as Gamaliel had put it together.

WHAT DID GAMALIEL DO? MOTIVE, MEANS, AND OPPORTUNITY

But what exactly did Gamaliel do? That he had some role in orchestrating a final version of the *Amidah* seems plain, but the nature of his contribution is not quite so obvious. Detective stories remind me here that people cannot be assumed to have done anything unless they have motive, means, and opportunity. Gamaliel was certainly motivated to canonize the *Amidah* as something for everyone to say. As we saw previously, he was bent on centralizing all authority at Yavneh following the war against Rome. Beyond that, it may be that by organizing the blessings the way he did, he encoded within the prayer as a whole a further message to his generation in the wake of defeat — a possibility that will engage us in just a minute. But first, we ought to inquire about means and opportunity.

Take opportunity first. Gamaliel had the opportunity too: he was the *Nasi,* the chief Rabbi of his era, supported in his position by Roman authority. The question is, however, given the technological competence and the social network of his time, did he also have the means? We should stop to consider what means he would have needed to compose a final version of the *Amidah* and then to disseminate it successfully for his rabbinic colleagues to use.

People rarely stop to consider how technology affects prayer books. At the very least, a prayer book editor needs the requisite means to write the prayers down on something. But in the time of Gamaliel, writing was rare. It has been estimated that only 2 to 4 percent of men in the ancient Mediterranean were literate, while the figure for women is even smaller. Jews may pride themselves on literacy and college attainment today, but in the first century, they were no different from anyone else in this regard. Elite groups, however — the rulers and their entourages, especially in cities — were almost all literate, since their education normally taught them how to read and write so that they might retain their class prerogatives. What social class, then, were the Rabbis in?

We should assume that a man like Gamaliel, an upper-class male and representative to the Roman authorities, was literate; and the same could probably be said for many, if not most, other leading Rabbis in the first and second centuries. But many Rabbis probably could not read, even though they could cite written works. They could work with scripture, in other words, even if they could not necessarily read it. We should take seriously the fact that they prided themselves on respecting an *oral* law, above and beyond the written one. It is clear also that they did not regularly look things up in books; instead, they relied on personal memorizers who mastered huge amounts of oral material and recited it when necessary. All the more so, the Jews to whom the Rabbis preached were not literate. So if Rabban Gamaliel was ordaining a prayer regimen for the masses, he certainly could not have been dictating precise wording that every Jew would read out of a prayer book day after day.

For that matter, even if people had been literate, cost would have prohibited prayer books in Gamaliel's time. Paper was still unavailable. All writing was done on parchment, animal skin. A single prayer book for the entire year would have taken the hides of some 150 sheep or calves to prepare. Even literate people had few books to read, therefore. What Gamaliel did not do, then, is dictate the words of the *Amidah* as a fixed text that everyone was duty bound to recite. As late as the fourteenth century, a Spanish rabbi writes that everywhere he goes the exact wording of the *Amidah* varies. All the more so, it varied in Gamaliel's day, when most people did not read and when even those who did, had no prayer books in which the prayers might be written.

Prayer was an oral thing in the first and second century. At most, the Rabbis shared wide-ranging agreement on the order of topics that the service should address. They had no such consensus on the exact words with which the topics should be covered. That is why to this day we have different versions of some prayers: two prayers for peace for instance, one at the end of the morning *Amidah* (see *Siddur Sim Shalom,* "Give us peace," p. 153) and a different one in the evening *(Shalom Rav,* "Great peace"); and two versions of the blessing that precedes the *Sh'ma* — again, one for the morning (See Volume 1, *The Sh'ma and Its Blessings,* p. 67) and one for the evening. When writing was more widespread in the Middle Ages, these alternatives were assigned different places in the service. But originally, they had existed side by side as alternative ways of saying the prayer in question. People had been able to choose either one; in fact, more accurately put, they were even allowed, if not encouraged, to make up new versions or to borrow others that they had heard, so that any given day and service might feature an altogether novel rendition of a given theme. (Hence the accent on the need to insert spontaneity into the service, known as *kavvanah* — see Volume 1, *The Sh'ma and Its Blessings,* pp. 3–5.)

So Gamaliel did not prescribe wording; he merely put the topics in order. When the Talmud says that eighteen benedictions were *arranged* before Rabban Gamaliel in Yavneh, the word "arranged" is carefully chosen. Before Gamaliel, there had been no mandated arrangement; now there was.

But if there was no mandated order, what blessings did people say prior to Gamaliel? Here is where the second necessity enters in: not just technological but social competence, meaning the limits inherent in any particular way that society is organized. Gamaliel could order a mandated set of blessings because his authority to rule was backed up by Rome. But his power to enforce his ruling was limited by the decentralized social structure that typified the rabbinic class. The Rabbis achieved authority among their own circle of students by virtue of their own knowledge and charisma. Like Chasidic masters in our own time, they shared a certain common universe of belief and of discourse, often talking about the same topics and doing so in similar ways; but, as we saw, they were not organized hierarchically — no one had an automatic right to enforce religious principles on anyone else. Editors of prayer books today enjoy an institutional system that supports what they do: a rabbinic organization with an executive to make decisions and committees to put them into practice. But none of that was in place in the first century. We should hardly imagine, therefore, that the *Amidah* developed in the simple linear fashion that Zunz and Elbogen imagined. Suppose, for the sake of argument, that blessings are sometimes composed in response to historical events; and suppose that one of them was the benediction calling for a return of Jewish judges, following the Roman replacement of the Sanhedrin with the Roman judicial system. How would the Rabbis have gotten together to write such a blessing? They were scattered throughout the country; they worked without committees; they had no meetings, took no minutes, used oral recollection only. They could hardly decide as a group to write a national blessing and then to circulate it by mail or by fax, as we do today. They couldn't even write it down.

What we should imagine instead is that over the course of time, long before Gamaliel, historical events prompted the desire to cry out to God. Any given event might have prompted hundreds of prayers, most of which disappeared as quickly as they came into being. Over the course of years, different communities developed their own preference for one prayer rather than another: this set, but not that one. Gamaliel inherited no single collection of blessings that everyone used. He inherited a practice of saying a proto-*Amidah* that varied from place to place, as well as examples of what these proto-*Amidot* contained: their typical topics, the kind of things people prayed for here and there, in as many different ways as there were people.

Gamaliel's accomplishment was, therefore, extraordinary. He managed to hammer together some form of organized structure out of complete chaos. And he did so despite the decentralized nature of the rabbinic class, which generated opposition. According to the Mishnah:

> Rabban Gamaliel said: Everyone must say eighteen benedictions every day. Rabbi Joshua said: A synopsis suffices. Rabbi Akiba said: Eighteen benedictions are desirable only if people know them fluently; if not, they should say a synopsis of eighteen benedictions. Rabbi Eliezer said: If you make your prayers a fixed task, your prayers are not genuine and real supplications. (M. Ber. 4:3–4)

While we cannot know what all the Rabbis thought of Gamaliel's innovation, we find Rabbis Joshua, Akiba, and Eliezer cited as typical of the spectrum of opinion available. Joshua agrees with the eighteen topics but prefers to fix them into a shorter composition made of a single benediction that synopsizes them all. Akiba compromises: eighteen separate blessings are preferable, but necessary only for those learned enough to say them all. Eliezer dismisses the whole idea of a fixed *Amidah*. Petitions should flow from the heart, not from a predetermined list of requests that someone else finds desirable. Any process of fixing what should be spontaneous is enough to destroy the very essence of acceptable petitionary prayer.

Although Gamaliel prevailed eventually, it probably took him a long time to do so. Since Akiba represents the next generation (he died in 135), the process did not occur overnight.

Finally, we are not even sure that *originally,* Gamaliel meant "literally" eighteen. Considerable evidence suggests that the number eighteen was used symbolically to say "a lot." Gamaliel might merely have meant that Jews should say a daily *Amidah* that comprised a lot of blessings, enough, at least, to reflect the flow of topics that he laid down. Joshua may have meant only that as long as the topical flow was adhered to, even one long blessing was sufficient. And Akiba reasoned that people of considerable textual competence might string the *Amidah* out as Gamaliel preferred, while the average person could make do with one single blessing that included the required topics.

We can now see what Gamaliel actually did. Only many years after his edict had become widespread did people interpret his idealized number eighteen literally. Until then, the *Amidah* was a loosely structured set of petitions that was as apt to be said in a single blessing as it was in several. As before (in the period that I called a proto-*Amidah)*, local differences remained common. What had changed, however, was the widespread acceptance of a set order of topics that every community accepted as mandatory — all of which takes us to the final, and most interesting, finding of our detective story: the motivation behind Gamaliel's edict. We should wonder what there was about Gamaliel's topics that even his opponents found compelling. In sum, we will see that they constituted a code. Taken in their proper order, the intermediate blessings constituted a message in which the whole is greater than the sum of the parts.

DECODING THE MESSAGE OF THE *AMIDAH*

Ever since Leopold Zunz, our premier detective of Jewish prayer, debate has raged over the degree to which Jewish national interests dominate the *Amidah*. Zunz had carefully disentangled what he thought to be "secondary" national concerns (like the messianic restoration of Jewish judges) from "primary" and "original" spiritual yearnings (petitions for wisdom, repentance, or health, for instance). But the distinction was always questionable, and it was only a matter of time until it was suggested that even the apparently personal benedictions are actually national. Perhaps the entire set of blessings could be seen as one lengthy prayer conditioned by the traumatic events of the war against Rome. Why else would Gamaliel have insisted on canonizing just this set of topics in just this order? Why else would his rabbinic colleagues have argued with the need for independent blessings for each topic, but (except for Eliezer) not for the topics themselves. The Palestinian Genizah fragments may differ from the Babylonian version that we follow today, but they both portray the same topical order. We even have a shortened version of the *Amidah* (called *Havineinu)*, which is reserved by Halakhah for occasions when there is insufficient time to say the *Amidah* in its entirety. It is clearly not a synopsis of the *Amidah* as we have it, but an independent composition, probably from the first or second century — and it too obeys the thematic flow demanded by Gamaliel. Apparently all the Rabbis came to agree on the need to include precisely these topics. Official rabbinic texts display plenty of room for diversity, but not on the issue of what topics the *Amidah* must contain, nor on their order, nor on the identification of this new prayer of Rabban Gamaliel as the most important prayer of all, *Hat'fillah* — that is, *"The* Prayer" *par excellence.*

The most intriguing version of this theory came from my own teacher, Leon Liebreich, *zikhrono liv'rakhah* ("May his memory be a blessing"), in whose name I repeat it. He taught it to his students year after year but never wrote it down, except in a course syllabus that outlined his ideas. Impressed with the Talmud's insistence that Gamaliel had "put the topics in order," he searched for the links that bind the blessings to each other. Some are obvious: for instance, Blessing 5 ("Repentance") leads naturally to Blessing 6 ("Pardon"). But the connection between others is less evident. Though presumably clear to worshipers in the post-70 era, the organizing principles have been forgotten over the centuries. We have to search them out by looking for allusions to them elsewhere in rabbinic literature.

Liebreich suspected that he could find them in the Rabbis' discussions on theology, so he combed through rabbinic texts looking for instances where allusions to the ideas of the *Amidah* are connected. When he was done, he was able to trace a progression of thought from the first of the intermediary benedictions through to the last one. The entire set of blessings constitutes the most coherent statement we have on the Rabbis' view of redemption.

One final look at the list will demonstrate what Liebreich meant:

4. For wisdom
5. For repentance
6. For forgiveness
7. For deliverance
8. For healing
9. For "years" (agricultural fertility in the Land of Israel)
10. For the gathering of the exiles
11. For justice (the restoration of just judges)
12. For punishment of heretics
13. For reward of the righteous
14. For the rebuilding of Jerusalem
15. For the coming of the messiah
16. For God to hear prayer

Redemption begins with wisdom (#4), not the wisdom of a single person trained in some academic specialty, but the wisdom of all Jews together, who realize the cardinal importance of repentance (#5). Repentance (#5) leads to forgiveness (#6). Believing that a national tragedy like the defeat at the hands of Rome was a consequence of sin, it followed (for the Rabbis) that if our sins are completely forgiven, redemption from Roman rule would result. The *Amidah* is first and foremost about the promise of redemption, a state of Jewish independence from all tyranny, when God and God alone will rule the world in perfect justice. National forgiveness (#6) thus leads inextricably to Israel's redemption (#7), which has a number of stages to it, all of which follow in Blessings 8 to 15.

First, human pain and suffering will cease (#8, the blessing for restored health). Human health is paralleled by a restoration of the health of the Land of Israel, once known as a "land of milk and honey," but by rabbinic times very largely a desert, with even its most arable land, the Galilee, largely destroyed as a result of the war. The benediction for health (#8) therefore leads to #9, a petition for "years" (agricultural fertility in the Land of Israel), a necessary next step in preparation for the most important part of the redemptive promise: the gathering of the exiles (#10), who would have to live off the produce of a restored land. The returning exiles were expected, first and foremost, to replace Roman rule with Jewish judges dedicated to the rule of justice (#11). The first act of the restored Jewish judiciary would be to level punishment upon the heretics who had so troubled Israel during Roman times (#12) and, equally, to reward the just who had suffered so, but who would be vindicated at the end of time (#13). With a land restored to its pristine productivity, ruled by God's just representatives, and populated only by the righteous, Jerusalem would at last be rebuilt (#14) and the scion of David restored to his rightful messianic throne (#15). The Palestinian version of the *Amidah,* the one with only eighteen blessings, combines the last two notions into a single culminating vision, but the idea is the same. Redemption ends with the restoration of the holy city under resumed messianic rule. The entire hope is capped by a final plea for it all to come to pass: "Oh God, hear our prayer" (#16).

Liebreich characterized the entire *Amidah* as Gamaliel's response to the final fall of the Second Jewish Commonwealth, in the year 70. A clearer statement of rabbinic political theory could not be imagined.

The theory is unprovable, of course. Who knows if some other order of blessings might equally be supported by connections located in midrash? But for years, I have taught my teacher's view to class after class of students at the Hebrew Union College, considering it as cogent an explanation as any for Gamaliel's codification of the *Amidah,* according a set order. I have suspected, however, that Professor Liebreich missed the significance of putting David's appearance last on the list without any mention in any blessing of a final messianic war against Rome. All the prophetic speculation on a final bloody battle was obviously passed over in this selective perception of the events that would mark the end of days. Given the disastrous consequences of the war of 70, it was clear why the Rabbis preferred to believe that redemption would come without a military uprising. The rabbinic class, as a whole, had probably resisted the militants' call to arms in the first place, then fought from within to cut the war short and sue for peace, and then been rewarded with authority to determine the next stage of Jewish history from their administrative center at Yavneh. Now Gamaliel was defining the final form of hope that would motivate Jewish minds and hearts for centuries. The messiah would come, all right, but only after all the messianic work was done. Should a messianic pretender arise again with the cry to arms, the proper Jewish response would be to examine the order of events portrayed in the *Amidah,* as a litmus test of determining whether the claim should be honored. Has human suffering come to an end (#8)? Is the Land of Israel again a "land of milk and honey" (#9)? Have the exiles returned, and Israel a place of perfect justice (#10–13)? If not, then, as Rabban Yochanan ben Zakkai (Gamaliel's predecessor) is reputed to have said, "Should you be on your way to plant a tree when the news of the messiah's arrival reaches you, first finish planting your tree, and only then go to meet the messiah." The Jewish way to redemption has historically become the long-term preparation of planting trees and awaiting their fruit to blossom, not the overnight miracle of all-out conflict.

JUDAISM AND THE MESSIAH

Others have now joined Liebreich in seeing the middle blessings of the *Amidah* as a sustained theological statement on redemption. The view that it is a counter-messianic manifesto has been demonstrated by Reuven Kimelman, for instance — a professor at Brandeis University and the most recent detective of the *Amidah* to find his way here. Kimelman reached this conclusion independently by contrasting the *Amidah* with non-rabbinic literature of the first and second centuries. It used to be commonplace to imagine the Rabbis as the dominant interpreters of the times — homogeneous keepers of some orthodox Jewish faith, surrounded on all sides by opponents whose heretical views they fought off successfully again and again. A more accurate picture would be to see many different kinds of Judaism equally prevalent then. The Rabbis were just one stream among many, trying to make sense of the tumultuous era of Roman occupation and the failure of the Temple to last forever. The Jews who lived in the caves of Qumran just south of Jerusalem, and whose views we now have in the Dead Sea Scrolls, were another such community. So too were early Christians, who actually constituted several communities, not just one. Many Jewish voices vied for the right to determine the shape of Judaism during the first and second centuries.

The shrillest voices of all belonged to apocalyptic denouncers of the status quo, who predicted an imminent and bloody messianic conflict as the way to hasten history's end. Such writers usually adopted pseudonyms from the biblical era: Barukh, for instance, the scribe who had written down the prophecies of Jeremiah, or even Ezra himself. The Bible was not yet fully canonized, so it was not clear which writings reflected God's will and which did not. In rabbinic circles, for instance, debate raged over whether to include the Song of Songs, which seemed divine to some, but mere erotic poetry to others. The Book of Esther too was questionable, since the name of God is never mentioned in it. The Jewish canon has 150 psalms, but there were many more around, some of which were put together into a separate book called the Psalms of Solomon but omitted from the Jewish Bible. Several accounts of the Maccabees existed, two of which made it into Christian scripture, but not Jewish. The Rabbis included Proverbs but omitted *The Wisdom of Ben Sirah,* which looks very similar. Our Bible did not so much reflect what Judaism taught as it defined it, by declaring some books to be sacred and others books not. By and large, the Rabbis omitted books with apocalyptic speculation.

They were unable to ignore the need to define a doctrine of the end of days, for that was a matter that every group grappled with, as the mighty Roman Empire seemed sometimes to be coming to an end. "Messiah" *(mashi'ach)* is just a passive participle meaning "anointed"; as a noun, *"the* messiah" *(hamashi'ach)* meant "the anointed one," that is, a ruler appointed by God to administer the divine kingdom that would displace foreign rule once and for all. Most Jewish writers believed in such a figure, therefore, but they differed on his role. The apocalypticists thought he would usher in the kingdom by a mighty act of war. The Rabbis, who remembered the war of 70, saw a second such conflict as anathema. Some of them would flirt with apocalyptic speculation one final time, in the Bar Kochba revolt of 135, which proved to be a the final gasp of militancy. Hadrian quashed the rebellion, killed its leaders, and made Jerusalem a pagan city off-limits for Jews. Ever after, Judaism survived by defining apocalyptic speculation outside the pale.

The *Amidah* reminded Jews of just how much Judaism was *not* a messianic religion, for it relegated the messiah to a mere afterthought of redemption. Deliverance would occur, but only in God's good time and in ways that God alone could know. As the years grew into centuries and Jews lost all military means of rebellion anyway, that message grew slowly irrelevant until eventually it was lost. All over the world, Jews so internalized the view of the Rabbis that they willingly, if not always happily, waited for the end of days to arrive in its own good time, unaided by messianic militarism. The *Amidah* no longer had to preach what Jews knew instinctively, so it never occurred to anyone to see the origins of the *Amidah* in a theological-political message that had saved rabbinic Judaism from becoming a dead-end faith like its apocalyptic rivals.

In our time, however, it seems to me that its anti-messianic message demands restatement. In an age when some extremists have revived apocalyptic militancy in Israel, we need more than ever to recall the conscious decision of Gamaliel's generation to declare active messianism beyond the Jewish ken. Jews do not hasten the messiah; instead, we pray and hope for better days, and we patiently perform *mitzvot*, the little acts of faith by which we slowly move the world along toward history's conclusion.

The Genizah Fragments

How Our Ancestors Prayed in the Ancient Land of Israel

Joel M. Hoffman

This translation of the *Amidah* found in the Cairo Genizah is designed to facilitate comparison with the present-day *Amidah*. Where the two versions contain identical text, the two translations are rendered identically also. However, because the translation of the present-day *Amidah* takes into account stylistic matters sometimes absent from the Genizah version, this translation at times ignores some nuances of the Genizah fragments. A historical approach would have begun with a translation of the Genizah fragments and then turned to our present-day version, whereas we have begun with the current text that everyone knows and then worked backward, at the cost of some of the finer details of what the older Genizah fragments may mean.

We have enhanced the Hebrew with vowels to facilitate reading and with superscript numbers to facilitate comparison with the English translation, but otherwise, the Hebrew appears as it does in the original manuscripts.

OPENING MEDITATION

[1] Adonai, open my lips, that my mouth may declare your praise.

אֲדֹנָי שְׂפָתַי תִּפְתָּח

[1]ה' שְׂפָתַי תִּפְתָּח וּפִי יַגִּיד תְּהִלָּתֶךָ:

BLESSINGS 1 TO 3: BLESSINGS OF PRAISE

BLESSING 1— AVOT: "ANCESTORS"

[1] Blessed are You, Adonai, our God and our ancestors' God, Abraham's God, Isaac's God, and Jacob's God, great, mighty, and revered God, supreme God, master of heaven and earth, our protector and our ancestors' protector, our security in each and every generation. [2] Blessed are You, Adonai, Abraham's protector.

אָבוֹת

[1]בָּרוּךְ אַתָּה י' אֱלֹהֵינוּ וֵאלֹהֵי אֲבוֹתֵינוּ אֱלֹהֵי אַבְרָהָם אֱלֹהֵי יִצְחָק וֵאלֹהֵי יַעֲקֹב הָאֵל הַגָּדוֹל הַגִּבּוֹר וְהַנּוֹרָא אֵל עֶלְיוֹן קוֹנֵה שָׁמַיִם וָאָרֶץ מָגִנֵּינוּ וּמָגֵן אֲבוֹתֵינוּ מִבְטַחֵינוּ בְּכָל דּוֹר וָדוֹר [2]בָּרוּךְ אַתָּה י' מָגֵן אַבְרָהָם:

BLESSING 2— G'VUROT: "GOD'S POWER"

[1] You are mighty, you humble the proud, you are strong, you judge the wicked, and you live forever; [2] You support the dead, cause the wind to blow and bring down the dew, and sustain life giving life to the dead; [3] in the blink of an eye you bring salvation. [4] Blessed are you, Adonai, who gives life to the dead.

גְּבוּרוֹת

[1]אַתָּה גִבּוֹר מַשְׁפִּיל גֵּאִים חָזָק וּמֵדִין עָרִיצִים חֵי עוֹלָמִים [2]מָקִים מֵתִים מֵשִׁיב הָרוּחַ וּמוֹרִיד הַטַּל מְכַלְכֵּל חַיִּים מְחַיֶּה הַמֵּתִים [3]כְּהֶרֶף עַיִן יְשׁוּעָה לָנוּ תַצְמִיחַ [4]בָּרוּךְ אַתָּה י' מְחַיֶּה הַמֵּתִים:

BLESSING 3— K'DUSHAT HASHEM: "SANCTIFICATION OF GOD'S NAME"

[1] Holy are You, and your name is revered; there is no god other than You. [2] Blessed are You, Adonai, the holy God.

קְדוּשַׁת הַשֵּׁם

[1]קָדוֹשׁ אַתָּה וְנוֹרָא שְׁמֶךָ וְאֵין אֱלוֹהַּ מִבַּלְעָדֶיךָ [2]בָּרוּךְ אַתָּה י' הָאֵל הַקָּדוֹשׁ:

BLESSINGS 4 TO 5: BLESSINGS OF PETITION

BLESSING 4— BINAH: *"KNOWLEDGE"*

[1] Favor us, with your knowledge, our father, and with your Torah's understanding and wisdom. [2] Blessed are you, Adonai, who favors people with knowledge.

בִּינָה

יָחָנֵּנוּ אָבִינוּ דֵּיעָה מֵאִתְּךָ וּבִינָה
וְהַשְׂכֵּל מִתּוֹרָתֶךָ ²בָּרוּךְ אַתָּה יְיָ חוֹנֵן
הַדָּעַת:

BLESSING 5— T'SHUVAH: *"REPENTANCE"*

[1] Bring us back to You, Adonai, that we shall return. [2] Renew our days as of old. [3] Blessed are You, Adonai, who takes pleasure in repentance.

תְּשׁוּבָה

יָהֲשִׁיבֵנוּ יְיָ אֵלֶיךָ וְנָשׁוּבָה ²חַדֵּשׁ יָמֵינוּ
כְּקֶדֶם ³בָּרוּךְ אַתָּה יְיָ הָרוֹצֶה בִּתְשׁוּבָה:

BLESSING 6— S'LICHAH: *"FORGIVENESS"*

[1] Forgive us, our father, for we have sinned before You; [2] wipe out and remove our transgressions from before your eyes, for great is your mercy. [3] Blessed are You, Adonai, who is quick to forgive.

סְלִיחָה

יָסְלַח לָנוּ אָבִינוּ כִּי חָטָאנוּ לָךְ ²מְחֵה
וְהַעֲבֵר פְּשָׁעֵינוּ מִנֶּגֶד עֵינֶיךָ כִּי רַבִּים
רַחֲמֶיךָ ³בָּרוּךְ אַתָּה יְיָ הַמַּרְבֶּה לִסְלוֹחַ:

BLESSING 7— G'ULAH: *"DELIVERANCE"*

[1] See our affliction and fight our fight; [2] redeem us for the sake of your name. [3] Blessed are You, Adonai, who redeems Israel.

גְּאוּלָה

יָרְאֵה בְעָנְיֵנוּ וְרִיבָה רִיבֵנוּ ²וּגְאָלֵנוּ
לְמַעַן שְׁמֶךָ ³בָּרוּךְ אַתָּה יְיָ גּוֹאֵל
יִשְׂרָאֵל:

Blessing 8—
R'fu'ah: "Healing"

[1] Heal us, Adonai, from the pains of our heart, and remove sorrow and complaint from among us. [2] Bring healing to our wounds. [3] Blessed are You, Adonai, who heals the sick among his people Israel.

רְפוּאָה

¹רְפָאֵנוּ יְיָ אֱלֹהֵינוּ מִמַּכְאוֹב לִבֵּנוּ וְיָגוֹן וַאֲנָחָה וְהַעֲבֵר מִמֶּנּוּ ²וְהַעֲלֵה רְפוּאָה לְמַכּוֹתֵנוּ ³בָּרוּךְ אַתָּה יְיָ רוֹפֵא חוֹלֵי עַמּוֹ יִשְׂרָאֵל:

Blessing 9—
Shanim: "Years"

[1] Bless this year for us for goodness through its produce, Adonai our God, and quickly bring the year near that ends our exile. [2] Grant dew and rain on the surface of the ground, and eternal abundance from the stores of your goodness, and grant blessing through the work of our hands. [3] Blessed are You, Adonai, who blesses our years.

שָׁנִים

¹בָּרֵךְ עָלֵינוּ יְיָ אֱלֹהֵינוּ אֶת הַשָּׁנָה הַזֹּאת לְטוֹבָה בְּכָל מִינֵי תְבוּאָתָהּ וְקָרֵב מְהֵרָה שְׁנַת קֵץ גְּאוּלָתֵנוּ ²וְתֵן טַל וּמָטָר עַל פְּנֵי הָאֲדָמָה וְשַׂבַּע עוֹלָם מֵאוֹצְרוֹת טוּבֶךָ וְתֵן בְּרָכָה בְּמַעֲשֵׂה יָדֵינוּ ³בָּרוּךְ אַתָּה יְיָ מְבָרֵךְ הַשָּׁנִים:

Blessing 10—
Kibbutz G'luyot: "Gathering the Exiles"

[1] Sound a great shofar for our freedom, and lift up a banner for the gathering of our exiles. [2] Blessed are You, Adonai, who gathers the dispersed among his people Israel.

קִבּוּץ גָּלִיּוֹת

¹תְּקַע בְּשׁוֹפָר גָּדוֹל לְחֵירוּתֵנוּ וְשָׂא נֵס לְקִבּוּץ גָּאֻלִיּוֹתֵינוּ ²בָּרוּךְ אַתָּה יְיָ מְקַבֵּץ נִדְחֵי עַמּוֹ יִשְׂרָאֵל:

Blessing 11—
Mishpat: "Justice"

[1] Restore our judges as in days of old, and our counselors as in former times, and reign over us, You alone. [2] Blessed are You, Adonai, who loves justice.

מִשְׁפָּט

¹הָשִׁיבָה שׁוֹפְטֵנוּ כְּבָרִאשׁוֹנָה וְיוֹעֲצֵינוּ כְּבַתְּחִלָּה וּמְלוֹךְ עָלֵינוּ אַתָּה לְבַדֶּךָ ²בָּרוּךְ אַתָּה יְיָ אוֹהֵב הַמִּשְׁפָּט:

BLESSING 12—
MINIM: "HERETICS"

[1] May there be no hope for apostates, and may You quickly uproot the insolent reign in our day, and may the Christians and heretics instantly perish. [2] May they be erased from the book of life, and may they not be written with the righteous. [3] Blessed are You, Adonai, who humbles the insolent.

BLESSING 13—
TSADIKIM: "THE RIGHTEOUS"

[1] Show compassion to righteous converts, and give us a good reward with those who do your will. [2] Blessed are You, Adonai, who is the trust of the righteous.

BLESSING 14—
Y'RUSHALAYIM V'DAVID:
"JERUSALEM AND DAVID"

[1] Have mercy, Adonai our God, in your great mercy, on Israel your people, and on Jerusalem your city, and on Zion where your presence dwells, and on your palace and on your habitation and on your righteous servant David's kingdom. [2] Blessed are You, Adonai, David's God, who builds Jerusalem.

BLESSING 15—
T'FILLAH: "PRAYER"

[1] Adonai our God, hear the voice of our prayers and have mercy on us, for You are the God who is gracious and merciful. [2] Blessed are You, Adonai, who hears prayer.

מִינִים

לַמְשׁוּמָּדִים אַל תְּהִי תִקְוָה וּמַלְכוּת¹ זָדוֹן מְהֵרָה תְעַקֵּר בְּיָמֵינוּ וְהַנֹּצְרִים וְהַמִּינִים כְּרֶגַע יֹאבֵדוּ ²יִמָּחוּ מִסֵּפֶר הַחַיִּים וְעִם צַדִּיקִים אַל יִכָּתֵבוּ ³בָּרוּךְ אַתָּה יֶי מַכְנִיעַ זֵדִים:

צַדִּיקִים

עַל גֵּירֵי הַצֶּדֶק יֶהֱמוּ רַחֲמֶיךָ וְתֶן לָנוּ¹ שָׂכָר טוֹב עִם עוֹשֵׂי רְצוֹנֶךְ ²בָּרוּךְ אַתָּה יֶי מִבְטַח לַצַּדִּיקִים:

יְרוּשָׁלַיִם וְדָוִד

רַחֵם יֶי אֱלֹהֵינוּ בְּרַחֲמֶיךָ הָרַבִּים עַל¹ יִשְׂרָאֵל עַמֶּךְ וְעַל יְרוּשָׁלַיִם עִירֶךָ וְעַל צִיּוֹן מִשְׁכַּן כְּבוֹדֶךָ וְעַל הֵיכָלֶךְ וְעַל מְעוֹנֶךְ וְעַל מַלְכוּת בֵּית דָּוִד מְשִׁיחַ צִדְקֶךְ ²בָּרוּךְ אַתָּה יֶי אֱלֹהֵי דָוִד בּוֹנֵה יְרוּשָׁלָ͏ִם:

תְּפִלָּה

שְׁמַע יֶי אֱלֹהֵינוּ בְּקוֹל תְּפִלָּתֵינוּ וְרַחֵם¹ עָלֵינוּ כִּי אֵל חַנּוּן וְרַחוּם אָתָּה ²בָּרוּךְ אַתָּה יֶי שׁוֹמֵעַ תְּפִלָּה:

Blessings 16 to 18: Blessings of Thanksgiving

Blessing 16— Avodah: "Sacrificial Service"

[1] Find favor, Adonai our God, and dwell in Zion that You may be served by your servants in Jerusalem. [2] Blessed are You, Adonai, whom we will serve with awe.

Blessing 17— Hoda'ah: "Grateful Acknowledgment"

[1] We gratefully acknowledge You—You are Adonai our God and our ancestors' God— for all the goodness, the kindness, and the mercy that you have shown and done for us and for our ancestors before us, and if we say our step has faltered, your kindness will support us. [2] Blessed are You, whom is it good to gratefully acknowledge.

Blessing 18— Birkat Kohanim: "The Priestly Blessing"

[1] Grant your peace on Israel your people and on your city and on your heritage, and bless all of us as one. [2] Blessed are you, Adonai, who brings peace.

Closing Meditation

[1] May the words of my mouth and the thoughts of my heart be favorable before You, Adonai, my rock and my redeemer.

עֲבוֹדָה

¹רְצֵה יְיָ אֱלֹהֵינוּ וּשְׁכוֹן בְּצִיּוֹן וְיַעַבְדוּךָ עֲבָדֶיךָ בִּירוּשָׁלַ͏ִם ²בָּרוּךְ אַתָּה יְיָ שֶׁאוֹתְךָ בְּיִרְאָה נַעֲבוֹד:

הוֹדָאָה

¹מוֹדִים אֲנַחְנוּ לָךְ אַתָּה הוּא יְיָ אֱלֹהֵינוּ וֵאלֹהֵי אֲבוֹתֵינוּ עַל כָּל הַטּוֹבוֹת הַחֶסֶד וְהָרַחֲמִים שֶׁגְּמַלְתָּנוּ וְשֶׁעָשִׂיתָ עִמָּנוּ וְעִם אֲבוֹתֵינוּ מִלְּפָנֵינוּ וְאִם אָמַרְנוּ מָטָה רַגְלֵינוּ חַסְדְּךָ יְיָ יִסְעָדֵינוּ ²בָּרוּךְ אַתָּה יְיָ הַטּוֹב לְךָ לְהוֹדוֹת:

בִּרְכַּת כֹּהֲנִים

¹שִׂים שְׁלוֹמֶךָ עַל יִשְׂרָאֵל עַמֶּךָ וְעַל עִירֶךָ וְעַל נַחֲלָתֶךָ וּבָרְכֵנוּ כּוּלָּנוּ כְּאֶחָד ²בָּרוּךְ אַתָּה יְיָ עוֹשֶׂה הַשָּׁלוֹם:

יִהְיוּ לְרָצוֹן

¹יִהְיוּ לְרָצוֹן אִמְרֵי פִי וְהֶגְיוֹן לִבִּי לְפָנֶיךָ יְיָ צוּרִי וְגוֹאֲלִי:

Introduction to the Commentaries

How to Look for Meaning in the Prayers

Lawrence A. Hoffman

THE ART OF JEWISH READING

I remember the day I looked at a manuscript of a prayer book that no one could identify. It had been smuggled out of Russia, then the Soviet Union, and was obviously the liturgy for Rosh Hashanah, but who had written it, and when? It was handwritten, so the style told us much, but in addition, someone had written marginal notes in another handwriting, and yet a third person had written comments to the comments — a third unknown scholar of years gone by whose name we wanted to rescue from oblivion.

Standing before the massive volume, I reflected on the sheer joy of studying a traditional Jewish text. I had seen printed versions before, but never a handwritten instance. What a wonderful habit we Jews developed once upon a time: writing a text in the middle of the page and then filling up the margins with commentaries. Every page becomes a cross-cut through Jewish history. Jewish Bibles come that way; so do the Talmud, the Mishnah, and the codes. We never read just the text. We always read it with the way other people have read it.

To be a Jewish reader, then, is to join the ranks of the millions of readers who came before us, leaving their comments in the margins, the way animals leave tracks in the woods. Go deep into the forest, and you will come across deer runs, for example: paths to water sources, carved out by hundreds of thousands of deer over time. The deer do not just inhabit the forest; they are part of the forest. They change the forest's contours as they live there, just as the forest changes them, by offering shelter, food, and water. There is no virgin forest, really; it is an ecosystem, a balance between the vegetation and the animals who live there.

So too, there are no virgin texts. They too are ecosystems, sustaining millions of readers over time. When we read our classic texts, we tread the paths of prior readers, in search of spiritual nourishment. *My People's Prayer Book* is therefore not just the Siddur text; it is the text as read by prominent readers from among the people. You are invited to share our path and even to break new ground yourself, passing on to others your own marginal notes, should you wish.

The Hebrew Text and Translation

For the Hebrew text, we have chosen the Ashkenazi edition favored by the renowned historian of the liturgy, the late E. D. Goldschmidt, perhaps the greatest master of liturgical text who ever lived. Born in Germany, later a refugee from the Nazis, Goldschmidt moved to Israel, where he assiduously collected and compared hundreds of manuscripts for the Siddur, to arrive at an authoritative version as free of scribal and printing error as possible.

The Goldschmidt text was then translated by Joel Hoffman so as to reproduce not only the content of the original Hebrew, but also its tone, register, and style, and to bring to modern readers the same experience (to the greatest extent possible) that the original authors would have conveyed with their words. In terms of content, we assume that, by and large, words have meaning only to the extent that they contribute to sentences and concepts — as, for example, "by and large," which has nothing to do with "by" or "large." We try to reproduce a tone and register similar to the original text: formal, but not archaic; prose or poetry, depending on the Hebrew. Where the Hebrew uses obscure words, we try to do the same, and where it uses common idiom, we try to use equally common idiom. Parallel structure and other similar literary devices found in the Hebrew are replicated in the English translation. We have not doctored the text to make it more palatable to modern consciousness. Blatant sexisms are retained, for instance, wherever we think the author intended them. We depend upon our commentaries to bridge the gap between the translation of the original and our modern sensibilities.

The Commentaries

The heart and soul of *Minhag Ami* is its choice of commentaries that surround the prayer book text. Translator Joel Hoffman explains his choice of words, provides alternatives, and compares his own translation with a selection of the most popularly used prayer books in the English-speaking world. Mark Brettler comments particularly on the way the Bible is embedded in the Siddur. Marcia Falk and Elliot Dorff provide theological reflections on what the prayers might mean, should mean, could mean, cannot mean, or have to mean (even if we wish they didn't). Judith Hauptman adds insight from the world of the Talmud and the rabbinic tradition that it spawned. Daniel Landes gives us the Halakhah of prayer, the rules and traditions by which this sacred liturgical drama has traditionally been carried out. Larry Kushner and Nehemia Polen supply a kabbalistic commentary, adding wisdom from the world of Chasidic masters. David Ellenson surveys liberal prayer books of the last 200 years to see how their writers agonized over attempts to update this book of Jewish books for modern times. My own contribution is a summary of what we know about the historical development of the liturgy: when prayers were written, what they meant in the context of their day — and to some extent, what later generations saw in them. I also provide some of the interesting textual variants between one tradition and another, especially between Sefardi tradition and Ashkenazi tradition (as represented here).

Some of the commentaries require some comments in advance.

Translator Joel Hoffman had to make a judicious selection of translations to compare with his own. For an Orthodox version, he relied on Philip Birnbaum's classic (1949) *Daily Prayer Book: Hasiddur Hashalem* ("Birnbaum") but looked also at *Siddur Kol Ya'akov* ("Artscroll," 1984). American Reform is represented by the *Gates of Prayer* (1975) and revisions since. Conservative Jews will find their *Siddur Sim Shalom* (1985) and Reconstructionists their *Kol Haneshamah* (1994) cited. Hoffman compared British liturgy too: *Forms of Prayer* (1977) from the Reform Synagogues of Great Britain and both *Service of the Heart* (1967) and *Siddur Lev Chadash* (1995) from the Union of Liberal and Progressive Synagogues. For biblical citations, he consulted the Jewish Publication Society Bible ("JPS") but compared it with the New Revised Standard Version of 1989 ("NRSV") and *The Five Books of Moses,* by Everett Fox ("Fox," 1995).

My own historical commentary had to deal with the fact that the Goldschmidt translation is only for Ashkenazi Jews, more specifically, the Ashkenazi version common in eastern Europe, often under the influence of Elijah ben Solomon of Vilna, known as the Vilna Gaon (1720–1797). To balance the picture, I cite "Sefardi" practice also.

But the word "Sefardi" has two distinct meanings.

Nowadays, it usually describes Jews whose liturgy was influenced by the specific brand of Kabbalah initiated by Isaac Luria (the "Ari"), in sixteenth-century Palestine. Goldschmidt compiled a scientific edition of this variant too, and I use that to represent "Sefardi practice." But "Sefardi" can also mean the old Spanish-Portuguese custom carried by Jews from Spain in 1492 and then brought to the Netherlands, whence it moved to England (among other places) and eventually to America as well. When I want to draw attention to this Spanish-Portuguese custom, I call it that, using as my guide the standard work published in England at the turn of the century by

Moses Gaster, *The Book of Prayer and Order of Service According to the Custom of the Spanish and Portuguese Jews.*

I try also to cite early prayer books of our tradition and commentators from the Middle Ages, as well as the Genizah fragments, manuscripts telling us how Jews prayed in Eretz Yisrael prior to the Crusades.

David Ellenson was asked to fill in the gap caused by the fact that even the standard Ashkenazi and Sefardi versions hardly represent the majority of Jews today. As Jews have evolved, so have our modern movements, each with its own version of what our forebears once considered normative. The last two hundred years have witnessed the composition of countless Jewish prayer books, and Ellenson surveys the most prominent of these for instances where the traditional text evoked debate.

For historical reasons, many are Reform, beginning with the *Hamburg Temple Prayer Book,* published in 1819 and 1841, the very first efforts to make the content of the classical liturgy comport with modern ideas. Ellenson's survey of the nineteenth century also included *Seder T'filah D'var Yom B'Yomo* (1854; republished 1870) by Rabbi Abraham Geiger, the preeminent leader of German Reform.

For early American liturgies, he turned to Rabbis Isaac Mayer Wise and David Einhorn. Wise's *Minhag America* (1857) was the most popular prayer book of its day, and Einhorn's *Olath Tamid* (1856) became the prototype for the *Union Prayer Book,* which was adopted in 1895 as the official liturgy for North American Reform Jews. In 1975, *Gates of Prayer* replaced the *Union Prayer Book,* and in 1996 the latest in a series of gender-inclusive editions of *Gates of Prayer* appeared. All three of these official movement books are cited here.

Among the non-American prayer books of the late 1900s, Ellenson made extensive use of *Ha'avodah Shebalev,* adopted by the Israeli Progressive Movement in 1982, and *Siddur Lev Chadash,* published by the Union of Progressive and Liberal Synagogues in London in 1995.

These Reform prayer books are supplemented by several Conservative and Reconstructionist volumes. The former include various prayer books produced since 1958 by the Rabbinical Assembly of the Conservative Movement, but especially the 1985 *Siddur Sim Shalom.* Since Conservative worship is in Hebrew, however, and since the Hebrew is generally unchanged, while the vernacular equivalent is usually a literal translation of it, Ellenson has less to say about Conservative books than he does of Reform volumes, where both Hebrew and English tend to vary widely. However, he has made careful use of the latest Conservative Siddur to appear in Israel: *Siddur Va'ani T'filati* (1998). Precisely because Hebrew *is* the vernacular in Israel, this prayer book offers insight into contemporary issues of belief within Israeli Conservative Judaism. The Reconstructionist Movement, which, like Reform, has tended toward considerable liturgical creativity, is represented primarily by *Kol Haneshamah,* published in 1996, but from time to time Ellenson discusses earlier work, especially by Mordecai Kaplan, the founder of the movement.

Ellenson gives priority to denominationally associated prayer books because they have been most widely disseminated but does include some others, notably *The Book of Blessings,* authored in 1996 by Jewish feminist Marcia Falk, one of our commentators here. He uses more liberal prayer books than Orthodox ones, because liberal books have been more readily altered to reflect modern ideas about God, the universe, and human nature. Orthodox volumes are cited here, but references to them are limited.

The halakhic commentary by Daniel Landes was included not just to explain how prayers should be said. Even without that abiding practical concern, it would have found its way here because Halakhah (Jewish law) is essential to Judaism. Frequently misunderstood as mere legalism, it is actually more akin to Jewish poetry, in that it is the height of Jewish writing, the pinnacle of Jewish concern, sheer joy to create or to ponder. It describes, explains, and debates Jewish responsibility, yet is saturated with spiritual importance. Jewish movements can be differentiated by their approach to Halakhah, but Halakhah matters to them all.

A short overview of its history and some of its vocabulary will be helpful in advance.

The topic of Halakhah is the proper performance of the commandments, said to number 613, and divided into positive and negative ones, numbering 248 and 365, respectively. Strictly speaking, commandments derived directly from Torah *(mid'o-ra'ita)* are of a higher order than those rooted only in rabbinic ordinance (called *mid'rabbanan),* but all are binding.

The earliest stratum of Halakhah is found primarily in the Mishnah, a code of Jewish practice promulgated about 200 C.E. The Mishnah is the foundation for further rabbinic discussion in Palestine and Babylonia, which culminated in the two talmuds, one from each center, and called the Palestinian Talmud (or the Yerushalmi), and the Babylonian Talmud (or the Babli). While dates for both are uncertain, the former is customarily dated to about 400 C.E., and the latter between 550 and 650.

With the canonization of the Babli, Jewish law developed largely from commentary to the talmuds and from responsa, applications of talmudic and other precedents to actual cases. These are still the norm today, but they were initiated by authorities in Babylonia called Geonim (sing., Gaon) from about 750 to shortly after 1000. By the turn of the millennium, other schools had developed in North Africa particularly, but also in western Europe. Authorities in these centers are usually called Rishonim ("first" or "early" [ones]) until the sixteenth century, when they become known as Acharonim ("last"or "later" [ones]).

The first law code is geonic (from about 750), but it was the Rishonim who really inaugurated the trend toward codifying, giving us many works, including three major ones that are widely cited here: the *Mishneh Torah,* by Maimonides (Moses ben Maimon, 1135–1204), born in Spain, but active most of his life in Egypt; the *Tur,* by Jacob ben Asher (1275–1340), son of another giant, Asher ben Yechiel, who had moved to Spain from Germany, allowing Ashkenazi and Sefardi practice to intertwine in his son's magnum opus; and the *Shulchan Arukh,* by Joseph Caro (1488–1575), who is technically the first generation of the Acharonim, but who wrote influential commentaries on both the *Mishneh Torah* and the *Tur* before composing what would become the most widely used legal corpus ever.

The halakhic commentary in this volume draws on all of the above. References to the *Tur* and the *Shulchan Arukh* usually are to the section called *Orach Chayim,* "The Way of Life," which contains most of the Halakhah on prayer and is shortened here to "O. Ch." The other references are either to standard halakhic works or to the authorities who authored them. In keeping with Jewish tradition, we refer to the authorities by acronyms that are formed by combining their title (usually, Rabbi) and their names, or by other titles that history has bestowed upon them. A list of the books and authorities follows:

Abudarham (David Abudarham [late thirteenth to fourteenth century], Spain)

Bach (short for *Bayit Chadash,* commentary to the *Tur* by Joel Sirkes [1561–1640], Poland)

Ben Ish Chai (The Chakham Joseph Chaim [1832–1909], Baghdad)

Chida (Chaim Joseph David Azulai [1724–1806], Jerusalem)

Gra (The Vilna Gaon, Rabbi Elijah of Vilna [1720–1797], Lithuania)

Har Zvi (Zvi Pesach Frank [d. 1961], Jerusalem)

Iggrot Moshe (Moshe Feinstein [1895–1986], Russia and New York)

Maharil (Jacob ben Moses Moelin [1360–1427], Germany)

Magen Avraham (commentary to the *Shulchan Arukh* by Abraham Gombiner [1637–1683], Poland)

Mishnah B'rurah (by Israel Meir HaCohen Kagan [1838–1933], Poland)

Rashi (Solomon ben Isaac [1040–1105], France)

Rashba (Solomon ben Abraham Adret [1235–1310], Spain)

Rema (Moses Isserles [1530–1575], Poland)

Riva (Isaac ben Asher [d. 1130], Germany)

Rivash (Isaac ben Sheshet Perfet [1326–1408], Spain)

Sefer Charedim (R. Eleazar ben Moses Azikri [1533–1600], Safed, Israel)

Sefer Chasidim (by Judah Hachasid [d. 1217] Germany)

Taz (short for *Turei Zahav,* commentary to the *Shulchan Arukh* by David ben Samuel Halevi [1586–1667], Poland)

Torat Habayit (commentary by Moses ben Nachman, better known as Nachmanides [1194–1270], Spain)

We have gone out of our way to provide a panoply of scholars, all students of the prayerbook text and all committed to a life of prayer, but representative of left, right, and center in the Jewish world. They represent all of us, all of *Am Yisrael,* all of those God had in mind when God said to Ezekiel (34:30) "They shall know that I, Adonai their God, am with them, and they, the House of Israel, are My People." Unabashedly scholarly and religious at one and the same time, *Minhag Ami,* "A Way of Prayer for My People," will be deemed a success if it provides the spiritual insight required to fulfill yet another prophecy (Isa. 52:6), that through our prayers,

> My People (ami) may know my name
> That they may know, therefore, in that day,
> That I, the One who speaks,
> Behold! Here I am.

1 Opening Meditation
אֲדֹנָי שְׂפָתַי תִּפְתָּח

1 Adonai, open my lips that my mouth
may declare your praise.

אֲֽדֹנָי שְׂפָתַי תִּפְתָּח וּפִי יַגִּיד תְּהִלָּתֶֽךָ.[1]

BRETTLER (BIBLE)

"Adonai, open my lips" Ps. 51:17, recited by David after being confronted by Nathan the prophet about his affair with Bathsheba. Its invocation here establishes the absolute dependence of human beings (who are fundamentally sinful) upon a beneficent God (see Ps. 51:7 — "I was brought forth in iniquity; my mother conceived me in sin") and the role of prayer as surpassing the efficacy of sacrifice (see v. 19: "True sacrifice to God is a contrite spirit; God, you will not despise a contrite and crushed heart").

———◆———

DORFF (THEOLOGY)

"Adonai, open my lips that my mouth may declare your praise" While we commonly think that prayer happens solely at the initiative of the person praying, this verse from Ps. 51:17, placed at the beginning of the *Amidah* — what the Rabbis call "The Prayer" — strongly proclaims another message. We are, as it were, dumb when we want to address God. We need God's help in what we are about to do. Prayer, in other words, is not the utterances of the person praying, as subject, to God, as object. Prayer is, rather, the interaction of the person praying with God. For prayer to work, God has to want to help us pray as much as we must want to pray.

———◆———

OPENING MEDITATION

אֲדֹנָי שְׂפָתַי תִּפְתָּח

[1] Adonai, open my lips that my mouth may declare your praise.

ELLENSON (MODERN LITURGIES)

"Adonai, open my lips" Many non-Orthodox prayer books, beginning with the classics, *Olath Tamid* of David Einhorn and *Minhag America* of Isaac Mayer Wise, but including also the *Union Prayer Book*, classical Reconstructionist liturgy, and *The Book of Blessings* by Marcia Falk, omit this line. Some consider it *(p. 54)*

FALK (FEMINISM)

"Adonai, open my lips that my mouth may declare your praise" What does it mean to ask that one's lips be opened to speech — opened, that is, not by the self but by an Other?

In her book *The Journey Is Home*, feminist theologian Nelle Morton tells a moving story about a woman who is "heard to speech" by a supportive community. In Morton's recounting, a reluctant *(p. 54)*

HAUPTMAN (TALMUD)

"Adonai, open my lips that my mouth may declare your praise" Printed right before the beginning of the *Amidah*, usually in small letters, is the verse "Adonai, open my lips that my mouth may declare your praise" (Ps. 51:17). Following the *Amidah* is a similarly inspirational verse, "May the words of my mouth and the thoughts of my heart be favorable before You, Adonai, my rock and redeemer" (Ps. 19:15). This bracketing of the *Amidah* with verses originated with R. Yohanan (Talmud Bavli, Ber. 4b; Yerushalmi Ber. 4:4, 8a). *(p. 54)*

KUSHNER & POLEN (Chasidism)

"Adonai, open my lips that my mouth may declare your praise" It seems odd that as a prelude to the *amidah*—a bouquet of prayers of praise, petition, and thanksgiving, the most intensely conversational script of the entire Siddur — someone thought to throw in Psalm 51:17: "God, open my lips so that my mouth may declare Your praise."

Wouldn't it make more sense to say something like, "Here I am God, ready to begin our conversation," or "Permit me to introduce myself," or "I know we haven't always seen eye to eye on certain things," something that would accentuate the dialogic nature of what will follow. For there to be a conversation, an intercession, there must be two discrete parties. It takes two to tango.

In much (but not all) of the Hebrew Bible and the Siddur, God and people are separate, *(p. 55)*

LANDES (Halakhah)

"Adonai, open my lips" The connection between the *G'ullah* (the blessing that completes the prior rubric, known as the *Sh'ma* and Its Blessings — see Volume 1, *The Sh'ma and Its Blessings*) and the *Amidah* cannot be broken. One can say "Amen" to the reader's recitation of the *G'ullah,* for it is considered an integral part of the blessing itself (and, therefore, not a real interruption), but we try to say the blessing with the reader, so as to obviate the need to say "Amen" separately. In addition, *(p. 56)*

L. HOFFMAN (History)

PS. 51:17 PROVIDES A SILENT MEDITATIVE MOMENT, BEFORE THE ACTUAL BLESSINGS OF THE AMIDAH BEGIN. THE FIRST THREE BLESSINGS, KNOWN TRADITIONALLY AS BLESSINGS OF PRAISE, THEN COMMENCE.

"Adonai, open my lips that my mouth may declare your praise" Despite the second-century ruling against inserting anything at all between the prayer preceding the morning *Amidah* and the *Amidah* itself, it became customary to preface the *Amidah* with this quotation from Psalms. The innovation is talmudic, and its apparent disregard for the earlier regulation led to considerable commentary through *(p. 56)*

¹ אֲדֹנָי שְׂפָתַי תִּפְתָּח וּפִי יַגִּיד תְּהִלָּתֶךָ.

J. HOFFMAN (Translation)

"Open my lips" In the Hebrew, "lips" precedes "open" and is thereby emphasized, in a way that English grammar cannot capture.

"That my mouth may declare your praise [t'hillah]" The Hebrew reads (literally), *"and* my mouth will declare. . . ." But Hebrew often uses conjunction where English prefers subordination. Other possibilities include "and let . . ." (*Kol Haneshamah* [Reconstructionist]) or "and my lips will . . ." (*Siddur Sim Shalom* [Conservative]). Birnbaum, *Kol Haneshamah* (Reconstructionist), *Siddur Sim Shalom* (Conservative), and *Service of the Heart* (Liberal, England) all agree with "praise." For *t'hillah, Gates of Prayer (p. 56)*

ELLENSON (MODERN LITURGIES)

extraneous. Others, however, whose naturalistic theology posits an impersonal deity, reject the reference to a personal God who hears supplicatory prayer. Both editions of the *Hamburg Temple Prayer Book* (1819 and 1841) retained it, however, and it has been reinserted in most modern liberal liturgies, including the American *Gates of Prayer,* the British *Siddur Lev Chadash,* the Israeli *Ha'avodah Shebalev,* and the current Reconstructionist *Kol Haneshamah.* The Hamburg authors were conservative regarding change and tended to keep things in if they had no serious objection. Modern decisions to restore it demonstrate the extent to which people have internalized a personalistic faith once again.

———◆———

FALK (FEMINISM)

participant in a women's conference is given an extraordinary kind of attention — a wholly attuned, uninterrupted listening — that allows her to break through her reticence and tell her own (as it happens, painful) story. Reversing the familiar model of speech as stimulus to hearing, Morton creates a new paradigm: hearing as stimulus to speech. This is, as Morton puts it, "a totally new understanding of hearing," hearing that can indeed open the lips. Is this, then, what the prayer asks of God in the opening line of the *Amidah?*

Perhaps. But in Morton's paradigm, the purpose of "hearing someone to speech" is not to evoke praise — indeed, it is not to elicit any particular predetermined outcome at all. Rather, Morton calls for a respectful receptivity that allows even one who is reticent to fully express *her own truths.*

I would have to say that Morton's story is more resonant for me than the deferential statement that opens the *Amidah.* Even if we view this statement as a request for God's aid or a declaration of one's intentions — rather than as a promise or a bargain being struck — it still rings false. For though one may be praying with fixed words, one can never predict or anticipate the true prayer of the heart — nor, it would seem, should one strive to. The sacrality that I sometimes experience in deep silence is one that allows truth to be seen and heard and recognized — in whatever form it takes.

———◆———

HAUPTMAN (TALMUD)

Although he gave no rationale for appending these deeply religious passages from Psalms, it seems clear that he wanted to enclose the rabbinic set of petitions with biblical verses on the subject of heartfelt prayer and its acceptance by God. These additions would "force" God to listen. It should be noted that a different sage, R. Judan, recited both verses before saying the *Amidah.* This, too, makes good sense.

The first verse, "open my lips," is a prayer for successful prayer, a request that the supplicant not stumble in their attempt to sing God's praises, and, as a result, fail to "grab God's ear." It is saying, in a self-effacing way, that the one who prays intends to praise God but may not find the appropriate words to do so. Petitioners may be so awed by coming into the presence of God that they find themselves tongue-tied. This verse expresses the hope that the words flow smoothly.

The second verse, "May the words of my mouth . . ." is the closing line of Psalm 19, a poem about the magnificence of nature and the excellence of God's Torah. This passage, too, is a prayer for successful prayer, a request that the petitions just uttered be accepted and answered. Over time, this second verse was incorporated into a closing paragraph, also of Talmudic origin (Bavli, Ber. 17a). We are told that when Mar, the son of Ravina, finished praying the *Amidah* he would append yet another petition, as we still do today, "My God, guard my tongue from evil . . ." and conclude with the verse "May the words of my mouth . . ." as recommended by R. Yohanan.

All of these supplements to the *Amidah* are written in the first person singular and not the first person plural, the mode of most paragraphs of the *Amidah* itself. They thus add a personal dimension to the *Amidah,* allowing the petitioner to feel more immediately involved in the prayer.

———◆———

KUSHNER & POLEN (CHASIDISM)

distinct, discrete, autonomous, independent and apart from one another. God says this, we say that. God does this, we do that. God's there, we're here. The energy of the whole thing comes precisely from our being separate from one another. So why begin our personal prayers with a denial of that mutual autonomy and free will?

The Psalm says, "God, would you please open my mouth." Hey, who's working my mouth anyway, me or God? Who's praising God, me or God? What's going on here?

What's going on here is another spiritual paradigm, one in which God and people are not only *not* distinct from one another but are literally *within* one another. God is the ocean and we are the waves. In the words of the Chasidic maxim, *"Alles ist Gott,* it's all God." My mouth is God's mouth. My praises are God's words. In the teaching of Rabbi Kalynomos Kalmish Shapira of Piesetzna (who perished in the Warsaw ghetto), "Not only does God hear our prayers, God prays them through us as well!"

The words of the *amidah* that will follow may *sound* like they come from me but in truth they come from a higher source. Prayer may ultimately be an exercise for helping us let go of our egos, hopelessly anchored to this world where one person is discrete from another and from God, and soar to the heavens where we realize there is a holy One to all being and that we have been an expression of it all along. "God, open my lips so that my mouth may declare Your praise."

———◆———

OPENING MEDITATION

LANDES (HALAKHAH)

we say, "Ado-nai, open my lips . . .," before commencing the *Amidah*, but we do it in an undertone. That practice is permitted because it was established by the Rabbis, and technically, it is considered an attachment to the *G'ullah*, not a separate liturgical entity that would constitute a separation between the *G'ullah* and the *Amidah*, the two of which belong together *(Turei Zahav* 101:2).

Say the sentence in an undertone while taking three short steps backward, beginning with the right foot, and then three steps forward, as if approaching a sovereign.

———◆———

L. HOFFMAN (HISTORY)

the centuries. This simple biblical line must contain a message so important that the Rabbis elected to include it.

Indeed, there is a message here, and it is astonishingly bold. The full citation from Psalms, of which this is but the beginning, is, "Adonai, open my lips that my mouth may declare your praise; for you have no delight in sacrifice. If I were to give a burnt offering, You would not be pleased" (Ps. 51:17–18). It is well known that the Rabbis proclaimed the *Amidah* to be the equivalent of the defunct sacrificial cult. Here, by innuendo, the Rabbis go even farther: the *Amidah* is not just equal to the sacrificial system that ceased with the Temple's destruction in 70; it is even better. God would not accept a sacrifice even if we were to offer it, whereas the words of our mouth are always acceptable on high. According to the Midrash, Israel said to God, "We are impoverished now that we cannot offer sacrifices." God answered, "I seek words from you now, as it is written, 'Take words with You when you return to God'" (Hos. 14:2).

So great is the power of words that Jewish philosophy customarily categorized human beings as *m'daber*, that is, the sole creation whose distinctive capacity is speech. As we open the *Amidah* with a prayer to use our speech wisely, so too we end it with such a hope. The final meditation reads, "My God, guard my tongue from evil, and my lips from speaking deceit." With speech we may curse or bless, slander or praise, hurt or heal. The Rabbis have instructed us to bracket the *Amidah* with the wish that we use the power of words only for good.

———◆———

J. HOFFMAN (TRANSLATION)

(Reform) offers "glory," perhaps for prosodic reasons: their translation may be sung to the same melody as the Hebrew.

————————— ◆ ◆ ◆ —————————

2 | *The* Amidah

עֲמִידָה

A. Blessings of Praise

1. *Avot* ("Ancestors")

¹ **B**lessed are You, Adonai, our God and our ancestors' God: Abraham's God, Isaac's God, and Jacob's God, great, mighty, and revered God, supreme God, who acts most piously, who is master of everything, who remembers the piety of our ancestors, and who brings a redeemer to their descendants for the sake of his name in love.

[From Rosh Hashanah to Yom Kippur, add:

² Remember us for life, our king who delights in life, and write us in the book of life, for your sake, our living God.]

³ Our king helps and saves and protects! ⁴ Blessed are You, Adonai, Abraham's protector.

2. *G'vurot* ("God's Power")

¹ **Y**ou are forever mighty, Adonai: giving life to the dead, You are a mighty savior.

[From Sh'mini Atseret to the first day of Passover, add:

² You cause the wind to blow and you cause the rain to fall.

אֲבוֹת

¹ בָּרוּךְ אַתָּה יְיָ אֱלֹהֵינוּ וֵאלֹהֵי אֲבוֹתֵינוּ אֱלֹהֵי אַבְרָהָם אֱלֹהֵי יִצְחָק וֵאלֹהֵי יַעֲקֹב הָאֵל הַגָּדוֹל הַגִּבּוֹר וְהַנּוֹרָא אֵל עֶלְיוֹן גּוֹמֵל חֲסָדִים טוֹבִים וְקֹנֵה הַכֹּל וְזוֹכֵר חַסְדֵי אָבוֹת וּמֵבִיא גוֹאֵל לִבְנֵי בְנֵיהֶם לְמַעַן שְׁמוֹ בְּאַהֲבָה.

[From Rosh Hashanah to Yom Kippur, add:

² זָכְרֵנוּ לְחַיִּים. מֶלֶךְ חָפֵץ בַּחַיִּים. וְכָתְבֵנוּ בְּסֵפֶר הַחַיִּים. לְמַעַנְךָ אֱלֹהִים חַיִּים.]

³ מֶלֶךְ עוֹזֵר וּמוֹשִׁיעַ וּמָגֵן. ⁴ בָּרוּךְ אַתָּה יְיָ מָגֵן אַבְרָהָם.

גְּבוּרוֹת

¹ אַתָּה גִּבּוֹר לְעוֹלָם אֲדֹנָי. מְחַיֵּה מֵתִים אַתָּה. רַב לְהוֹשִׁיעַ.

[From Sh'mini Atseret to the first day of Passover, add:

² מַשִּׁיב הָרוּחַ וּמוֹרִיד הַגָּשֶׁם.

3 You bring down the dew.]

4 You sustain life with kindness, giving life to the dead with great mercy, supporting the fallen, healing the sick, and freeing the captive, and keeping faith with sleepers in the dust. 5 Who is like You, master of might, and who resembles You, a King who causes death and causes life, and causes salvation to flourish!

[From Rosh Hashanah to Yom Kippur, add:

6 Who is like you, father of mercy, who in mercy remembers his creatures for life!]

7 You faithfully give life to the dead. 8 Blessed are You, Adonai, who gives life to the dead.

3. K'DUSHAT HASHEM ("SANCTIFICATION OF GOD'S NAME")

[This version is said individually during the period of silent prayer that precedes the repetition by the prayer leader:]

1 You are holy and your name is holy, and holy beings will praise You every day forever. *2 Blessed are You, Adonai, the holy God.

*[*From Rosh Hashanah to Yom Kippur,
say instead:*

3 Blessed are You, Adonai, the holy king.]

‪מוֹרִיד הַטָּל]‬ ³

‪מְכַלְכֵּל חַיִּים בְּחֶסֶד מְחַיֵּה מֵתִים‬ ⁴
‪בְּרַחֲמִים רַבִּים. סוֹמֵךְ נוֹפְלִים וְרוֹפֵא‬
‪חוֹלִים וּמַתִּיר אֲסוּרִים. וּמְקַיֵּם אֱמוּנָתוֹ‬
‪לִישֵׁנֵי עָפָר. מִי כָמוֹךָ בַּעַל גְּבוּרוֹת וּמִי‬ ⁵
‪דּוֹמֶה לָּךְ. מֶלֶךְ מֵמִית וּמְחַיֶּה וּמַצְמִיחַ‬
‪יְשׁוּעָה.‬

‪[From Rosh Hashanah to Yom Kippur, add:]‬

‪מִי כָמוֹךָ אַב הָרַחֲמִים זוֹכֵר יְצוּרָיו‬ ⁶
‪לַחַיִּים בְּרַחֲמִים.]‬

‪וְנֶאֱמָן אַתָּה לְהַחֲיוֹת מֵתִים. בָּרוּךְ אַתָּה‬ ⁷ ⁸
‪יְיָ מְחַיֵּה הַמֵּתִים.‬

‪קְדוּשַׁת הַשֵּׁם‬

‪אַתָּה קָדוֹשׁ וְשִׁמְךָ קָדוֹשׁ וּקְדוֹשִׁים‬ ¹
‪בְּכָל־יוֹם יְהַלְלוּךָ סֶּלָה. *בָּרוּךְ אַתָּה יְיָ‬ ²
‪הָאֵל הַקָּדוֹשׁ.‬

*[*From Rosh Hashanah to Yom Kippur,
say instead:*

‪בָּרוּךְ אַתָּה יְיָ הַמֶּלֶךְ הַקָּדוֹשׁ.]‬ ³

[This version is reserved for the public repetition of the Amidah by the prayer leader:]

[Prayer leader]

4 Let us sanctify your name on earth, as it is sanctified in the heavens on high, as written by your prophet, "They called out one to another:

⁴ נְקַדֵּשׁ אֶת־שִׁמְךָ בָּעוֹלָם כְּשֵׁם שֶׁמַּקְדִּישִׁים אוֹתוֹ בִּשְׁמֵי מָרוֹם כַּכָּתוּב עַל יַד נְבִיאֶךָ וְקָרָא זֶה אֶל זֶה וְאָמַר.

[Congregation and Prayer leader]

5 'Holy, holy, holy is the Lord of hosts. The whole earth is full of his glory.'

⁵ קָדוֹשׁ קָדוֹשׁ קָדוֹשׁ יְיָ צְבָאוֹת מְלֹא כָל־הָאָרֶץ כְּבוֹדוֹ.

[Prayer leader]

6 From across the way they offer blessing:

⁶ לְעֻמָּתָם בָּרוּךְ יֹאמֵרוּ.

[Congregation and Prayer leader]

'The glory of Adonai is blessed from his place.' "

בָּרוּךְ כְּבוֹד יְיָ מִמְּקוֹמוֹ.

[Prayer leader]

7 In your holy scriptures it is written:

⁷ וּבְדִבְרֵי קָדְשְׁךָ כָּתוּב לֵאמֹר.

[Congregation and Prayer leader]

"Adonai will reign forever, your God, Zion, for all generations. Halleluyah."

יִמְלֹךְ יְיָ לְעוֹלָם אֱלֹהַיִךְ צִיּוֹן לְדֹר וָדֹר הַלְלוּיָה.

[Prayer leader]

8 For all generations we will tell of your greatness and for all of eternity proclaim your holiness. 9 Your praise, our God, will never depart our mouths, for You are a sovereign God, great and holy. *10 Blessed are You, Adonai, the holy God.

⁸ לְדוֹר וָדוֹר נַגִּיד גָּדְלֶךָ וּלְנֵצַח נְצָחִים קְדֻשָּׁתְךָ נַקְדִּישׁ. ⁹ וְשִׁבְחֲךָ אֱלֹהֵינוּ מִפִּינוּ לֹא יָמוּשׁ לְעוֹלָם וָעֶד כִּי אֵל מֶלֶךְ גָּדוֹל וְקָדוֹשׁ אָתָּה. *¹⁰ בָּרוּךְ אַתָּה יְיָ הָאֵל הַקָּדוֹשׁ.

[*From Rosh Hashanah to Yom Kippur, say instead:

[*From Rosh Hashanah to Yom Kippur, say instead:

11 Blessed are You, Adonai, the holy king.]

¹¹ בָּרוּךְ אַתָּה יְיָ הַמֶּלֶךְ הַקָּדוֹשׁ.]

59

BRETTLER (BIBLE)

"Abraham's God, Isaac's God, and Jacob's God" An infrequent biblical formula, never found in biblical prayers, but central to God's self-revelation to Moses in Exod. 3:6, 15, 16, and 4:5. Its prominence here reflects a rabbinic theological doctrine known as "merits of the ancestors" *(z'khut avot)*, according to which the righteous actions of the patriarchs continue on to benefit their descendants. In biblical thought, it is the *promise* inherent in the *covenant* that continues through time, not the specific meritorious *deeds* of Abraham, Isaac, and Jacob.   *(p. 62)*

ELLENSON (MODERN LITURGIES)

"Our ancestors' God" The word *avot*, as Joel Hoffman notes, "in general, is clearly inclusive" and should be translated as "ancestors," not "fathers." Older non-Orthodox prayer books, however (Einhorn's *Olath Tamid*, the *Union Prayer Book*, and Reconstructionist and Conservative liturgies prior to *Kol Haneshamah* and *Siddur Sim*   *(p. 65)*

FALK (FEMINISM)

"Our ancestors' God" As Joel Hoffman notes, *avot* may also be read as "fathers" or "patriarchs," and (contrary to Hoffman) I believe these are closer in meaning to the original *in its context* than the gender-neutral "ancestors." Although one would *like* to think   *(p. 67)*

DORFF (THEOLOGY)

Traditionally, the *Amidah* is recited silently and then repeated by the prayer leader (= *chazarat hashatz*, literally, "the repetition by the agent of the community"). This enables those who do not know the prayers to fulfill their obligation to pray by answering "Amen" after each of the reader's blessings. But repeating the *Amidah* that way takes time, and people are tempted to talk or let their minds wander during the repetition.

As a result, during the last several centuries, an alternative method for reciting the *Amidah* has emerged: the *Hoeche K'dushah* (pronounced HAY-chee k'-DOO-shah). This method eliminates the need to repeat   *(p. 63)*

1. AVOT ("ANCESTORS")

אָבוֹת

¹ Blessed are You, Adonai, our God and our ancestors' God: Abraham's God, Isaac's God, and Jacob's God, great, mighty, and revered God, supreme God, who acts most piously, who is master of everything, who remembers the piety of our ancestors, and who brings a redeemer to their descendants for the sake of his name in love.

HAUPTMAN (TALMUD)

Theoretically, we are in the section of the *Amidah* that is called *Shevach*, "Praise." But the very first blessing introduces the notion of a redeemer who has not yet appeared and whose task is still ahead. This means that even in this opening section, God *is* being petitioned for help. The second blessing too seems on the face of it merely to be describing God's attributes or ongoing activities, like sustaining life, healing the sick, and giving life to the dead. But here too, the entire blessing is a petition that is just worded so as to give   *(p. 68)*

KUSHNER & POLEN (CHASIDISM)

"Abraham's God, Isaac's God, and Jacob's God . . . Abraham's protector" The *Amidah* is an anthology of blessings designed to walk us through a comprehensive spiritual regimen: parents, divine power, holiness, service, gratitude, peace. Much has been written about the importance of each theme and its place in the larger sequence, but Nosson Sternhartz, the amanuensis of Nachman of Bratslav, in his *Likkutei Halakhot* (O. Ch., section 1), asks, why begin with parents, specifically Abraham? Could it perhaps be because of some particularly "prayerful" characteristic of the first Jewish father? And does the unconditional, selfless love of a parent teach us something about the nature of prayer itself?

We know that the patriarchs *(p. 69)*

L. HOFFMAN (HISTORY)

THE FIRST THREE BLESSINGS, KNOWN TRADITIONALLY AS BLESSINGS OF PRAISE, NOW COMMENCE.

THE FIRST OF THE THREE ESTABLISHES OUR COVENANTAL CLAIM ON GOD, WHOM WE APPROACH KNOWING THAT WE ARE SPIRITUAL DESCENDANTS OF THE BIBLICAL ANCESTORS WHO ESTABLISHED THE COVENANT IN THE FIRST PLACE.

"Our God and our ancestors' God" From time to time, the question has arisen as to whether converts may recite this blessing, in that they are not descended from Abraham as (presumably) born Jews are.
(p. 70)

בָּרוּךְ אַתָּה יְיָ אֱלֹהֵינוּ וֵאלֹהֵי אֲבוֹתֵינוּ¹
אֱלֹהֵי אַבְרָהָם אֱלֹהֵי יִצְחָק וֵאלֹהֵי יַעֲקֹב
הָאֵל הַגָּדוֹל הַגִּבּוֹר וְהַנּוֹרָא אֵל עֶלְיוֹן
גּוֹמֵל חֲסָדִים טוֹבִים וְקֹנֵה הַכֹּל וְזוֹכֵר
חַסְדֵי אָבוֹת וּמֵבִיא גוֹאֵל לִבְנֵי בְנֵיהֶם
לְמַעַן שְׁמוֹ בְּאַהֲבָה.

J. HOFFMAN (TRANSLATION)

"Our ancestors' God" Others, "fathers," not "ancestors." The list of names makes it clear that the author meant only the "fathers," but the word *avot* can mean either "patriarchs" in the technical sense or "ancestors," depending on the context. Some versions (e.g., *Gates of Prayer* [Reform], *Siddur Lev Chadash* [Liberal, England]) insert *imoteinu*, giving us "our God and our fathers' and mothers' God," or "our patriarchs' and matriarchs' God."

Others, "God of our ancestors," but this translation misses the parallel structure in the Hebrew: *elohei-nu*, "God-[of]-us" and *elohei avoteinu*, *(p. 71)*

LANDES (HALAKHAH)

"Blessed [Barukh] *are You* [atah], *Adonai"* At *Barukh*, bend the knees. At *atah*, bow from the waist with upper body and head (but not as far as the belt, for that would connote the arrogance of a prideful piety). At Ado-nai (God's name), bend back up straight, for it is written: "The Lord [Ado-nai] raises up those who are bowed down."

The *avot* (literally, "fathers," but here, as evidenced by the old Yiddish rabbinic-influenced translations that translate *avotainu* as *dic eltern* or *(p. 70)*

[From Rosh Hashanah to Yom Kippur, add:

[From Rosh Hashanah to Yom Kippur, add:

² Remember us for life, our king who delights in life, and write us in the book of life, for your sake, our living God.]

³ Our king helps and saves and protects! ⁴ Blessed are You, Adonai, Abraham's protector.

²זָכְרֵנוּ לְחַיִּים. מֶלֶךְ חָפֵץ בַּחַיִּים. וְכָתְבֵנוּ בְּסֵפֶר הַחַיִּים. לְמַעַנְךָ אֱלֹהִים חַיִּים.]

³מֶלֶךְ עוֹזֵר וּמוֹשִׁיעַ וּמָגֵן.
⁴בָּרוּךְ אַתָּה יְיָ מָגֵן אַבְרָהָם.

BRETTLER (BIBLE)

"Great, mighty, and revered God" From Deut. 10:17, but quoted in the late biblical prayer of Neh. 9:32, and then used again here. Since there are other cases too where parts of the *Amidah* are found in Deuteronomy and/or Nehemiah 9, it has been suggested that some form of the *Amidah* goes back to the late biblical era; more likely, however, the similarities occur because the *Amidah* stands in a continuum of developing prayer language from the Bible to the Rabbis. In both Deuteronomy 10 and Nehemiah 9, "great, mighty, and revered" occurs in a context referring to the patriarchs (Deut. 10:15) or the covenant that God made with them (Neh. 9:32), so it was natural to include the phrase here.

According to biblical use, these attributes are listed in ascending order: *gadol* ("great") is a general term; *gibor* ("mighty") applies to God and humans; *nora* ("revered" or "awe-inspiring") is reserved for God.

"Supreme God [el elyon], who acts most piously, who is master of everything" A modification of the name through which Melchizedek blessed Abram (Gen. 14:19) — "Supreme God *[el elyon],* creator of heaven and earth" — and probably borrowed from the Canaanite deity El. In its biblical context, "Supreme God" elevates God over other deities, although by the time of the liturgy, this was no longer its sense, since by then a "purely" monotheistic context was taken for granted.

The biblical phrase "creator of heaven and earth" is an example of a literary device called a "merism," that is, two opposite terms that express totality by referring to the opposites as well as everything in between. Our blessing changes the initial phrase from Genesis into "master" (or "creator") *"of everything,"* so as to avoid the possible misunderstanding that God has created *only* the heaven and earth. It also breaks the biblical epithet apart by inserting "who acts most piously" in the middle, a reference to God's *chesed. Chesed* is a biblical concept related to the idea of the covenant and denotes actions of loyalty performed by a strong party for a weaker one.

In sum, this phrase "Supreme God, who acts most piously, who is master of everything" is a remarkable example of how a pre-biblical phrase used of the Canaanite deity

El came to be applied to God by a biblical author and was then further reinterpreted and modified in rabbinic liturgy.

"Who remembers the piety of our ancestors" It is assumed that, in a measure for measure way, we are the recipients of God's *chesed* ("steadfast love") because God was once the recipient of the patriarchs' *chesed.* We may therefore ask for God's beneficence, in the *Amidah* that follows, even if we believe that we do not deserve it through our own actions or merits.

"Remember us for life" The first of several insertions added during the ten days of repentance (the period between Rosh Hashanah and Yom Kippur), a period with no special significance in the Bible, but very important to the Rabbis. Its main theme is God as judge; as such, God is depicted here as a king, since one of the king's main roles in antiquity was judicial. The notion of God's controlling our destiny through a book of life is biblical (Exod. 32:32–33; Isa. 4:3; Ps. 69:29; Mal. 3:16–18; Dan. 12:1), most likely borrowed from Mesopotamia.

"Abraham's protector" More literally "shield." God is often depicted as the psalmist's shield (e.g., Ps. 3:4), and "shield of Abraham" comes from Gen. 15:1, where God makes a covenant with Abraham, saying, "I am a shield to you." "Shield of Abraham" *(magen avraham)* was probably a frozen epithet for God even before the blessing was composed, since it is found in a prayer in a second-century B.C.E. extra-biblical work called Ben Sirah (51:12): "Praise the shield of Abraham."

———◆———

DORFF (THEOLOGY)

the entire *Amidah,* but preserves the communal recitation of the third blessing, the *K'dushah,* a matter about which the Rabbis felt very strongly, because of the biblical mandate that they read in Prov. 14:28: "The glory of the Sovereign is in the multitude of people" — that is (as the Rabbis interpreted it), "Group sanctification honors God more than individual prayer does" (Ber. 53a).

The way it works is that in the morning services *(Shacharit),* the congregation and cantor sing the first two blessings together and chant the third one (the *K'dushah*) antiphonally, with the congregation joining in for (1) *Kadosh, kadosh, kadosh . . .,* (2) *Barukh k'vod . . .,* (3) *Yimlokh Adonai l'olam . . .,* and (4) the final line (the *chatimah*), *Barukh atah Adonai, ha'el hakadosh.* Everyone then continues silently to the end of the *Amidah.*

This method is consistent with the Rabbis' instructions that we not interrupt the flow that joins the first major rubric (the *Sh'ma* and Its Blessings) to the following one (the *Amidah*). Attuned as they were to the emotional — almost musical — quality of the service, they ruled that nothing intercede between the blessing following the *Sh'ma* and the blessing that begins the *Amidah.* In the morning, therefore, congregations who use the *Hoeche K'dushah* go directly from the end of the *Sh'ma* and Its Blessings into a communal singing of the first two blessings of the *Amidah,* as described.

The recitation of the *Amidah* for *Minchah* (the afternoon service) and *Musaf* (the additional service) differ. Since no *Sh'ma* precedes them, the concern to maintain continuity between the *Sh'ma* and the *Amidah* does not apply. In those services, then, if the *Hoeche K'dushah* is applied, the leader usually begins alone; the congregation (1) joins in for the *K'dushah* as described above, (2) recites the first two blessings (which it has not yet said) silently, (3) skips the public *K'dushah* (which it has already said) but says the private and silent version of it including the third blessing, and (4) recites the rest of the *Amidah* silently through to the end.

Proper recourse to the *Hoeche K'dushah* should be limited to congregations where there is reason to believe that people know how to pray the *Amidah* on their own. It is inappropriate also for *Shacharit* of Shabbat and Festivals, when there is no need to shorten prayer so as to rush off to work. Conservative congregations often use it for *Musaf,* however, partly to save time and partly to offset the discomfort that many Conservative rabbis and congregants have with a public and cantorial rendering of the middle blessing of *Musaf,* which requests (in the traditional liturgical text) the restoration of the sacrifices or (in the revised version of Conservative prayer books) at least the recollection of them.

Shevach: Blessings of Praise

Though the Rabbis explain the logic behind the paragraphs of the *Sh'ma,* they nowhere do so regarding the *Amidah.* It is a fact, however, that every *Amidah* begins and ends with the same two triads of blessings, while only the intermediary ones change. Moreover, the very name for our prayer book —*Siddur* (meaning "order") — suggests that the Rabbis were conscious of sequence. I suggest three interpretations of why the Rabbis chose these particular prayers in this particular order to begin every *Amidah.*

1. *Temporal order:* The first blessing speaks of our link to God in the past; the second, of our hopes for salvation in the future; and the third, of how we experience God as holy and awesome in the present.

2. *The order of our relationships to God:* The first (*Avot* = "ancestors") describes God as an old and familiar ancestral deity who shielded Abraham and who will remember his love for our ancestors in loving and protecting us. The second (*G'vurot* = "power") describes a God who supports, sustains, and even revives us. The third (*K'dushah*) speaks of God as separate and apart from us, as wholly other, and as therefore deserving of respect and awe. The *Amidah* begins, then, by recognizing God's manifestation to us in all three of these ways.

3. *Identifying the players in the prayer to follow:* The three blessings identify the parties involved in prayer and the relationship among them. In the *Avot,* we are descendants of the patriarchs (and matriarchs), not mere strangers who appear before God with nothing to speak for us except our own merits; we come, rather, with *chasdei avot,* our ancestors' acts of loyalty and loving-kindness, that we hope God will remember for our good. The third blessing acknowledges God as the *mysterium tremendum,* the mystery before whom even the angels quake in fear, and whose honor (*kavod*— literally, "heaviness") fills the earth. Our reaction to this God, though, is not just fear, but praise, as we pray that He reign in Zion forever. The

first blessing identifies us; the third blessing acknowledges God; and the second blessing describes our primary relationship together: God can and does use His power to make it possible for us to live and thrive, perhaps even after death. Indeed, while only the second blessing speaks specifically of God's power, the other two refer to it obliquely, thus indicating that it is that aspect of the relationship between God and us that will be most invoked in the prayers that follow.

"Our ancestors' God . . . master of everything" This God of our ancestors is "master of everything" in the sense that He created and owns everything (the two meanings of the Hebrew verb *koneh),* and thus has supreme power, enough even to bring to the descendants of those ancestors a messianic redeemer. Jewish consciousness of time is not measured by moving repetitively from one day to the next, making each day identical to the one before. It operates with eras, from the past through the present to the anticipated redemptive future, providing roots to our present and hope for what is yet to come.

———◆———

ELLENSON (MODERN LITURGIES)

Shalom), followed Orthodox custom and said "our fathers." Even the relatively modern *Service of the Heart,* the British predecessor to *Siddur Lev Chadash* and the first of the many liberal prayer books that have emerged since the 1970s, still offered "God of our fathers" as its English translation.

All contemporary liberal prayer books thereafter have rejected this option, preferring "our ancestors" or sometimes the poetic "God of all generations." Their unanimous commitment to gender inclusivity in prayer stands in sharp contrast to Orthodox prayer books like Artscroll and Birnbaum, which still say either "our forefathers" or "our fathers."

The latest change in many books (the gender-sensitive edition of *Gates of Prayer, Kol Haneshamah,* and *Siddur Lev Chadash)* is to add *v'imoteinu,* "and our mothers," not only in English but in Hebrew as well, followed by the names of the matriarchs, to match the patriarchs.

The Israeli Reform *Ha'avodah Shebalev* and the new Israeli Conservative Movement Siddur (1998), *Va'ani T'filati,* have no translation from the Hebrew, of course, but treat the Hebrew as the vernacular it is for Israeli worshipers. In a way, however, each does provide a "translation." Both prayer books divide the page in half and offer two options to their worshipers. Alongside the traditional text (which appears in large print), there appears, in the Israeli Reform text (in Hebrew), "God of our fathers and our mothers, God of Abraham, Isaac, and Jacob, God of Sarah, Rebekah, Rachel, and Leah." In *Va'ani T'filati,* the same egalitarian alternative is offered, though the text in the Conservative prayer book appears in the same-sized print as the traditional formula. The former option bespeaks the traditionalism that distinguishes liberal Judaism in Israel, while the latter choice indicates that the same forces that inform liberal Diaspora Judaism are present in Israel as well.

"Who remembers the piety of our ancestors." Isaac Mayer Wise found the rabbinic doctrine of *z'khut avot* ("the merit of the ancestors") morally repugnant because it assumed that God rewards us on account of the good deeds performed by our ancestors. As a follower of the moral philosophy of Immanuel Kant, Wise believed that individuals could acquire merit only by their own autonomous moral stands. But Wise also clung fervently to the idea of covenant as the "immovable center" of Judaism. He held that the covenant between God and Israel is eternal, calling each generation and every individual Jew to strive to fulfill its conditions. Wise therefore substituted *b'rit* ("covenant") for "piety" and arrived at "and rememberest Thy covenant with our ancestors." He thereby managed to retain the rhythm of the traditional Hebrew while transforming its meaning to accord with his own principles.

On a different note, gender-inclusive prayer books like *Siddur Lev Chadash* and *Kol Haneshamah* have added *imahot* ("matriarchs") to *avot* ("patriarchs") in the Hebrew, lest Hebrew readers mistakenly think *avot* is "fathers" alone, rather than the more inclusive "ancestors," as we render it here.

"Redeemer" Since most liberal Jews have affirmed the ideal of a messianic era instead of the traditional belief in a personal messiah, all liberal liturgies of the past two hundred years have found this word problematic. A few, like the 1819 and 1841 editions of the *Hamburg Temple Prayer Book,* retained the traditional word *go'el* ("redeemer") for the Hebrew, but translated it *Erlosung,* German for "redemption." Their pattern is often followed to this day, namely, to leave the Hebrew text intact, while employing creative translations that remove or mute meanings that their authors find objectionable.

Others, however, too numerous to cite, reject this approach, preferring (at least here) to have the Hebrew say exactly what the translation does. They therefore substitute *g'ullah* ("redemption") for *go'el* ("redeemer") and translate accordingly, making Hebrew and English equally consistent with their belief. Interestingly, both Israeli non-Orthodox prayer books, *Ha'avodah Shebalev* and *Va'ani T'filati,* have opted for *g'ullah* as opposed to *go'el* in the texts of their liturgies.

"Abraham's protector" In response to the modern demand for gender equality, most liberal liturgies nowadays (Israel's *Ha'avodah Shebalev,* one of two optional versions of *Va'ani T'filati,* the British Liberal *Siddur Lev Chadash,* North American Reform's gender-sensitive *Gates of Prayer,* the Reconstructionist *Kol Haneshamah*) add the name of Sarah to that of Abraham. Some *(Ha'avodah Shebalev)* couple *magen Avraham* with *poked Sarah* ("who remembers Sarah"), a reference to Gen. 21:1, "And Adonai remembered *(pakad)* Sarah." This option achieves the symmetry of using biblical prototypes for both Abraham and Sarah, since *magen Avraham* reflects Gen. 14:20, where, however, *magen* is not just "shield" but the more aggressive "the One who delivers your enemies into your hand." Others, however, prefer *ezrat Sarah,* which they translate as "protector" or "help" of Sarah. They avoid *poked* ("remember") because the root meaning of *poked* is "to visit" and need not imply "visit in memory." It can also mean to visit for the sake of giving an order (hence, *pakid,* modern Hebrew for a clerk who takes orders), or to punish, or even to have sexual relations.

FALK (FEMINISM)

the Rabbis saw God as the protector of *all* our ancestors, the text itself, which goes on to enumerate the *avot* by name, including only the forefathers in the list, contradicts this reading. Sadly, there is not much evidence that the Rabbis gave thought to the foremothers when they composed or said these prayers; there is almost no mention of the foremothers by name anywhere in the liturgy.

Today, of course, many congregations add the names of the patriarchs' wives — Sarah, Rebekah, Rachel, and Leah — into this part of the *Amidah,* an insertion that is sanctioned by all the non-Orthodox branches of Judaism. Despite more than ample authorization, however, many congregations still resist this first step toward recording the presence of Jewish women in history. This resistance is a telling sign of the tenacity with which patriarchal attitudes can pervade communal consciousness, such that the invisibility of women is taken to be normative, and even minimal attempts to address absences in the liturgy are regarded as intolerable. It tells us that, indeed, we need to go far beyond the token gesture of making four of our foremothers an optional reference in our prayers; we need to go beyond even making their inclusion mandatory. We need to bring women's lives *fully into the foreground* of our awareness in order to begin to correct the imbalance in our liturgy and, ultimately, to move toward the creation of a genuinely inclusive community.

Toward this end, I believe it is imperative that we begin to include the words of Jewish women in our synagogue prayers. For example, in my own prayer book *(The Book of Blessings),* I have incorporated the poems of Yiddish and Hebrew women poets into the body of the *Amidah,* where they serve as a form of *k'rovot* (supplementary liturgical poems). The first section of that *Amidah* includes the twentieth-century Yiddish poet Malka Heifetz Tussman's *Ikh Bin Froy,* "I Am Woman," which offers a sweeping account of the history of Jewish women reimagined in a personal voice. Opening each stanza with the words "I am . . . ," Tussman claims her identity in a sequence of historical images, from "the exalted Rachel / whose love led the way for Rabbi Akiba" to the twentieth-century Zionist pioneer, the "pampered girl / who set herself behind a plow / to force the gray desert into green life." To complete the catalogue, Tussman offers an image from her own life; referring to her experience as a teacher of Yiddish, she writes: "I am the one who stubbornly / carries around a strange alphabet / to impart to children's ears." The poem concludes with this affirmation: "I am all these and many more. / And everywhere, always, I am woman" (translations mine).

The recitation of Tussman's poem — or other writings by Jewish women — as part of communal prayer can be a powerful experience for both women and men. Saying or hearing these words read aloud, Jewish women may, for the first time, recognize themselves — or, at least, some reflection of their lives — within the tradition. Jewish men, too, can benefit by this more inclusive vision of Jewish history. Though it may sound jarring, at first, for a man to hear (or himself say) words like "I am woman," the effect can be both edifying and liberating. Attempting to read oneself into the voice of the "other" gives men an opportunity to experience what women have had to do as a matter of course. At the same time, it can be affirming to women to hear men in the congregation willing to speak in a female voice.

Of course, the poem *Ikh Bin Froy* will not speak to everyone — any more than *any* words speak to everyone; and this is as true for rabbinic texts as for those we introduce today. Bringing new voices into our prayers often serves to highlight the need for even *more* — not less — liturgical variation; adding women's poetry into the *Amidah* is just one example of how to keep the liturgy evolving and alive.

If we really intend the *Avot* section to refer to our "ancestors," and if we want the whole community to feel connected to ancestral sources, we ought to begin by recalling *all* the biblical foremothers — including Bilhah and Zilpah, the concubines who bore four of Jacob's sons — and proceed from there to retracing the trail of their forgotten female descendants. We must do whatever we can to retrieve the lost stories of all the generations of foremothers and foresisters — including, of course, our own — if Jewish women's history is to be appreciated as a significant part of our heritage and if Jewish women today are to find points of nexus with the tradition.

———◆———

HAUPTMAN (TALMUD)

the impression of being praise. When we say that God heals the sick, supports the fallen, or frees the captive, we are implicitly saying that this is what we expect God to continue to do. We even slip into the paragraph the fact that God gives life (or can give life) to the dead, clearly a statement about the future.

"Abraham's God, Isaac's God, and Jacob's God" This is God's means of self-identification in the Bible, most notably upon appearing to Moses to discuss the imminent fulfillment of the promise to take the Jewish People out of Egypt and bring them to the Land of Israel. We invoke the patriarchs to remind God of that divine promise, since it was to these three men that the promise was made. But, in addition, since God is all-powerful, we imply that God should remember the kind deeds (or *chesed*) for which they were responsible, credit that kindness to their children's children, their descendants (that is, us), and redeem them. If these descendants do not quite measure up on their own to merit God's intervention in history, then their forefathers can make up for their shortcomings.

Merit is apparently calculated collectively and cumulatively over time.

"Ancestors" Though translated here as "ancestors," the word *avot* generally denotes "fathers" to modern readers. Perhaps, therefore, we should amend the blessing to say what it originally meant: forefathers. The question is, however, should we add the names of the *imahot,* the foremothers, to the blessing? Can we not also turn to God and claim special treatment because of the merit stored up by them? It might be that our blessing has in mind a series of acts that only the *fathers* did (like attempting to save Sodom from destruction). But it is more likely that the special piety in question is something more general: the way (we presume) that the *avot* and the *imahot* (the forefathers and the foremothers) lived their lives. Surely Sarah, Rebekah, Rachel, and Leah

also believed in God and did whatever God asked them to do. A reference to both would be a good way to express the totality of the Jewish People back then.

When our blessing was written, mentioning only the forefathers may have been sufficient because their wives were automatically included as members of the ancient household, who, like children and slaves, were cared for by the head of household. However, to make the same point today it is necessary to list the counterparts of the *avot,* Sarah, Rebekah, Rachel, and Leah. If we are asking God to be kind to us today because of the merit of our progenitors, then mentioning the matriarchs is critical.

"Who brings a redeemer to their descendants for the sake of his name in love" Stylistically, the first blessing builds to a crescendo as the phrases grow longer and longer. At first God's attributes are described in single words, like "great" and "mighty"; then we get an entire phrase, "Supreme God"; and finally, the blessing climaxes with the lengthy claim, "who brings a redeemer to their descendants for the sake of his name in love." As we see from later paragraphs, the reference here is to a messiah from the house of David who will lead the People back to Israel.

———◆———

KUSHNER & POLEN (CHASIDISM)

(and matriarchs), according to the Talmud (Ber. 26b), established the three daily services: Abraham "arose early" (Gen. 22:3), and so he initiated *Shacharit;* Isaac "walked in the afternoon" (Gen. 24:63) and began the *Minchah* prayers; and Jacob "came upon a place as the sun set" (Gen. 28:11) and was the first to pray *Ma'ariv.* But this only raises a larger problem. How could our fathers and mothers have known how to pray if the Torah had not yet been given? The answer, suggests Rabbi Nosson, was that even before the Torah was revealed at Sinai, there was divine *chesed* or love, which is the basis of Torah and therefore of creation itself. And our "parents," Abraham and Sarah and their children and grandchildren, were therefore able to "pray" directly through loving service. And the core of this "service" was *chesed chinam,* or "freely given love," love without any thought of return.

According to a similar tradition, not only was Abraham the first to begin to teach the world about the unity of God, but he is the very foundation of the world. In Gen. 2:4 we read, "These are the generations of the heavens and the earth when He [God] created them" *(b'hibaram).* And according to Midrash Genesis Rabbah 12:9, the Hebrew letters that make up *b'hibaram* בהבראם can be rearranged to spell *"b'Avraham"* באברהם, or, "with Abraham." In such a way, Abraham and his service of "freely given love" are the very basis of creation itself!

Indeed, in Gen. 12:2, God blesses Abraham by saying, "Be a blessing." What this means, says Nosson, is not merely that Abraham will bless other people, but that Abraham's name will be used to literally conclude the first blessing of the *Amidah,* "Blessed are You, Adonai, *Abraham's* protector." So, this one, who knew of *chesed chinam,* "freely given love," *even before* the Torah and who was also the first to understand that there was only one God, is therefore the one in whose name we commence the *Amidah*. And when we, Abraham and Sarah's progeny, rise to recite the *Amidah,* our great, great-grandfather stands with us as we too invoke the source of all prayer: unconditioned, freely given love.

———◆———

LANDES (HALAKHAH)

grandparents, thereby implicitly including the foremothers as well) are connected to all Israel, by lineage *(yichus),* which is a central and prized halakhic category of status. What is maintained here is that all Jews share equally in that status. Indeed, Maimonides insists that the righteous convert shares it too, because such a person is literally, not just figuratively, a child of Abraham. As a meta-halakhic category, this passage on the *avot* refers to the concept of *z'khut avot,* "the merit of the ancestors," matriarchs as well as patriarchs, which constitutes a legal source of defense of Israel, on high.

"Blessed [Barukh] *are You* [atah], *Ado-nai, Abraham's protector"* At "Blessed are You" *[Barukh atah],* bow, and at Ado-nai, stand erect — as before, in the opening line of the blessing (see "Blessed are You, Ado-nai" above). We thus bow at both the beginning and end of the introductory blessing.

———◆———

L. HOFFMAN (HISTORY)

Maimonides says they should, "for Abraham is also your father." He acknowledges further that becoming the spiritual offspring of Abraham does not demean life prior to conversion. "Do not think poorly of your own beginnings," he cautions. "We may be descended from Abraham, Isaac, and Jacob, but you are descended from the Creator, as Isaiah writes, 'One shall say: I am the Lord's; and another shall use the name Jacob'" (Isa. 44:5).

"Abraham's God, Isaac's God, and Jacob's God." Why is the word "God" repeated three times? We might more easily have said, "The God of Abraham, Isaac, and Jacob." The most common explanation is that each patriarch knew God personally. The *Sh'ma* is philosophical, while the *Amidah* is personal — a conversation with God about our lives.

"Great, mighty, and revered" The adjectives are roughly synonymous, so seem redundant, but David Abudarham (fourteenth century, Spain) says we need all three because God's power (the subject of this blessing) is known differently by each of the three different categories of creation in which medieval Jews believed: the angels, the heavenly bodies, and earth-bound human beings.

Humans know God's power through the last attribute, *nora* ("awesome"), implying the miracles that God performs. The problem for us is that most of us do not believe in miracles any more. The *Amidah* will therefore return to the topic of miracles in the second to last blessing, indicating that miracles need not be extraordinary, like burning bushes or falling manna. Miracles may equally be everyday things where God's presence is manifest: "miracles that are with us on each day . . . wonders and goodness at every time" (see below, Blessing 18, "Grateful Acknowledgment").

"For the sake of his name in love" The theological point of the prayer is that God will send us a redeemer not necessarily because we deserve it, but because our ancestors did. But if God will save us for the sake of our ancestors, why add, "For the sake of his name in love"? Maimonides actually omits the phrase, so as to give more credit to our ancestors.

———◆———

J. HOFFMAN (TRANSLATION)

"God [of] our ancestors." Using "God of our ancestors" would require "God of us," but that is not English.

"Great, mighty [gibor], *and revered God* [el], *supreme God* [el]" "God" here is *el*, whereas until now we have had *elohim*. *El* seems to denote "god" (with a lowercase "g") and *elohim* is "God." Both words come from the same root, *elohim* probably being the plural of *el*, with the Hebrew letter *heh* stuck in the middle. It was not uncommon to insert the letter *heh* to symbolize the change of a name from a non-Jewish to a Jewish one. Abraham and Sarah too (originally Abram and Sarai) have their names changed by the insertion of a *heh*.

For *gibor*, *Kol Haneshamah* (Reconstructionist) uses "heroic," which is a nice thought based loosely on the Hebrew, but probably inaccurate as translation.

"Who acts most piously . . . who remembers the piety of our ancestors" A radical departure from the usual translations, such as Birnbaum (Orthodox), "who bestow[s] lovingkindness," or *Kol Haneshamah* (Reconstructionist), "imparting deeds of kindness." At issue is the verb *g.m.l* and the noun *chesed*. Taken separately they mean, respectively, something like "reward" and "pious deeds," but together these seem to form a technical term in rabbinic thought, having something to do with rewarding pious deeds. According to the Mishnah (Pe'ah, 1:1), *g'milut chasadim* is one of the things "without measure." It also appears on one of the lists of the three things on which the world depends (Avot 1:2). *Gomel chasadim* likely means one who does *g'milut chasadim*, but we lack a term for that in English. Terms like "pious," "honorable," "charitable," "with lovingkindness," "in mercy," and "magnanimous" all approximate the original intent, but in isolation fail to convey the idea entirely.

Whatever the case, it cannot be accidental that the very next thought in the prayer is that God "remembers the *chesed* of our ancestors." Our translation should capture the connection by using the same word in English in both cases.

———◆ ◆ ◆———

BRETTLER (BIBLE)

"You are forever mighty" The primary theme of this blessing is God's might — an appropriate notion early on in the *Amidah,* where we recount God's strength before requesting its use on our behalf (see, e.g., 2 Sam. 22:2–3; Ps. 18:3–4). God's power is manifest in "supporting the fallen," but also, following a biblical tradition that is especially predominant in wisdom texts such as Job (e.g., 38:28–30), in the meteorological world ("You cause the wind to blow. . . . You bring down the dew"). A similar list highlighting God's power is found in a prayer from Qumran: "He will heal the badly *(p. 74)*

DORFF (THEOLOGY)

"Supporting the fallen . . . healing the sick" While the ability to determine life and death may be the most dramatic evidence of God's power, we recognize it also in more common occurrences, like supporting the fallen and healing the sick. In all such areas, we are called to imitate God.

A later blessing turns specifically to the role of healing, but the theme is already struck here, where it is the image of "the fallen" that stands out. When people fall — physically, intellectually, or emotionally — it is necessary, though often difficult, to help them regain their standing. Recognizable, and often dramatic, examples include orthopedists and physical therapists who help people walk again; teachers who painstakingly teach those who have difficulty *(p. 75)*

2. *G'VUROT* ("GOD'S POWER") גְּבוּרוֹת

1 You are forever mighty, Adonai: giving life to the dead, You are a mighty savior.

[From Sh'mini Atseret to the first day of Passover, add:

2 You cause the wind to blow and you cause the rain to fall.

ELLENSON (MODERN LITURGIES)

"Giving life to the dead (m'chayei hametim)" Several times this blessing cites bodily resurrection as the prime example of God's power. Modern Orthodoxy, from its German founder, Samson Raphael Hirsch, to the American Artscroll Siddur, retains the notion, translating faithfully as *(p. 76)*

FALK (FEMINISM)

"Giving life to the dead" The second blessing of the *Amidah* is known as *G'vurot,* "God's Power." An important aspect of divine power mentioned three times in this blessing — once in the opening, once in the middle, and once in the eulogy — is that of "giving life to (or reviving) the dead," *m'chayeh metim* — an attribution that has been eliminated from recent Reform and Reconstructionist prayer books. In place of the words *m'chayeh metim, Gates of Prayer* offers the more general phrase *m'chayeh hakol, (p. 78)*

HAUPTMAN (TALMUD)

"You are forever mighty" The first blessing talks about the past, God's special relationship with the progenitors of the Jewish People. The second tries to gain God's attention in the present with an eye on the activities that we expect of God in the future.

———◆———

KUSHNER & POLEN (Chasidism)

"Who gives life to the dead" We have a tradition never to push away anyone no matter what he might have done nor how far away she might have strayed (2 Sam. 14:14). Indeed, when we say that God's compassion extends to all creatures (Ps. 145:9), it means even to those who seem to be hopelessly lost, spiritually dead. But how does this compassionate energy reach them?

According to one tradition *(Divrei Shmuel, Sha'arei T'fillah, Y'sod Ha'avodah,* pp. 36–37), the Hebrew letters are not merely signs for sounds but the very instruments through which the world comes into being. Words literally make reality; we create as we speak. (Abracadabra is an Aramaic contraction of *avara b'davara,* meaning "I create as I *(p. 79)*

LANDES (Halakhah)

"You cause the wind to blow and . . . rain to fall/You bring down the dew" "You cause the rain to blow . . ." is recited during the winter months, from *Musaf* of Sh'mini Atseret (the eighth day of Sukkot) until the *Musaf* of the last day of Passover. For the thirty days after Sh'mini Atseret, if you finish the *Amidah* and are not sure if you said it, you should assume that you have not done so and start the *Amidah* again, this time including it. If, however, doubt occurs *after* thirty days have elapsed, *(p. 80)*

L. HOFFMAN (History)

THE SECOND BLESSING CELEBRATES GOD'S POWER IN SUSTAINING THE NATURAL CYCLE OF RAIN, VEGETATION, AND REBIRTH. BY EXTENSION, WE ARE REMINDED OF A PARALLEL HUMAN CYCLE OF REBIRTH: THE PROMISE OF LIFE AFTER DEATH.

"Giving life to the dead" When we say that we "take something on faith," we mean that we believe in something that we have not seen. There are degrees of faith therefore. When someone I trust reports something outlandish, I may still believe it on faith, but only the lowest level of faith, since I do have *(p. 80)*

1 אַתָּה גִבּוֹר לְעוֹלָם אֲדֹנָי. מְחַיֵּה מֵתִים אַתָּה. רַב לְהוֹשִׁיעַ.

[From Sh'mini Atseret to the first day of Passover, add:

2 מַשִּׁיב הָרוּחַ וּמוֹרִיד הַגָּשֶׁם.

J. HOFFMAN (Translation)

"Giving life [m'chayeh] *to the dead* [metim]" or "a giver of life." The question is whether God actually gives life ("giving life") or is one who can or might give life ("giver of life"). This same distinction can be seen more clearly in the English "you are an executioner" (on a par with "a giver of life") and "you execute = you kill people" ("giving life"). The official executioner may or may not actually kill anyone; similarly, a giver of life may not actually give life. "You are a doctor" and "you heal people," respectively, demonstrate the same point.

The question is crucial to our theological understanding of this prayer, but the Hebrew is ambiguous. If we assume that the word *atah* ("You") that *(p. 82)*

*From the first day of Passover to
Sh'mini Atseret, add:*

³ You bring down the dew.]

⁴ You sustain life with kindness, giving life to the dead with great mercy, supporting the fallen, healing the sick, and freeing the captive, and keeping faith with sleepers in the dust. ⁵ Who is like You, master of might, and who resembles You, a King who causes death and causes life, and causes salvation to flourish!

[From Rosh Hashanah to Yom Kippur, add:

⁶ Who is like you, father of mercy, who in mercy remembers his creatures for life!]

⁷ You faithfully give life to the dead. ⁸ Blessed are You, Adonai, who gives life to the dead.

*From the first day of Passover
to Sh'mini Atseret, add:*

מוֹרִיד הַטָּל.] ³

מְכַלְכֵּל חַיִּים בְּחֶסֶד מְחַיֵּה ⁴
מֵתִים בְּרַחֲמִים רַבִּים. סוֹמֵךְ
נוֹפְלִים וְרוֹפֵא חוֹלִים וּמַתִּיר
אֲסוּרִים. וּמְקַיֵּם אֱמוּנָתוֹ
לִישֵׁנֵי עָפָר. ⁵ מִי כָמוֹךָ בַּעַל
גְּבוּרוֹת וּמִי דוֹמֶה לָּךְ. מֶלֶךְ
מֵמִית וּמְחַיֶּה וּמַצְמִיחַ יְשׁוּעָה.

[From Rosh Hashanah to Yom Kippur, add:

מִי כָמוֹךָ אַב הָרַחֲמִים ⁶
זוֹכֵר יְצוּרָיו לְחַיִּים בְּרַחֲמִים.]

וְנֶאֱמָן אַתָּה לְהַחֲיוֹת מֵתִים. ⁷
בָּרוּךְ אַתָּה יְיָ מְחַיֵּה הַמֵּתִים. ⁸

BRETTLER (**BIBLE**)

wounded and will make the dead live; He will proclaim good news to the meek, give lavishly [to the need]y . . ." (F. G. Martinez, *The Dead Sea Scrolls Translated,* p. 394, from 4Q521=4Q Messianic Apocalypse).

"Giving life to the dead" Similar phrases are used in Akkadian prayers of a deity, where "reviving the dead" means restoring the gravely ill to good health, the original sense of the phrase here too. Eventually, however, the benediction was expanded to incorporate a belief in resurrection of the dead, and "giving life to the dead" was reinterpreted accordingly.

"And keeping faith with sleepers in dust" From Dan. 12:2, "Many of those that sleep in the dust of the earth will awake," one of the latest biblical passages and the only one that unequivocally refers to the resurrection of the dead. Resurrection is a late and

peripheral biblical idea, which became more significant during the persecutions perpetrated by Antiochus IV (in the war against the Hasmoneans, or Maccabees) and appears quite centrally in rabbinic literature.

"Who causes death and causes life" From Hannah's prayer (1 Sam. 2:6), where, however, it means that God kills certain people while sustaining others. Here, however, with the theme of resurrection emphasized, it is reinterpreted to mean that God brings death and then life renewed to the same individual — a remarkable example of how a biblical phrase changes meaning when it is put into a new context.

"And causes salvation to flourish" An additional manifestation of God's power, referring to the arrival of the messianic age and connecting the two central rabbinic beliefs of the messianic age and the resurrection, ideas that never appear together in the Bible.

——◆——

DORFF (THEOLOGY)

learning; and friends, relatives, or counselors who help the bereaved cope with loss. Support for the fallen is often a normal and too little noticed part of day-to-day life; as an exercise of both power and goodness, it is nothing short of a godly act.

"Freeing the captive" The phrase conjures up instances of redeeming captives and prisoners, and it certainly denotes that. The same words, though, are used in the early morning blessings, where, according to the Talmud (Ber. 60b), they denote the ability just to sit up in bed on the way to getting up in the morning. Anyone who has ever been bedridden or seen someone else in that state will recognize the poignancy of the blessing in that context: we who can get up bless God for freeing us from being chained to our beds. The phrase can also be interpreted metaphorically to refer to releasing someone from intellectual or psychological bonds — superstitious beliefs, for example, or prejudice toward others. All of these instances of liberating the bound require both power and goodness — two of God's chief characteristics — and therefore, these too are godly acts.

"Giving life to the dead" The most controversial part of this blessing is the assertion that God is faithful in "giving life to the dead." The Talmud speaks of resurrection metaphorically also, by mandating the recitation of the blessing "Blessed are You . . . who revives the dead" upon seeing someone for the first time in over a year (Ber. 58b). The term occurs also in the early morning liturgy, just before the fourteen morning blessings, where we thank God for the renewed energy and consciousness we feel upon waking up, by saying, "Blessed are You . . . who restores souls to dead corpses *(hamachazir n'shamot lifgarim metim)."*

The Rabbis also believed that there is life after death, however, and most Jews today doubt that. In 1991, for instance, a *Los Angeles Times* poll found that 67 percent of Christians and 45 percent of those with no religious identity at all, but only 30 percent of Jews, believed in an afterlife. Most Jews prefer to interpret "life after death" as living on in the influence that they have on others, possibly through their children. Even fewer Jews believe in a devil or a hell to which sinners are condemned: 58 percent of Christians accept these doctrines, but only 4 percent of Jews do. True, we have evidence each spring for life springing forth from what appears to be dead, and we see also how new plants sprout from the ashes of a forest fire. With regard to human beings, though, nobody has returned from the land of the dead to tell us whether there is postmortem life or not.

The Rabbis actually had two different views on the matter. Some claimed that the whole person dies and then is resurrected at some future time, while others maintained that only the body dies and the soul lives on until it is rejoined with the body at the time of resurrection. Louis Finkelstein (1895–1991) claimed that the phrasing here — "who gives life to the dead" — is deliberately ambiguous in order to accommodate both rabbinic views.

Even those who doubt that God's power extends to restoring life to the dead can appreciate the assertion here that God is manifest in the many things that transcend our understanding and control. They can also accept the model of a human life dedicated to imitating God in sustaining the hungry, supporting the fallen, healing the sick, and freeing the bound. At worst, then, they may hold that resurrection of the dead is a logical though exaggerated claim, a literary flare, perhaps, intended to emphasize the power of God.

In all philosophical honesty, however, we must admit that while we have no experiential evidence to prove resurrection, we also have no evidence to disprove it. Saadiah Gaon (882–942, Babylonia; *Book of Doctrines and Beliefs,* chapter 7, section 1) argued that if we concede that God created us to begin with, we should further grant that for God to do so again is a cinch, since originally, we had to be created *ex nihilo,* "out of nothing," whereas at resurrection, God can use our remains as raw materials. (This traditional view does *not* preclude organ donation, by the way, because God inevitably will need to reshape our remains from the way we died, if we are to live again. Indeed, according to the Conservative Movement's Committee on Jewish Law and Standards, making one's organs available for transplant is a *mitzvah,* a positive obligation.) Perhaps, then, far from being unreasonable, the doctrine of resurrection is a logical acknowledgment of God's unique power.

———◆———

ELLENSON (MODERN LITURGIES)

"revives . . .," "resurrects . . .," or "resuscitates the dead." Reform, British Liberal, Reconstructionist, and Conservative Jews, however, have generally rejected the belief in bodily resurrection and replaced it with faith in the immortality of the soul; they have therefore found this blessing's repeated assurances of resurrection problematic. Rather than comment separately on each occurrence of the phrase, I will summarize the various solutions to all of them here. The authors are not always consistent, however. They sometimes adopt different strategies at different points in the benediction or within different services or editions of their prayer books.

Many liturgies simply remove the Hebrew altogether, although Isaac Mayer Wise left it in his 1866 High Holy Day service, saying of God (in the English), "who killeth and reviveth. . . . Blessed be Thou who grantest perpetual life after death." In this instance, he leaves open the question of whether life after death is resurrection of the body or mere spiritual immortality, but we can see what he believed by the fact that elsewhere he provided *m'chayeh nishmot hametim* and offered as its English translation, "Thou art faithful to the living and the dead. Praised be Thou, O God, who keepest alive the souls of dying mortals."

A completely unambiguous solution can be found in the *Union Prayer Book,* which followed David Einhorn in replacing *m'chayeh metim* with another traditional phrase, one that Einhorn remembered from the blessing that is recited after reading Torah, *notei'a b'tokheinu chayei olam,* "who hast implanted within us immortal life." (In 1896, Einhorn's son-in-law, Emil Hirsch, reedited his father-in-law's German *Olath Tamid* for English readers and translated more loosely, "dispenser of life eternal.") Earlier in the prayer, Einhorn had inserted *podeh nefesh avadav mimavet,* saying in translation, "with infinite kindness Thou redeemest the souls of Thy servants from death spiritual." He thus testified to his comfort with the idea of spiritual immortality while simultaneously signaling his rejection of the doctrine of bodily resurrection.

More recently, several liberal liturgies have shied away from any sense of an afterlife at all. Two pioneer prayer books of the 1970s *(Gates of Prayer* and the British *Service of the Heart)* — both of which were edited in part by Chaim Stern — substituted *m'chayeh hakol* (literally, "giving life to everything") and translated it freely as "all life is your gift," or more literally, "gives life to all," or even "Source of Life." Sometimes, the issue is bypassed completely by offering an altogether different prayer in the English suggested by the theme of the Hebrew. All these emendations expurgate the idea of bodily resurrection or even spiritual eternality and instead praise God as the force that sustains all life.

Reconstructionist liturgy has been especially careful to avoid any notions that do not accord with the rationalistic sensibilities of its founders. The *Daily Prayer Book* (1963) removed "You faithfully give life to the dead," from both Hebrew and English, and substituted the geonic interpolation for the Ten Days of Repentance, "Who in mercy remembers His creatures for life." Its current *Kol Haneshamah* inserts *m'chayeh kol chai,* translated as "nurturing the life of every living thing," and goes on to describe God not as "the One who gives life to the dead" but as "the fount of life, who gives and renews life."

In the same naturalistic vein, *The Book of Blessings* compresses this entire benediction into "Let us bless the well eternally giving — the circle of life ever-dying, ever-living."

At the same time, some very recent books have restored the original. *Siddur Lev Chadash* put back the Hebrew *m'chayeh hametim,* but translates it "You are the source of eternal life" — an example once again of the contemporary proclivity of the Reform and British Liberal Movements to retain an old Hebrew text for emotional reasons while employing translation to mute or transform ideologically objectionable elements. Most

Reform Jews do not realize that even the 1975 *Gates of Prayer* experimented with keeping *m'chayeh hametim* in its service for Israel's Independence Day (p. 599). In honor of the occasion, the text for the *Amidah* was drawn largely from the Genizah fragments, the ancient *minhag* of Eretz Yisrael, which the editors were loath to alter, especially since resurrection seemed a fitting way to think about the founding of the modern state of Israel.

Finally, Israel's *Ha'avodah Shebalev* displays another Reform tendency — to retain the latent emotional content of the service by reproducing the rhythm of the traditional text, albeit in different Hebrew words. Instead of *m'chayeh metim atah,* we have *mashpil af m'romem atah* ("You humble, even as You elevate" — a citation from 1 Sam. 2:7). The sound or feel of the language is similar, but the meaning is altogether new.

The mantra-like power of the Hebrew for Jewish worshipers is retained also in the prayer books of the Conservative Movement. While its 1974 *Weekday Prayer Book* appears to be comfortable with the notion of bodily resurrection, translating the phrase "With great mercy You bring the dead to life again," the other Conservative precursor to *Siddur Sim Shalom, Sabbath and Festival Prayer Book,* opts for spiritual immortality by saying, "Faithful art Thou, O Lord, who callest the dead to life everlasting." Elsewhere, the same precursor prefers to call God "Master over Life and Death," a strategy adopted by *Siddur Sim Shalom* as well.

"You cause the wind to blow . . . the rain to fall / You bring down the dew" Traditional practice mandates these lines only during certain months of the year, corresponding to the seasonal cycle in the Land of Israel. As such, they not only affirm God as the master of nature, but do so particularistically with regard to Eretz Yisrael. The contemporary Israeli Reform prayer book, *Ha'avodah Shebalev,* therefore happily includes them. However, classical Reform liturgists (beginning with David Einhorn), who opposed Zionistic sentiments, removed these lines from their services. The North American *Union Prayer Book* and *Gates of Prayer* as well as the British *Service of the Heart* followed suit. So too did the 1963 Reconstructionist *Daily Prayer Book,* not because the movement's founder rejected Zionism, but because he rejected a personal deity who micromanages nature.

Isaac Mayer Wise, however, took a different tack and inserted these lines as a permanent part of this benediction without variation depending on Israel's climatic cycle. He could thus affirm God's responsibility for nature everywhere, not just in Israel. Great Britain's Liberal *Siddur Lev Chadash* does the same thing, even adding *mazr'iach hashemesh* — God is "the One who causes the sun to shine."

◆

FALK (FEMINISM)

literally, "who revives all," while *Kol Haneshamah* substitutes *m'chayeh kol chai,* literally, "who revives all that lives." The substitution of *hakol,* "all," or *kol chai,* "all that lives," for *metim,* "the dead," is, of course, a euphemism — for, after all, what can be "given life" or "revived" except that which is lifeless or dead? — and one that seems unnecessarily evasive. Presumably, contemporary objections to the phrase *m'chayeh metim* have to do with the literal interpretation of it as referring to the resurrection of the dead in messianic times. While that may once have been its primary meaning, there are a number of other ways to read it and to reconstruct the idea behind it. Indeed, of all theological concepts, that of *t'chiyat hametim,* "revival of the dead," seems especially worth grappling with, since it addresses one of the monumental concerns of human life — our relationship to mortality.

I find *t'chiyat hametim* to be especially meaningful when it is understood to be an affirmation of death as an integral part of life. For what is life without death? And what life is not part of the circle of dying, and what death is not part of the circle of living? I have tried to express this in a meditation for this section of the *Amidah* (found in *The Book of Blessings*):

> To celebrate life is to acknowledge the ongoing dying, and ultimately to embrace death. For although all life travels toward its death, death is not a destination: it too is a journey to beginnings: all death leads to life again. From peelings to mulch to new potatoes, the world is ever-renewing, ever-renewed.

Unlike Ezekiel's vision of the dry bones rising from their graves or Daniel's prophecy of the sleepers roused from the dust, the understanding of *t'chiyat hametim* as life in continuous regenerative movement, continually dying and renewing itself, is neither apocalyptic nor fantastic; rather, it is based on simple observation of the natural world. Yet it addresses an age-old spiritual quest — the need to understand our origins and accept our finitude — through an awareness of our lives as part of a greater, ongoing whole. For those of us who do not find comfort in the realm of the supernatural — in concepts that we cannot embrace with full intellectual integrity — the discovery of meaning and mystery within the natural world can be all we need of miracles. Indeed, it may be for us just as sustaining as the visions of the biblical prophets were in their own time.

———◆———

KUSHNER & POLEN (CHASIDISM)

speak!") *Divrei Shmuel* suggests that similarly, when we pray, we are able to activate the creative divine power residing in the letters and words of the prayer.

In just this way, we are able to bring those who seem to be hopelessly lost, spiritually dead, "back to life." We begin with the purity of intention and focus on ourselves, then we shift our attention to the letters themselves, awakening the power latent within them, and finally, we share this life-giving energy with "sleepers in the dust." We become agents of the divine in spreading God's life-giving power in and through the letters. "Blessed are You, O God, who gives life to the dead!"

———◆———

LANDES (HALAKHAH)

the presumption is that you are used to saying it and that you therefore did so, whether you noticed it or not, so that you may continue praying without repeating anything.

The alternative prayer regarding dew is inserted in summer (the other half of the year), in accord with the climate of the Land of Israel. Various rules exist regarding what to do if a mistake is made regarding these insertions:

1. If you mention dew instead of rain during the winter months:
    a. If you catch the error before finishing the blessing, go back and recite the prayer, this time mentioning rain, and then repeat the rest of the blessing.
    b. If you catch the error after concluding the blessing, do not return; just proceed to the next blessing.

2. If you forget to say any insertion at all during the winter months:
    a. If you catch the error before finishing the blessing, go back and recite the prayer, this time mentioning rain, and then repeat the rest of the blessing (as above, 1a).
    b. If you have actually finished the blessing but not yet begun the next one (the *K'dushah*), just insert the missing prayer, with "rain," and continue with the next blessing.
    c. If you catch the error after beginning the *K'dushah,* stop and return to the very beginning of the *Amidah* and say the whole prayer over again correctly.

3. If you mention rain instead of dew in the summer months:
    a. If you catch the error before completing the blessing, go back to the beginning of the blessing and say it over again with the right insertion.
    b. If you catch the error after the blessing has been completed, stop and return to the very beginning of the *Amidah* and say the whole prayer over again correctly (Gra).

Technically, this is an instance of "mentioning" God's gifts of rain and dew, as instances of God's power. It is not intended as a petition for them. The petitions are inserted in Blessing 9, "Years" (see below, "Grant blessing/dew and rain for blessing").

"Freeing the captive" Of all the great, heroic acts of God that we can emulate, the freeing of Jewish prisoners (the *mitzvah* of *pidyon sh'vuyim)* is the greatest. As an act of *ts'dakah,* it is of primary importance (Maimonides, "Laws of Gifts to the Poor" 8:10).

L. HOFFMAN (HISTORY)

something to go on: my prior experience with the person doing the reporting. The highest level of faith is belief in something that no one has ever seen — like a God who provides eternal life, especially where the eternal life that is pictured is patently "unbelievable": resurrection of the dead. Resurrection became a central doctrine among the Rabbis and was carried over into Christianity, where the resurrection of Jesus represented the core around which everything else revolved. Church Father Augustine knew how outlandish the idea of resurrection was and affirmed, "I believe because it is absurd." Echoing a similar point of view, among Jews, the medieval halakhist called the Roke'ach says that it is a special merit that we continue to believe in resurrection, the one point of faith to which, by definition, no one can ever attest.

But Jews have often had difficulty believing in bodily resurrection. The Mishnah (San. 10:1, c. 200) says that eternal life will be withheld from anyone who denies that resurrection is attested in the Torah. This is no argument against pagans, obviously, since only other believing Jews would have been likely to debate what the Torah attests. Even in rabbinic circles, therefore, some people questioned the reality of resurrection.

In the Middle Ages, the doctrine underwent further critique. In his commentary on the Mishnah, Maimonides calls it a "cardinal doctrine," but the way he glosses over it in his code ("Laws of Repentance" 8) made his critics think he really disbelieved it, preferring instead the talmudic notion (Ber. 17a) of a world to come that is wholly spiritual, a state reserved for the soul while the body decomposes forever. The critics may have been right. Maimonides championed a Jewish version of Aristotle's view, whereby it is a person's acquired intellect that is eternal; it joins with God's own intellect, as it were, making disembodied knowledge the only thing that lasts forever. Hell is the absence of such a glorious future, the death of a body without any eternal wisdom attained by the soul.

Did Maimonides also believe in bodily resurrection? In a later letter, he says he does, but guardedly, and not as an end in itself. First, he reaffirms his belief in a disembodied world-to-come for the soul's acquired intellect. It exists already, he says, parallel to the world of the senses that we inhabit, and our soul goes there immediately after we die. The sensory world, however, exists in time (unlike the disembodied world of eternity, which does not), and the history of this time bound world will climax with the coming of the messiah. At that point, resurrection of the righteous will take place. But after living for a long time under wonderful messianic conditions, the resurrected bodies will die a second time, and then the souls of those bodies will have a second chance to enter the ultimate goal of the disembodied world-to-come. Our goal, then, should not be resurrection, though that may occur, but mastery of wisdom, which alone is eternal.

Spanish commentator Abudarham (fourteenth century) says the whole point of the service is the affirmation of matters of faith like this one: things no one has ever seen. Whenever the prayer leader of his day would come to such blessings, the whole congregation would shout, "Amen," affirming faith in the possibility that what no one had ever seen would nonetheless come to pass. Our hope is buttressed by a belief in a Presence in the universe totally beyond ourselves such that even the outlandish may come to pass.

With the rise of science, resurrection was attacked anew, leading liberal Jews to make their benediction reflect some other image of eternal life (see Ellenson). The particular image we choose matters less than the underlying point that all the images have in common: the denial of the view that we are born by accident, live out our years by chance, and then die without significance. Less than we need to affirm the precise nature of the alternative, we need to believe that an alternative is possible, and toward that end, our liturgy gives us many traditional images, including resurrection. The important thing is to believe that our life has eternal value in one way or another and then to live so that we affirm that value daily.

Maimonides would have agreed. He urges his readers, "Concerning these things [matters of the world-to-come, resurrection, and the messianic age] no one knows how they will come to pass until they actually occur. For the prophets record them only as veiled allusions, and the only traditions our sages have are those that come from Scripture, so opinion is divided. Whatever turns out to be the case, the order and details of what will happen do not belong to the essence of religion. It is wrong, then, to ponder tales that may be legend, or midrashic accounts on such matters. One should avoid making them central since they cannot lead us to reverence and love of God."

———◆———

J. HOFFMAN (TRANSLATION)

follows is part of this phrase (i.e., the phrase would read *m'chayeh metim atah*), *atah* ("You") being the subject of *m'chayeh metim,* the sense would be that "You [God] are a life-giver," but elsewhere in the prayer we have no way of knowing.

"Dead" could also be "dying." Taken with the ambiguity inherent in *m'chayeh,* we have a variety of possible meanings supported by the original Hebrew: "You give life to the dying" (i.e., You do not let people die, to begin with); "You are the life-giver to the dying" (any help that arrives for people who would otherwise die comes from God, though in fact, they may not actually get any); "You give life to the dead" (resurrection); and "You are the life-giver to the dead" (any potential resurrection comes from God, though there may not be any). Here we take one likely interpretation and use it throughout, recognizing that the Hebrew is ambiguous. Our translation accords with the assumption that the Rabbis believed in resurrection as an event that would actually occur, not just something within God's power to bring about, in theory. See also "You faithfully give life to the dead," below.

"You sustain life with kindness [b'chesed]" Above ("Who acts most piously") we used "piety" for *chesed,* primarily to preserve parallel structure. Here we use the more common "kindness." The Hebrew, like the English, is ambiguous as to whether "kindness" here is an attribute of God or a tool in sustaining life.

"Sleepers in the dust" Presumably meaning those who have died, akin to the modern English colloquialism "bit the dust."

"Causes death and causes life, and causes salvation [memit, um'chayeh, umatzmi'ach]" *M'chayeh* above (see "Giving life") is translated as "giving life," but it is changed here to convey the parallelism in the Hebrew. *Gates of Prayer* (Reform) offers the particularly poetic "author of life and death."

"You faithfully give life to the dead" Probably meaning "You can be counted on to."

"Who gives life" This odd transition from second-person "You" to third-person "who gives" typifies the rabbinic blessing style, and so we retain it in the English.

◆ ◆ ◆

BRETTLER (BIBLE)

"Let us sanctify" The community's recitation of "Let us sanctify" reflects the human desire to parallel the divine retinue's act of sanctifying God. Although the Bible knows nothing of the idea of *sanctifying* God on earth to match what is done in heaven, Ps. 148:1–12 calls upon God *to be praised* from the heavens and earth, equally (cf. Ps. 103:20–22). A Dead Sea Scroll hymn likewise suggests that people praise God alongside the angels (F. G. Martinez, *The Dead Sea Scrolls Translated,* p. 332; 1QH XI21–22).   *(p. 87)*

FALK (FEMINISM)

"You are holy and your name is holy" The third blessing of the *Amidah, K'dushat Hashem,* "Sanctification of God's Name," is concise and emphatic: "You are holy and your name is holy, and holy beings praise You every day forever. Blessed are You, Adonai, the holy God." The key words here — "holiness" and "name" — are integrally connected to each other, for the way in which we name something is the way we differentiate it — set it apart — from other things; and holiness, according to rabbinic teaching, is the very quality of being set apart,   *(p. 88)*

DORFF (THEOLOGY)

"Let us sanctify" God is inherently holy; we do not make Him so. We announce his holiness in the world so that all may note it and respond accordingly.

"Your praise, our God, will never depart our mouths" We invoke three attributes of God: God's holiness, God's heaviness, and God's greatness. God's holiness (from the root *kadosh)* refers to God's otherness, the distinctive characteristic that makes God different from all other beings. God's heaviness *(kavod)* denotes God's significance, the quality that makes us give God honor *(kavod* = "honor" comes from the root *kaved* = "heavy"). "Your greatness" *(godlekha)* refers to God's power. These three qualities combine to make   *(p. 88)*

3. *K'DUSHAT HASHEM* ("SANCTIFICATION OF GOD'S NAME")

קְדוּשַׁת הַשֵּׁם

[This version is said individually during the period of silent prayer that precedes the repetition by the prayer leader:]

1 You are holy and your name is holy, and holy beings will praise You every day forever. *2 Blessed are You, Adonai, the holy God.

HAUPTMAN (TALMUD)

"You are holy" Aside from one verb that talks about holy beings who "will praise You every day forever," the other verbs in this blessing are all in the present tense. The tense we find in the rest of the *Amidah* is the imperative or the future: we command God, in no uncertain terms, to save us, bless us, sound a shofar, and so on; and we think about the distant future, saying, for instance, "May there be no hope for slanderers." This future orientation is fitting because those blessings are all on national themes. The present tense here stands out, therefore, claiming an immediacy of attention on the part of the worshiper.

———◆———

KUSHNER & POLEN (CHASIDISM)

"Holy, holy, holy" According to *Keter N'hora*, associated with the circle of Levi Yitzchak of Berditchev (1740–1810), the recitation of "The Sanctification of God's Name" (or the *K'dushah*) is to be accompanied by a meditative and bodily sacred choreography. We should, first of all, intend to fulfill the injunction "And I [God] shall be sanctified *among* the children of Israel" (Lev. 22:32). And during the *chazarat hashatz* (the prayer leader's repetition), we should close our eyes. Everything in the blessing should be spoken quietly, except for the "holy, holy, holy" *(kadosh, kadosh, kadosh)*, which should be pronounced in a loud voice. And while doing so, we should look upward but with closed eyes!

We should also contemplate Isa. 6:3, from *(p. 89)*

LANDES (HALAKHAH)

"Let us sanctify" During the prayer reader's repetition of the *Amidah*, the *K'dushah* is recited with great intention to fulfill the Torah command, *V'nikdashti*, "I shall be sanctified among the children of Israel" (Lev. 22:32). This *mitzvah*, uniquely Israel's (Maimonides, "Positive Commandments" No. 9), is perhaps the greatest of communal commandments and is fulfilled here by the recital of the *K'dushah (Torat Habayit*, p. 77).

The congregation says the *K'dushah* while standing with feet *(p. 91)*

L. HOFFMAN (HISTORY)

THE FINAL BLESSING IN THE OPENING TRIAD INVOKES THE PROPHETIC IMAGE OF THE ANGELS PRAISING GOD, ESPECIALLY WITH THE FAMILIAR LINE FROM ISAIAH: "HOLY, HOLY, HOLY IS THE LORD OF HOSTS. THE WHOLE EARTH IS FULL OF HIS GLORY."

"Holy, holy, holy" This is one of three places in the liturgy where the paradigmatic vision of Isaiah 6:3 is held up as ideal for human spiritual aspirations. Its full title is *K'dushat Hashem* ("Sanctification of God's Name"), but that title is usually shortened to *"K'dushah."* *(p. 92)*

¹אַתָּה קָדוֹשׁ וְשִׁמְךָ קָדוֹשׁ וּקְדוֹשִׁים בְּכָל־יוֹם יְהַלְלוּךָ סֶּלָה. *2* בָּרוּךְ אַתָּה יְיָ הָאֵל הַקָּדוֹשׁ.

J. HOFFMAN (TRANSLATION)

"Forever [selah]" From the way it is used in Psalms, it appears that the word *selah* was a technical musical term, perhaps an instruction to those who would sing this text. But *selah* appears only at the end of certain passages, and so it cannot have been anything so common as "sharp," "flat," "forte," etc.

Later, the word is held to have meant "forever."

We can reconcile these two uses if we assume that *selah* always meant "for a long time / forever" and that its musical meaning was the same as the modern-day *fermata* ⌒, which indicates that a note is to be held longer than normally.

"It is sanctified" Literally, "they sanctify," but English typically *(p. 93)*

<table>
<tr>
<td>

[*From Rosh Hashanah to Yom Kippur, say instead:

³ Blessed are You, Adonai, the holy king.]

</td>
<td>

[*From Rosh Hashanah to Yom Kippur, say instead:

³ בָּרוּךְ אַתָּה יְיָ הַמֶּלֶךְ הַקָּדוֹשׁ.]

</td>
</tr>
</table>

[This version is reserved for the public repetition of the Amidah by the prayer leader:]

[Prayer leader]

<table>
<tr>
<td>

⁴ Let us sanctify your name on earth, as it is sanctified in the heavens on high, as written by your prophet, "They called out one to another:

</td>
<td>

⁴ נְקַדֵּשׁ אֶת־שִׁמְךָ בָּעוֹלָם כְּשֵׁם שֶׁמַּקְדִּישִׁים אוֹתוֹ בִּשְׁמֵי מָרוֹם כַּכָּתוּב עַל יַד נְבִיאֶךָ וְקָרָא זֶה אֶל זֶה וְאָמַר:

</td>
</tr>
</table>

[Congregation and Prayer leader]

<table>
<tr>
<td>

⁵ 'Holy, holy, holy is the Lord of hosts. The whole earth is full of his glory.'

</td>
<td>

⁵ קָדוֹשׁ קָדוֹשׁ קָדוֹשׁ יְיָ צְבָאוֹת מְלֹא כָל־הָאָרֶץ כְּבוֹדוֹ.

</td>
</tr>
</table>

[Prayer leader]

<table>
<tr>
<td>

⁶ From across the way they offer blessing:

</td>
<td>

⁶ לְעֻמָּתָם בָּרוּךְ יֹאמֵרוּ:

</td>
</tr>
</table>

[Congregation and Prayer leader]

<table>
<tr>
<td>

'The glory of Adonai is blessed from his place.'"

</td>
<td>

בָּרוּךְ כְּבוֹד יְיָ מִמְּקוֹמוֹ.

</td>
</tr>
</table>

[Prayer leader]

<table>
<tr>
<td>

⁷ In your holy scriptures it is written:

</td>
<td>

⁷ וּבְדִבְרֵי קָדְשְׁךָ כָּתוּב לֵאמֹר:

</td>
</tr>
</table>

[Congregation and Prayer leader]

<table>
<tr>
<td>

"Adonai will reign forever, your God, Zion, for all generations. Halleluyah."

</td>
<td>

יִמְלֹךְ יְיָ לְעוֹלָם אֱלֹהַיִךְ צִיּוֹן לְדֹר וָדֹר הַלְלוּיָהּ.

</td>
</tr>
</table>

[Prayer leader]

<table>
<tr>
<td>

⁸ For all generations we will tell of your greatness and for all of eternity proclaim your holiness. ⁹ Your praise,

</td>
<td>

⁸ לְדוֹר וָדוֹר נַגִּיד גָּדְלֶךָ וּלְנֵצַח נְצָחִים קְדֻשָּׁתְךָ נַקְדִּישׁ.

</td>
</tr>
</table>

our God, will never depart our mouths, for You are a sovereign God, great and holy. *[10] Blessed are You, Adonai, the holy God.

⁹וְשִׁבְחֲךָ אֱלֹהֵינוּ מִפִּינוּ לֹא יָמוּשׁ לְעוֹלָם וָעֶד כִּי אֵל מֶלֶךְ גָּדוֹל וְקָדוֹשׁ אֱתָּה. [10] בָּרוּךְ אַתָּה יְיָ הָאֵל הַקָּדוֹשׁ.

[*From Rosh Hashanah to Yom Kippur, say instead:

[*From Rosh Hashanah to Yom Kippur, say instead:

[11] Blessed are You, Adonai, the holy king.]

[בָּרוּךְ אַתָּה יְיָ הַמֶּלֶךְ הַקָּדוֹשׁ.]¹¹

BRETTLER (BIBLE)

"On earth" [ba'olam] See "Adonai will reign forever" *[l'olam]*, below.

"Heavens [sh'mei] *on high* [marom]" Literally "heavens of heavens." This is typical biblical style: two words that are largely synonymous (*shamayim* = "heavens" and *marom* = "on high" or "heavens") are juxtaposed to express a superlative.

"As written by your prophet" From Isa. 6:3. (See comments on "Be blessed our rock" in Volume 1, *The Sh'ma and Its Blessings,* p. 56.)

"From across the way" Suggesting, perhaps, an antiphonal response between the earth-bound sanctification of God and the angelic praise in heaven.

"Adonai will reign forever [l'olam], *your God, Zion, for all generations. Halleluyah."* Alternatively, "May Adonai reign forever . . . ," meant to express a wish or desire that God will be forever sovereign. The previous two verses (from Isaiah 6 and Ezekiel 3) were chosen because they were understood to be part of the libretto of the heavenly praise of God. This verse, taken from the conclusion to Psalm 146, suggests praise also because it pictures God as a reigning monarch and, by implication, receiving praise from his angelic servants. Additionally, *l'olam* ("forever") nicely mirrors the word *ba'olam* ("on earth") in the opening sentence of the blessing.

"For all generations we will tell of your greatness" Although a conclusion specifically of the *K'dushah,* this paragraph functions also as a summary for all three of the first blessings, as it refers to God's greatness, the theme of the first and second blessings, and his holiness ("your greatness . . . your holiness"; "great and holy"). Traditionally, the first three blessings are seen as a unit. They follow biblical style in that they offer God praise before the petitions that will follow.

AMIDAH: BLESSINGS OF PRAISE

DORFF (THEOLOGY)

God awesome, and even an object of fear, but for all the respect and awe he feels, the author of this prayer is convinced that the proper response should be praise: "Your praise, our God, will never depart our mouths." Though powerful, significant, and other, God is nevertheless to be trusted as One worthy of praise.

———◆———

FALK (FEMINISM)

distinct, distinguished. It is not coincidental that another sanctification of God's name, the *Kaddish*—whose opening words read *Yitgadal v'yitkadash sh'meih rabba,* "May his great name be magnified and sanctified"—also makes this connection.

What is the relationship, for us today, between the domain of the sacred and the human act of naming? One way to think about this is to consider how we acquire our own "names"—that is, our individual (human) identities—and then to compare this to how we "name toward" God, attaching words and images to our experience of the divine. In a moving incantatory poem, widely adopted for use in memorial services in Israel, the twentieth-century Hebrew poet Zelda explores naming as a way to understand the multifaceted nature of the individual human life. Each stanza in the poem begins "Each of us has a name" (my translation, as found in *The Book of Blessings)* and then goes on to list the numerous circumstances and forces that give a person her or his *many* names—from parents to neighbors to enemies, from one's stature, clothing, and smile to the mountains, the seasons, and death.

Zelda's poem appears to be an elaboration on a rabbinic theme. In the Midrash (Koh. Rab. 7:1), the Rabbis teach, "A person is called by three names: one that his father and his mother call him by, one that others call him by, and one that he is called in the book telling the story of his creation." The Midrash Tanchuma (Parashat Vayak'hel) reads, "One finds three names by which a person is called: one that his father and his mother call him by, one that people call him by, and one that he acquires for himself. The best of all is that which he acquires for himself." The Rabbis recognize here that a human life is not containable in a single stage of development, nor is it sufficiently understood or reflected by a single viewpoint, as represented by a single name. Zelda elaborates on this insight by suggesting the multitude of aspects that come to define or name a life.

So too, the human experience of the divine cannot be captured by any single name—whether that name be the enshrined and liturgically dominant *Adonai* or one of the many alternatives that have arisen over the course of Jewish history, including, of course, in our own generation. The core revelation that contemporary Jewish feminism brings to theological naming is not the need to introduce feminine names for God to counterbalance God's overwhelming maleness in the liturgy—although this surely *is* important as a first step toward creating inclusive Judaism. The deeper insight to which feminist awareness logically leads is that we need to expand our theological naming in a multiplicity of directions, so that we can begin to genuinely recognize and reflect the diversity of our lives. By means of many different images and perspectives, and a variety of liturgical voices and genres, we may come to honor diversity not only in the context of our theology and our liturgy, but — ultimately and most important — in our daily dealings with the world.

———◆———

KUSHNER & POLEN (CHASIDISM)

which the prayer is taken, in its Aramaic translation (another version of the *K'dushah* called the *K'dushah D'sidra*, and recited near the conclusion of the morning service, actually contains this translation). From here we learn that the first "holy" refers to God's holiness in the heaven above, the residence of the divine. The second "holy" is God's holiness on earth, the handiwork of divine creativity. And the third "holy" evokes God's holiness in time, for ever and ever. This then is the meaning of the next phrase in the Isaiah verse, "The whole world is filled with the radiance of the divine Glory!" God's holiness is heavenly, earthly, and temporal.

The Isaiah passage goes on to describe how the prophet saw a seraf (a fiery angel) "fly" with a pair of wings, "And with two the seraf would fly." Thus, through our own sacred choreography we literally "fly" just like the angels themselves! And this is the origin, suggests Rabbi Levi Yitzchak of Berditchev, of "fluttering" on one's feet, standing on our tiptoes with each mention of *kadosh,* "holy."

"The holy God" Rabbi Yehuda Aryeh Leib of Ger, author of the *S'fas Emes* (1895, p. 165, *K'doshim),* suggests that there are not one but three modes of holiness. Leviticus Rabbah (24:8) tells us, "Rabbi Abin observed that it is like a case wherein the citizens of a province made three crowns for the king. What did the king do? He placed one on his own head and two on the heads of his sons. Similarly, every day the celestial beings crown the Holy One, blessed be He, with the three sanctities of 'Holy, holy, holy.' What does the Holy One do? God places one on his own head and two on the head of Israel." But God's holiness is unlike ours. The commandment in Lev. 19:2, "You shall be holy, for I, the Lord your God, am holy," might reasonably lead us to think that we are able to be *like* God. For this reason the text says, "I, the Lord your God, am holy," meaning "My God-like holiness is utterly beyond your human holiness."

We find this same idea echoed in 1 Sam. 2:2, "There is no holiness like God, for there is nothing other than You." Holiness is more than merely separating oneself from this world. For while God is beyond and separate from all creation (as it is written in Ps. 92:9, "You, God, are always beyond everything"), God also creates everything and continuously gives it life — even while remaining utterly beyond and separate from it. And just this is the essence of the mystery of the divine holiness, for even though "there is nothing other than You," nevertheless, You, God, sustain everything. For this reason God is unique, remaining in a state of unattainable divine holiness.

And this also bears witness to the essential nature of God's holiness as we have it from Isaac Luria where he talks about how God brought us out from Egypt. Luria notes that the Passover Haggadah says, "I and not an angel." (See also Mekhilta, Pis'cha, chapter 7.) For not even an angel could survive entering the terrible defilement of Egypt. Only God, whose holiness is utterly beyond and "other" than this world in every way, could make it happen, as it says, "And You [God] remain exalted beyond everything, forever" (Ps. 92:9), meaning "Even when You are in the world You are still exalted beyond it." The psalm says, "*And* You . . . " with a superfluous conjunction, "and," thereby implying that the pious, or *tsadikim,* who become one with God, are also exalted and merit this quality of holiness. Even though they remain *in* the world, they are not *of* the world.

Like the *tsadikim,* Israel too has some of this quality of being in the world while also being beyond it. For this reason, Israel is above the angels. Although the children of Israel went down into Egypt, they were nevertheless able to remain holy. And just this is what is hinted at in our midrash. While the angels are described as holy only once, Israel is called holy twice. Angelic holiness is ethereal, separate and distinct from the physical body. But another kind of holiness is bestowed upon Israel. Even though they have bodies and are clothed in physical form, they are able nonetheless to remain in a state of holiness!

And this is the meaning of "And you shall *be* holy . . .," meaning that you must remain in your state of holiness, just as we read in Pesachim 23a, "in their being, they shall be. . . ." Each Jew needs to guard that inner holy spark from becoming contaminated. As it is written in Ps. 101:3, "I will set no base thing before my eyes; I hate the doing of things crooked; it shall not *cleave* unto me." We are to watch over ourselves, thereby fulfilling Lev. 11:44 and 20:7, "You shall make yourselves holy," meaning that we will merit holiness and protect our souls from all contamination. This is the meaning of the praise that Song of Songs (2:2) bestows on Israel, "As a lily among the thorns." Even though Israel is mixed up in this world, nevertheless they are like a tightly enfolded rose, whose innermost holiness is guarded always.

And this is why Isa. 6:3 says, "Holy, holy, holy, is the Lord of Hosts, the whole world is full of God's glory." This threefold repetition of "holy" reflects a tripartite hierarchy of holiness! The first level of holiness is what we find with the angels: they are simply separated from anything physical. The second level of holiness is what we find with Israel: even though they are entangled with the physical world and frequently find themselves in impure situations, they nevertheless remain separate, distinct, and tightly enfolded. But God's holiness is even beyond these two. Even though "the whole world is full of God's glory," and even though God continually gives life to everything and brings everything into being, nevertheless — even though it is beyond human comprehension — God remains unique in God's holiness. God is *in* the world and *of* the world, yet *still* holy.

We could summarize the teaching thus: Angels are neither *in* nor *of* the world; they are utterly ethereal. That is how they remain holy. Israel is *in* the world but not entirely *of* it, as we were in Egypt. That is how we remain holy. God, in a way that is necessarily and logically incomprehensible to human beings, is totally *in* and *of* the world, yet nevertheless, still beyond it *and* holy!

And this is what our midrash is talking about when it speaks of our being holy like God. You might think that when it says "like Me," that it means that a person might be able to do whatever the heart desires and still remain in a state of holiness. Indeed this was precisely the perverse argument of the snake (Gen. 3:5) when he said, "And you shall be like God, knowing good and evil." But God had warned us (Gen. 2:17), "On the day that you eat from it, you will surely die." For it was known to God that Adam and Eve were not permitted to be in such a state of heightened holiness. For this reason, the children of Israel need to continue to protect their holiness by observing the Torah's commandments, which describe both what we are able to do in holiness as well as those things that we must shun. If we do so, then the promise of our sages (Baba Batra 75b) will at last come true. We shall be called "holy," just as God is called "holy."

———◆———

LANDES (HALAKHAH)

together and eyes heavenward. If you have already prayed earlier but find yourself in the presence of a *minyan* where the *K'dushah* is being repeated, it is necessary to join in the repetition. If you have not finished your private recitation yet, stop and concentrate on the *K'dushah* as it is repeated, but do not actually recite it yourself.

Technically (Gra, *Ma'aseh Rav* 44), the proper way to repeat the *K'dushah* is as follows:

1. *N'kadesh* ("Let us sanctify . . ."): The prayer leader alone recites this introductory section through *v'kara zeh el zeh v'amar* ("They called out one to another").
2. The congregation responds with *Kadosh kadosh kadosh* ("Holy, holy, holy") to *m'lo khol ha'arets k'vodo* (". . . full of his glory").

    It is customary, however, for the congregation to recite the introductory section *(N'kadesh,* 1 above) with the prayer leader *(Shulchan Aruch,* O. Ch. 25, *Mishnah B'rurah,* subsection 102).
3. The prayer leader and congregation then alternate, with the congregation concluding the end of each section that the prayer leader says: i.e., *Barukh k'vod Ado-nai mim'komo* ("The glory of Ado-nai is blessed from his place") and *Yimlokh Ado-nai l'olam . . . hall'luyah* ("Ado-nai will reign forever . . . Halleluyah"). The three congregational responses *(Kadosh . . ., Barukh k'vod . . .,* and *Yimlokh . . .)* are said in a loud voice with great enthusiasm. The reader joins in with an equal, but not dominant, voice (Maimonides, "Order of Prayer," end of "Laws of Prayer").

At *v'kara zeh,* bow to the left; at *el zeh,* bow to the right.

We rise on our toes at each mention of *kadosh.* Some people do so once also at *Barukh k'vod* and again at *Yimlokh* (Ben Ish Chai, *T'rumah* 4–6), but Halakhah forbids any attempt to jump into the air (Rema 122:2, *Mishnah B'rurah* 7). It is best to retain a full, reverential posture until the reader has completed the blessing *(Darchei Moshe,* quoting the practice of the Maharil), but if need be, you may move after reciting *Yimlokh.*

AMIDAH: BLESSINGS OF PRAISE

L. HOFFMAN (HISTORY)

This is the *K'dushah* of the *Amidah*. There is also a *K'dushah D'sidra* (which appears near the end of the service) and a *K'dushah* of the *Yotser*, a recitation of "Holy, holy, holy" in the first blessing preceding the daily *Sh'ma* (see Volume 1, *The Sh'ma and Its Blessings*, p. 42).

The Rabbis believed in angels the way we believe in a conscience — that is, they used projective language, while we prefer introjective language. They saw God without; we like to think of God within. The goal of worship for many moderns is to go "deep down inside ourselves" or to "get in touch with ourselves"; in antiquity, the same thing was expressed by the desire to get out of ourselves and to join the realm of the angelic host.

The angels' praise of God therefore became the most important part of the *Amidah*. Poets wrote complex nine-part poems for the *Amidah*, called *k'dushta'ot* (sing., *k'dushta*). The first two parts were inserted into the first and second blessings of the *Amidah*, where they generally combined the theme of the Torah and *Haftarah* portion with the theme of the blessings in question, but the other seven were placed in the third blessing, the *K'dushah*, from which the name of the poem as a whole *(k'dushta)* was derived. These complex poems were written in fifth- and sixth-century Palestine for every single Torah reading, and since the Palestinian cycle took some three to four years, rather than just one year, as is our custom today, we can only marvel at the prodigious output of poets who sometimes managed to complete entire cycles of poems for the synagogues of their day.

Only a fraction of the *k'dushta'ot* once available are still extant today, because Jewish tradition adopted the Babylonian, not the Palestinian, version of our liturgy (see introductory essay, Volume 1, *The Sh'ma and Its Blessings*). Our liturgy for Shabbat is altogether devoid of them. But the holiday liturgy is greatly expanded, precisely because the old poetry is still there. Perhaps the most famous example is the *Un'taneh Tokef*, a poem that we say on the High Holy Days. Its theme is that on Rosh Hashanah our fate is written and on Yom Kippur it is sealed, but "penitence prayer and charity annul the decree's severity." The *Un'taneh Tokef* is popularly held to have been written in Ashkenaz during a period of persecution but is actually the work of a Byzantine poet who may have lived as early as the fifth century, possibly in Palestine. It is the climactic section of what was probably a much lengthier *k'dushta*, once upon a time.

Ashkenazi and Sefardi wording for the *Amidah* is generally similar, but not here. Of the many *K'dushah* versions that existed in antiquity, the two traditions adopted different ones. The Spanish-Portuguese and the Lurianic Sefardi version for the daily morning service is as follows:

> *Let us sanctify and adore you, as the beautiful utterances of the assembly of holy Serafim, who thrice repeat "holy," as written by your prophet, "They called out one to another: 'Holy, holy, holy is the Lord of hosts. The whole earth is full of his glory.' From across the way they offer praise: 'The glory of Adonai is blessed from His place.'" In your holy scriptures it is written: "Adonai will reign forever, your God, Zion, for all generations. Halleluyah. You are holy and your name is holy, and holy beings will praise you every day forever. Blessed are You, Adonai, the holy God.*

נַקְדִּישָׁךְ וְנַעֲרִיצָךְ כְּנֹעַם שִׂיחַ סוֹד שַׂרְפֵי־קֹדֶשׁ הַמְשַׁלְּשִׁים לְךָ קְדֻשָּׁה וְכֵן כָּתוּב עַל יַד נְבִיאֶךָ וְקָרָא זֶה אֶל זֶה וְאָמַר קָדוֹשׁ קָדוֹשׁ קָדוֹשׁ יְיָ צְבָאוֹת מְלֹא כָל־הָאָרֶץ כְּבוֹדוֹ: לְעֻמָּתָם מְשַׁבְּחִים וְאוֹמְרִים בָּרוּךְ כְּבוֹד יְיָ מִמְּקוֹמוֹ: וּבְדִבְרֵי קָדְשְׁךָ כָּתוּב לֵאמֹר: יִמְלֹךְ יְיָ לְעוֹלָם אֱלֹהַיִךְ צִיּוֹן לְדֹר וָדֹר הַלְלוּיָהּ: אַתָּה קָדוֹשׁ וְשִׁמְךָ קָדוֹשׁ וּקְדוֹשִׁים בְּכָל־יוֹם יְהַלְלוּךָ סֶּלָה בָּרוּךְ אַתָּה יְיָ הָאֵל הַקָּדוֹשׁ.

———◆———

J. HOFFMAN (TRANSLATION)

uses the passive where Hebrew uses the third-person plural; the Hebrew is like the French *on* or the German *man*.

"Let us sanctify your name [shimkha] . . . *as* [k'shem she] *it is sanctified in the heavens* [sh'mei] *on high"* It is difficult to capture the beauty of the Hebrew, which relies on the threefold use of the root *sh.m,* first in *shimkha* ("your name"), then in *k'shem she* ("as"), and finally in *sh'mei,* a form of the noun *shamayim* ("heavens"). *Gates of Prayer's* rendition, "we sanctify Your name on earth even as all things to the ends of time and space proclaim your holiness," is also poetically written, but in a different way.

"The whole earth is full of his glory" "His glory fills the whole earth" might seem more natural but would not convey the same emphasis as the Hebrew, which deliberately makes "the whole earth" *(m'lo khol ha'arets)* the subject of the sentence. *Gates of Prayer* (Reform) suggests the more literal "the fullness of the whole earth is his glory," according to which the glory comes from the fact that the whole earth is full — an interesting idea, supported by the Hebrew.

"From across the way [l'umatan]*"* Or "in response."

"Your holy scriptures" Or "your holy words."

"For all generations [l'dor vador]*"* Better, "in each and every generation" or "from generation to generation," but the Hebrew provides a set of idioms here, each representing eternity, and each one beginning with the Hebrew preposition *l': l'dor vador, l'netsach n'tsachim,* and *l'olam.* Our English mirrors the parallelism by starting each phrase with "for": "for all generations," "for all of eternity," and "forever" (above). "Forever" appears in the next line also, but in the negative, forcing us to abandon the parallel structure, since "forever" necessarily becomes "never" in English.

"Halleluyah" That is, "praise God."

"Proclaim your holiness" As in Birnbaum (Orthodox). *Siddur Sim Shalom* (Conservative) offers "hallow your holiness," which better mimics the Hebrew but seems devoid of meaning in English.

———◆ ◆ ◆———

B. Blessings of Petition

4. *Binah* ("Knowledge")

[1] You favor people with knowledge and teach mortals understanding. [2] Favor us with your knowledge, understanding, and wisdom. [3] Blessed are You, Adonai, who favors people with knowledge.

בִּינָה

[1] אַתָּה חוֹנֵן לְאָדָם דַּעַת וּמְלַמֵּד לֶאֱנוֹשׁ בִּינָה. [2] חָנֵּנוּ מֵאִתְּךָ דֵּעָה בִּינָה וְהַשְׂכֵּל. [3] בָּרוּךְ אַתָּה יְיָ חוֹנֵן הַדָּעַת.

5. *T'shuvah* ("Repentance")

[1] Bring us back to your Torah, our father, draw us near to your service, our king, and turn us back, in perfect repentance before You. [2] Blessed are You, Adonai, who takes pleasure in repentance.

תְּשׁוּבָה

[1] הֲשִׁיבֵנוּ אָבִינוּ לְתוֹרָתֶךָ וְקָרְבֵנוּ מַלְכֵּנוּ לַעֲבוֹדָתֶךָ וְהַחֲזִירֵנוּ בִּתְשׁוּבָה שְׁלֵמָה לְפָנֶיךָ. [2] בָּרוּךְ אַתָּה יְיָ הָרוֹצֶה בִּתְשׁוּבָה.

6. *S'lichah* ("Forgiveness")

[1] Forgive us, our father, for we have sinned. [2] Pardon us, our king, for we have transgressed, for You forgive and pardon. [3] Blessed are You, Adonai, who is gracious and quick to forgive.

סְלִיחָה

[1] סְלַח־לָנוּ אָבִינוּ כִּי חָטָאנוּ. [2] מְחַל־לָנוּ מַלְכֵּנוּ כִּי פָשָׁעְנוּ כִּי מוֹחֵל וְסוֹלֵחַ אָתָּה. [3] בָּרוּךְ אַתָּה יְיָ חַנּוּן הַמַּרְבֶּה לִסְלוֹחַ.

7. *G'ulah* ("Redemption")

[1] See our affliction, and fight our fight; redeem us quickly for the sake of your name, for You are a mighty redeemer. [2] Blessed are You, Adonai, who redeems Israel.

גְּאוּלָה

[1] רְאֵה בְעָנְיֵנוּ וְרִיבָה רִיבֵנוּ וּגְאָלֵנוּ מְהֵרָה לְמַעַן שְׁמֶךָ כִּי גּוֹאֵל חָזָק אָתָּה. [2] בָּרוּךְ אַתָּה יְיָ גּוֹאֵל יִשְׂרָאֵל.

[On fast days, add:

[3] Answer us, Adonai, answer us on our fast day, for we are greatly distressed. [4] Do not regard our wickedness, do not hide your face from us, and do not hide from our

[On fast days, add:

[3] עֲנֵנוּ יְיָ עֲנֵנוּ. בְּיוֹם צוֹם תַּעֲנִיתֵנוּ. כִּי בְצָרָה גְדוֹלָה אֲנָחְנוּ. [4] אַל־תֵּפֶן אֶל־רִשְׁעֵנוּ. וְאַל־תַּסְתֵּר פָּנֶיךָ מִמֶּנּוּ. וְאַל־תִּתְעַלַּם מִתְּחִנָּתֵנוּ.

supplication. [5] May You be near to our cry; may your kindness be a comfort to us. [6] Before we call to You, answer us, as it is written, "Before they call, I will answer. While they are still speaking, I will hear." [7] For You, Adonai, who answers in time of distress, redeems and delivers in every time of distress and woe. [8] Blessed are You, Adonai, who answers in time of distress.]

[5] הֱיֵה נָא קָרוֹב לְשַׁוְעָתֵנוּ. יְהִי נָא חַסְדְּךָ לְנַחֲמֵנוּ. [6] טֶרֶם נִקְרָא אֵלֶיךָ עֲנֵנוּ. כַּדָּבָר שֶׁנֶּאֱמַר וְהָיָה טֶרֶם יִקְרָאוּ וַאֲנִי אֶעֱנֶה. עוֹד הֵם מְדַבְּרִים וַאֲנִי אֶשְׁמָע. [7] כִּי אַתָּה יְיָ הָעוֹנֶה בְּעֵת צָרָה. פּוֹדֶה וּמַצִּיל בְּכָל־עֵת צָרָה וְצוּקָה. [8] בָּרוּךְ אַתָּה יְיָ הָעוֹנֶה בְּעֵת צָרָה.]

8. *R'fu'ah* ("Healing")

[1] Heal us, Adonai, that we shall be healed. [2] Save us that we shall be saved, for You are our praise. [3] Bring complete healing to all of our wounds.

[If praying for a specific individual, add:

[4] May it find favor before You, my God and my ancestors' God, that You speedily send complete healing from the heavens, spiritual healing and physical healing to _____ who is sick, along with others who are sick among Israel.]

[5] For You are our sovereign, steadfast, merciful healing God. [6] Praised are You, Adonai, who heals the sick among his People Israel.

רְפוּאָה

[1] רְפָאֵנוּ יְיָ וְנֵרָפֵא. [2] הוֹשִׁיעֵנוּ וְנִוָּשֵׁעָה כִּי תְהִלָּתֵנוּ אָתָּה. [3] וְהַעֲלֵה רְפוּאָה שְׁלֵמָה לְכָל־מַכּוֹתֵינוּ.

[If praying for a specific individual, add:

[4] יְהִי רָצוֹן מִלְּפָנֶיךָ יְיָ אֱלֹהַי וֵאלֹהֵי אֲבוֹתַי שֶׁתִּשְׁלַח מְהֵרָה רְפוּאָה שְׁלֵמָה מִן הַשָּׁמַיִם רְפוּאַת הַנֶּפֶשׁ וּרְפוּאַת הַגּוּף לַחוֹלֶה/לַחוֹלָה _____ בְּתוֹךְ שְׁאָר חוֹלֵי יִשְׂרָאֵל.]

[5] כִּי אֵל מֶלֶךְ רוֹפֵא נֶאֱמָן וְרַחֲמָן אָתָּה. [6] בָּרוּךְ אַתָּה יְיָ רוֹפֵא חוֹלֵי עַמּוֹ יִשְׂרָאֵל.

9. *Shanim* ("Years")

[1] Bless this year for us along with all its various produce for goodness, Adonai our God,

[From Passover to December 4, say:

and grant blessing]

[From December 4 to Passover, say:

and grant dew and rain for blessing]

שָׁנִים

[1] בָּרֵךְ עָלֵינוּ יְיָ אֱלֹהֵינוּ אֶת־הַשָּׁנָה הַזֹּאת וְאֶת־כָּל־מִינֵי תְבוּאָתָהּ לְטוֹבָה

[From Passover to December 4, say:

וְתֵן בְּרָכָה]

[From December 4 to Passover, say:

וְתֵן טַל וּמָטָר לִבְרָכָה]

upon the surface of the earth, and satisfy us with its goodness, and bless our year like the best of years. [2] Blessed are You, Adonai, who blesses our years.

10. KIBBUTZ G'LUYOT ("GATHERING OF THE EXILES")

[1] Sound a great shofar for our freedom, and lift up a banner to gather our exiles, and gather us together from the four corners of the earth. [2] Blessed are You, Adonai, who gathers the dispersed among his People Israel.

11. MISHPAT ("JUSTICE")

[1] Restore our judges as in days of old and our counselors as in former times. [2] And remove sorrow and complaint from among us, and reign over us, You alone, Adonai, in kindness and mercy, and acquit us in trial. *[3] Blessed are You, Adonai, our king who loves righteousness and justice.

[*From Rosh Hashanah to Yom Kippur, say instead:

[4] Blessed are you, Adonai, the king of justice.]

12. MINIM ("HERETICS")

[1] May there be no hope for slanderers, and may all wickedness instantly perish, and may all your enemies quickly be destroyed. [2] May You quickly uproot, smash, destroy, and humble the insolent quickly in our day. [3] Blessed are You, Adonai, who smashes his enemies and humbles the insolent.

עַל פְּנֵי הָאֲדָמָה וְשַׂבְּעֵנוּ מִטּוּבָהּ וּבָרֵךְ שְׁנָתֵנוּ כַּשָּׁנִים הַטּוֹבוֹת. [2] בָּרוּךְ אַתָּה יְיָ מְבָרֵךְ הַשָּׁנִים.

קִבּוּץ גָּלֻיּוֹת

[1] תְּקַע בְּשׁוֹפָר גָּדוֹל לְחֵרוּתֵנוּ וְשָׂא נֵס לְקַבֵּץ גָּלֻיּוֹתֵינוּ וְקַבְּצֵנוּ יַחַד מֵאַרְבַּע כַּנְפוֹת הָאָרֶץ. [2] בָּרוּךְ אַתָּה יְיָ מְקַבֵּץ נִדְחֵי עַמּוֹ יִשְׂרָאֵל.

מִשְׁפָּט

[1] הָשִׁיבָה שׁוֹפְטֵינוּ כְּבָרִאשֹׁנָה וְיוֹעֲצֵינוּ כְּבַתְּחִלָּה. [2] וְהָסֵר מִמֶּנּוּ יָגוֹן וַאֲנָחָה וּמְלֹךְ עָלֵינוּ אַתָּה יְיָ לְבַדְּךָ בְּחֶסֶד וּבְרַחֲמִים וְצַדְּקֵנוּ בַּמִּשְׁפָּט. *[3] בָּרוּךְ אַתָּה יְיָ מֶלֶךְ אוֹהֵב צְדָקָה וּמִשְׁפָּט.

[*From Rosh Hashanah to Yom Kippur, say instead:

[4] בָּרוּךְ אַתָּה יְיָ הַמֶּלֶךְ הַמִּשְׁפָּט.]

מִינִים

[1] וְלַמַּלְשִׁינִים אַל־תְּהִי תִקְוָה וְכָל־הָרִשְׁעָה כְּרֶגַע תֹּאבֵד וְכָל־אוֹיְבֶיךָ מְהֵרָה יִכָּרֵתוּ. [2] וְהַזֵּדִים מְהֵרָה תְעַקֵּר וּתְשַׁבֵּר וּתְמַגֵּר וְתַכְנִיעַ בִּמְהֵרָה בְיָמֵינוּ. [3] בָּרוּךְ אַתָּה יְיָ שׁוֹבֵר אֹיְבִים וּמַכְנִיעַ זֵדִים.

13. Tsadikim ("The Righteous")

[1] Show compassion to the righteous, to the pious, to the leaders of your People, the House of Israel, to the remnants of their sages, to righteous converts, and to us, Adonai our God. [2] And give a good reward to all who truly trust in your name, and let our lot be among them forever that we will not be shamed, for we put our trust in You. [3] Blessed are You, Adonai, who is the support and trust of the righteous.

14. Y'rushalayim ("Jerusalem")

[1] Return to Jerusalem your city in compassion, and dwell in its midst as You promised You would, and rebuild it soon in our day into an eternal structure, and quickly establish David's throne within it. [2] Blessed are You, Adonai, who rebuilds Jerusalem.

15. David ("David")

[1] Cause the progeny of David, your servant, to blossom quickly. [2] Let him shine in your deliverance, for we await your salvation every day. [3] Blessed are You, Adonai, who causes the light of salvation to blossom.

צַדִּיקִים

[1] עַל־הַצַּדִּיקִים וְעַל־הַחֲסִידִים וְעַל־זִקְנֵי עַמְּךָ בֵּית יִשְׂרָאֵל וְעַל־פְּלֵיטַת סוֹפְרֵיהֶם וְעַל גֵּרֵי הַצֶּדֶק וְעָלֵינוּ יֶהֱמוּ רַחֲמֶיךָ יְיָ אֱלֹהֵינוּ. [2] וְתֵן שָׂכָר טוֹב לְכֹל הַבּוֹטְחִים בְּשִׁמְךָ בֶּאֱמֶת וְשִׂים חֶלְקֵנוּ עִמָּהֶם לְעוֹלָם וְלֹא נֵבוֹשׁ כִּי־בְךָ בָּטָחְנוּ. [3] בָּרוּךְ אַתָּה יְיָ מִשְׁעָן וּמִבְטָח לַצַּדִּיקִים.

יְרוּשָׁלַיִם

[1] וְלִירוּשָׁלַיִם עִירְךָ בְּרַחֲמִים תָּשׁוּב וְתִשְׁכֹּן בְּתוֹכָהּ כַּאֲשֶׁר דִּבַּרְתָּ וּבְנֵה אוֹתָהּ בְּקָרוֹב בְּיָמֵינוּ בִּנְיַן עוֹלָם וְכִסֵּא דָוִד מְהֵרָה לְתוֹכָהּ תָּכִין. [2] בָּרוּךְ אַתָּה יְיָ בּוֹנֵה יְרוּשָׁלָיִם.

דָּוִד

[1] אֶת־צֶמַח דָּוִד עַבְדְּךָ מְהֵרָה תַצְמִיחַ. [2] וְקַרְנוֹ תָּרוּם בִּישׁוּעָתֶךָ כִּי לִישׁוּעָתְךָ קִוִּינוּ כָּל־הַיּוֹם. [3] בָּרוּךְ אַתָּה יְיָ מַצְמִיחַ קֶרֶן יְשׁוּעָה.

16. T'FILLAH ("PRAYER")

[1] **H**ear our voice, Adonai our God. [2] Have pity and mercy on us, and accept our prayer with favor, for You are the God who hears our prayers and supplications. [3] Do not turn us away from You, our ruler, empty-handed, for You hear the prayer of your People Israel in mercy. [4] Blessed are You, Adonai, who hears prayer.

[1] שְׁמַע קוֹלֵנוּ יְיָ אֱלֹהֵינוּ. [2] חוּס וְרַחֵם עָלֵינוּ וְקַבֵּל בְּרַחֲמִים וּבְרָצוֹן אֶת־תְּפִלָּתֵנוּ כִּי אֵל שׁוֹמֵעַ תְּפִלּוֹת וְתַחֲנוּנִים אָתָּה. [3] וּמִלְּפָנֶיךָ מַלְכֵּנוּ רֵיקָם אַל תְּשִׁיבֵנוּ, כִּי אַתָּה שׁוֹמֵעַ תְּפִלַּת עַמְּךָ יִשְׂרָאֵל בְּרַחֲמִים. [4] בָּרוּךְ אַתָּה יְיָ שׁוֹמֵעַ תְּפִלָּה.

BRETTLER (BIBLE)

"You favor people with knowledge" The blessing opens with a poetic couplet in typical biblical style: "You favor people with knowledge / and teach mortals understanding." Unlike almost all of the following blessings, moreover, it is a declarative sentence, not an imperative — although an imperative ("Favor us with your knowledge . . .") follows next. Its declarative form, "You favor," creates a stylistic link with the conclusion of the preceding blessing, "You are holy," while the imperative in the second sentence anticipates the blessings that follow, most of which open similarly. The second and third sentences extensively reuse words used (p. 102)

FALK (FEMINISM)

Petitions: The Middle Benedictions As traditionally understood, the *Amidah* has three sections: an introduction consisting of three blessings of praise, a concluding section of three blessings containing thanksgiving, and a middle section that (except on Shabbat and holy days) comprises thirteen blessings of petition. In the Talmud (Ber. 34a), Rabbi Chanina describes this structure with an analogy: "In the first [blessings], he [the worshiper] resembles a servant who is delivering praise to his master; in the middle ones, he resembles a servant who is requesting a largesse from his master; in the last ones, he resembles a servant who has received a largesse from his master, and goes on his way." In Rabbi Chanina's account, the focus of the prayer would (p. 103)

DORFF (THEOLOGY)

"You favor people with knowledge" With the fourth blessing, we begin the middle, or petitionary, section of the daily *Amidah*. In many congregations, it is customary, during the prayer leader's repetition of this section, to pass around a box to collect charity. As we ask God to help us, we demonstrate our commitment to helping others. We thereby model the behavior that we associate with God, while showing God that we are worthy of having our own requests granted.

"Who favors people with knowledge" All other blessings that we might offer — and indeed, all (p. 102)

4. *BINAH* ("KNOWLEDGE")   בִּינָה

[1] You favor people with knowledge and teach mortals understanding. [2] Favor us with your knowledge, understanding, and wisdom. [3] Blessed are You, Adonai, who favors people with knowledge.

HAUPTMAN (TALMUD)

The blessings of the *Amidah* are fixed. The topic of each one is noted in the Talmud (Ber. 29a), but the wording is not. The specific words we say developed over time, with their fluidity of formulation lasting at least until the advent of printing in the fifteenth century. By contrast, nowadays, the whole text is fixed.

Mishnah Berakhot (chapter 4), which discusses the *Amidah* at length, inserts into the middle of its discourse a statement about the ongoing struggle between fixed and spontaneous (p. 104)

KUSHNER & POLEN (CHASIDISM)

"Wisdom" The *Degel Machaneh Ephraim (Parashat Sh'mini)* of Rabbi Moshe Hayyim Ephraim of Sudilkov (1748–1800) cites a tradition from his grandfather, the Baal Shem Tov: wisdom is like water issuing forth from a well-spring. The more one draws, the stronger the flow. And like life-sustaining water, wisdom too increases with the space in which it can spread out. In this way, when wisdom is allowed to flow into one's personality and behavior, one becomes both physically and spiritually purified. Such intellectual purification goes beyond its source in the individual. Wisdom also nurtures one's friends and students, even as they, by paying attention and taking it into themselves, provide it with an ever-growing expanse in which it can spread out and increase. For this reason, can this blessing should be understood as a *(p. 104)*

L. HOFFMAN (HISTORY)

WITH THE THREE BLESSINGS OF PRAISE BEHIND US, WE BEGIN THE PETITIONARY PART OF THE AMIDAH. THE FIRST REQUEST IS FOR KNOWLEDGE.

"Knowledge, understanding, and wisdom" (de'ah binah v'haskel) The Ashkenazi and old Spanish-Portuguese versions are identical here, but under the influence of the Kabbalah, the Sefardi prayer book exchanged these three Hebrew words for three other ones that also denote different types of knowledge: *chokhmah, binah,* and *da'at.* These are taken to refer to the upper three *s'firot* of the kabbalistic diagram and the three stages of divine wisdom prior to the emergence *(p. 105)*

1אַתָּה חוֹנֵן לְאָדָם דַּעַת וּמְלַמֵּד לֶאֱנוֹשׁ בִּינָה. 2חָנֵּנוּ מֵאִתְּךָ דֵּעָה בִּינָה וְהַשְׂכֵּל. 3בָּרוּךְ אַתָּה יְיָ חוֹנֵן הַדָּעַת.

J. HOFFMAN (TRANSLATION)

"You favor people [adam]" The Hebrew is the generic "man," but, in context, it is clearly inclusive of all people.

"Your knowledge" Or, more literally, "knowledge from You." It is not clear whether we get part of the same divine knowledge that God has or whether God merely doles out our human knowledge to us. The theological implications are great, but the solution will not be found in the choice of words here.

"Who favors people" The object "people" is missing from the Hebrew but required in English. In this case, it is particularly unfortunate that "who favors with knowledge" is not *(p. 105)*

LANDES (HALAKHAH)

"Knowledge" Each of the middle petitionary blessings has ethical consequences for us who pray it. Since we ask God to do these things, it must be in God's nature to do them; and since we are made in God's image, it must be our nature also to do them, when we act in a godly way. The middle blessings are, therefore, more than requests we make of God. They are equally a catalogue of our own responsibilities. "Knowledge," for instance, refers to *talmud* *(p. 104)*

BRETTLER (BIBLE)

in the first, such as "favor," "knowledge," and "understanding," creating a density that also typifies biblical poems.

The worshiper asks God to provide knowledge — an odd notion to us, for we view knowledge as a combination of genetics and environment. In the biblical view, however, God "instructs people in knowledge" (Ps. 94:10), and Solomon was wise because he had asked God for wisdom (1 Kings 3:9) and God granted it (v. 12).

The threefold use of the verb *chanan,* "to favor," is especially noteworthy. The verb is usually used by a lamenting individual making supplication in the face of enemies or illness but is used here to reflect the fact that God graces people with knowledge. Given the centrality of wisdom in general, but most especially for observing Torah (Ps. 119:66: "Teach me good sense and knowledge, for I have put my trust in your commandments"; cf. Deut. 4:6), it is not surprising to find a quest for knowledge as the first petition of the *Amidah.*

———◆———

DORFF (THEOLOGY)

requests that we might voice — depend on our ability to know ourselves and God's world in the first place.

There are three kinds of knowing: "Knowledge" *(de'ah)* is factual information. "Discernment" *(binah)* denotes the ability to analyze things and to distinguish between them — its root, *b.y.n,* means "between." "Wisdom" (referred to here by the verb *haskel,* like the Yiddish *sekhel)* means experiential knowledge.

Had God not created us as He did, we would have no knowledge in the first place. Moreover, liturgically speaking, knowledge is an additional boon because it enables us to do distinctly human things like praying. Three times, therefore, the prayer calls God *chonan,* "gracious."

Finally, a special virtue of God's is divine omniscience. God knows even the secrets of the world and of people's hearts, for Deut. 29:28 maintains, "The secrets belong to the Lord, our God." The liturgy of Yom Kippur emphasizes, "You know the mysteries of the world and the hidden secrets of every living thing. You search out all the areas of the stomach and examine [each person's] emotions and thoughts" (literally, each person's kidneys and heart, the kidneys being the seat of emotions and the heart the seat of thought, as most ancient texts assumed). We become God-like by virtue of our knowledge — the characteristic that Maimonides describes as the image of God within us *(Guide for the Perplexed,* part I, chapter 1).

———◆———

FALK (FEMINISM)

seem to be the middle section, that is, the petitioner's requests: What precedes is preparation; what follows is denouement.

The basic tripartite structure of the weekday *Amidah* is also found in the *Amidah* for Sabbaths and holy days; however, there is one major difference in the content. On Sabbaths and holy days, the middle section of the prayer consists of a single blessing sanctifying the day. While scholars do not agree on the historical reasons for this difference between weekday and holy day forms of the *Amidah,* the accepted traditional (interpretive) explanation is that holy days represent a state of perfection; hence, petitions are inappropriate. But, we might ask, if part of the purpose of prayer is to bring us closer to a state of holiness, what is the place of petition in prayer at all?

Of course, it is human to hope and desire and wish. But there are other ways — besides petitioning God — to express these needs in prayer. One could say, for instance (as I do, in *The Book of Blessings),* "May our hearts be lifted" or "May the month of Nisan be a month of blessings." Petitionary prayers — direct requests made to a listener — are especially problematic for those of us who do not conceive of, or encounter, God by means of personal (anthropomorphic) images, be they traditional ones, like Rabbi Chanina's portrayal of God as master, or newer ones, such as the image of God as friend. For many Reconstructionists and other Jews who experience the divine as immanent presence in the world, personal imagery for God can be uncomfortable and even dishonest, and the petitionary mode of prayer can feel artificial and strained. Indeed, for some Jews (myself among them), this mode actually gets in the way of spiritual union with God or — to use a phrase that expresses my own theology — a sense of participation in the greater whole of being.

In my personal use of the *Amidah* in weekday prayer, I replace the middle section of thirteen petitionary blessings with a contemplative poem, which I think of as a "daily psalm" *(shir shel yom,* as tradition calls it). Choosing a different poem for each day of the week is a way to acknowledge the uniqueness of each day and, by extension, the individuality and preciousness of each moment. I follow the reading of the daily psalm with a period of silence, during which I try to allow myself not to focus on my desires but to let go of them; not to wish but simply to accept what is. For me, silent meditation provides a satisfying transition from the first part of the *Amidah* to the last, moving me from a state of awareness and appreciation — the cognitive or sensory recognition of life's gifts — to a feeling of deep acceptance and wholeness — that state of mind and heart that we call gratitude. I will say more about gratitude (which I believe to be the self's best gift to itself) and about silence in a discussion of the "Blessing of Gratitude" *(Hoda'ah)* below (see "We gratefully acknowledge").

———◆———

HAUPTMAN (TALMUD)

prayer. Fixed prayer lacks the intensity and directedness of spontaneous prayer. But spontaneous prayer alone is insufficient because knowing how to pour out one's heart in prayer is an art that needs to be learned and practiced.

There is a third kind of prayer, also spoken about in the Mishnah in the very same place: prayer triggered by an occasion. The Mishnah reports that when R. Nechunya ben Hakanah entered and exited the *Bet Hamidrash* (the "House of Study"), he would utter a short prayer. Upon entering, he would say, "May it be God's will that no one stumble because of me," and upon leaving, he would say, "Thank God for my lot in life." These private prayers look simple on the surface. But when we read them in conjunction with other similar prayers, formulated in similar terms (as in Mishnah Berakhot, chapter 9), we discover that prayers like these are said when a person senses danger and feels the need for God's help in surviving the experience in question. Other examples include visiting a big city, a place of evil and corruption in the world, in the view of the Rabbis, or just going to sleep at night and waking up in the morning (Ber. 60b) because there was no assurance that one would return safely from a sleeping state to wakefulness and life. These are all examples of making a transition in and out of a dangerous state.

If Rabbi Nechunya saw the *Bet Hamidrash* as dangerous, however, it could not have been in the physical sense, obviously, but in the spiritual and intellectual sense: he needed to arrive at correct decisions about Jewish law so that he would not lead people astray. When the Rabbis debated points of Halakhah with each other, they had no way, other than majority vote, to establish truth. In his role as legislator, Nechunya asks God, therefore, to give him the ability to determine Jewish law without mistakenly declaring the pure impure and the forbidden permitted. It is as if his personal wholeness — his "safety" — were dependent on his being the best judge of fact that he could possibly be. R. Nechunya is praying that he cast his vote responsibly.

Petitions like these did not enter into the fixed liturgy of the *Amidah,* but they are part of Jewish prayer.

———◆———

KUSHNER & POLEN (CHASIDISM)

request that our wisdom flow forth — both within ourselves and our circle of friends and students. One's wisdom only increases as it flows forth and ultimately is given to others.

———◆———

LANDES (HALAKHAH)

torah, Torah study, one of the greatest *mitzvot* because it brings along all others in its wake.

———◆———

L. HOFFMAN (HISTORY)

of creation. The initials of the three *(ch.b.d)* are the basis for *ChaBaD,* the title by which Lubavitch Chasidim are known.

———◆———

J. HOFFMAN (TRANSLATION)

English because the general pattern of the blessings in the *Amidah* is that God's role is mentioned specifically at first (in this case, "You favor people with knowledge") and then repeated in general terms in the *chatimah* (in this case, "You favor with knowledge"). Our translation necessarily strays from this pattern here, but it can be seen more clearly in the blessings that follow, where the pattern is always, "You do this for us. . . . Blessed are you who does this."

BRETTLER (BIBLE)
"Bring us back"

Here too the poetic structure is obvious, as the first two phrases in the Hebrew are parallel to each other in meaning and in style. The third phrase is slightly longer but otherwise is similar to the first two. *Avodah* probably means specifically ritual or cultic sacrifice, following the use of that word in the late biblical texts that reflect priestly interests (e.g., Num. 4:24; 1 Chron. 23:24; 2 Chron. 31:21). Two types of return to God are thus envisioned: study of Torah and ritual. *(p. 108)*

ELLENSON (MODERN LITURGIES)
"Bring us back to your Torah, our father . . . our King" While most non-Orthodox liturgies have left this prayer untouched, *Kol Haneshamah* objects to the "image of an external God pronouncing individual judgments" as too hierarchical. Wanting to do away also with the masculine "father" and "king," it has adopted, instead, *m'korienu*, "our Source," and *a'tarteinu*, "our Sovereign."

———◆———

DORFF
(THEOLOGY)
"Who takes pleasure in repentance . . . who is gracious and quick to forgive" (Blessings 5 and 6) The movement from Blessing 4 (knowledge) to Blessings 5 and 6 (repentance and forgiveness) implies that the first aspect of awareness is the revelation that we sin and that we therefore need forgiveness. In Greek philosophy, knowledge evokes pride; here it results in recognition of our moral brokenness and our need for reinstatement.

It is hard to ask for forgiveness and hard also to accept it. Either or both parties may feel violated. In all but the most trivial cases — like harmlessly bumping into someone in a crowd — the offender must overcome embarrassment just to request forgiveness, and the one injured may feel angry and in no mood to forgive. The victim may

5. T'SHUVAH ("REPENTANCE") תְּשׁוּבָה

[1] Bring us back to your Torah, our father, draw us near to your service, our king, and turn us back, in perfect repentance before You. [2] Blessed are You, Adonai, who takes pleasure in repentance.

also suspect that the transgressor is not seriously remorseful or that granting forgiveness will look weak in the eyes of the perpetrator, thus adding to one's vulnerability to future attack. If both parties are partially at fault, they both must confront the difficulties of both asking for forgiveness and forgiving. Both asking and granting forgiveness therefore demand considerable strength of character.

It matters therefore that God is portrayed as one "who takes pleasure in repentance," because at stake is a fundamental tenet of Jewish theology: God is not mean or vindictive; God has standards, but deals compassionately with those who do not meet them, as long as they honestly try to return to the right path. God's compassion enables us to make amends, to get past *(p. 108)*

KUSHNER & POLEN (CHASIDISM)

"Perfect repentance" In his *K'tonet Passim*, Yakov Yosef of Polnoye (d. 1782), one of the Baal Shem Tov's principal disciples, cites Yoma 86b, which draws the famous distinction between *t'shuvah miyirah*, "repentance motivated by fear," and *t'shuvah me'ahavah*, "repentance motivated by love." Repentance from love not only makes expiation for the sin but actually, says the Talmud, transforms the sin into a merit! While the fact of the sin's having been committed remains unchanged, atonement transforms its meaning. Yakov Yosef draws on what will become a primary tenet of Chasidic spirituality (and the reason Chasidism's opponents called it heretical): since God's glory fills the whole world, everything must be "full of the divine" — even sin!

Chemdah ("yearning, desire") is the source of all creative energy, but also the source of all sin as well. With this in mind, Yakov Yosef reminds us that there are two names for God. Before *chemdah* gets us to act, God's name is the infinite and eternal *shem havayah*, that is, the four-letter *yod, heh, vav, heh* יהוה, but after we have acted and sinned from *chemdah* ("desire"), God's name becomes *Adonai* (again four letters: *alef, dalet, nun, yod* אדני), which, according to tradition, implies divinity in the physical and all the necessary limitations that come along with it. *(p. 108)*

L. HOFFMAN (HISTORY)

TRUE KNOWLEDGE (THE OBJECT OF BLESSING 4) LEADS US NOW TO SEE THE VALUE IN TURNING TO GOD. BLESSING 5, THEREFORE, SEEKS REPENTANCE.

———◆———

J. HOFFMAN (TRANSLATION)

"Bring us back" Or "cause us to return," but our English captures the parallel structure of the Hebrew, which displays three verbs in parallel: "bring us back" *(hashiveinu)*, "draw us near" *(korveinu)*, and "turn us back" *(hachazireinu)*.

"To your Torah" Or, perhaps, "to your law."

"In perfect repentance" From the same root as "to bring back," above, a fact not captured in the English.

———◆———

הֲשִׁיבֵנוּ אָבִינוּ לְתוֹרָתֶךָ וְקָרְבֵנוּ מַלְכֵּנוּ¹ לַעֲבוֹדָתֶךָ וְהַחֲזִירֵנוּ בִּתְשׁוּבָה שְׁלֵמָה לְפָנֶיךָ. ²בָּרוּךְ אַתָּה יְיָ הָרוֹצֶה בִּתְשׁוּבָה.

LANDES (HALAKHAH)

"Turn us back" The human dimension of the request that God "turn us back" is the *mitzvah* of confessing our sins *(vidui hacheit)*, one of the 613 *mitzvot* (the *taryag mitzvot*) as enumerated by Maimonides ("Laws of Repentance" 1).

———◆———

BRETTLER (BIBLE)

We think of repentance as following solely from human initiative, but here it is portrayed as divinely caused — as in Deut. 30:6–8, "Then Adonai your God will open up your heart . . . and you will again heed Adonai and obey all his command-ments. . . ." Other biblical texts modify that God-dependent stand by suggesting that only if Israel begins to return, God will support the process (e.g., Hos. 14:2–9). God is thus, in the words of this blessing, a God "who takes pleasure in repentance," because "it is not my desire that anyone shall die, declares the Lord God. Repent, therefore, and live!" (Ezek. 18:32).

———◆———

DORFF (THEOLOGY)

wrongdoing, and to get on with our lives. We need not remain stuck in the disabling guilt and the despair of sin.

Here again, God serves as model for us. "Do not avenge or hold a grudge," the Torah admonishes (Lev. 19:18). According to rabbinic law, if I assault you, not only must I pay you for your injuries, time lost, medical expenses, embarrassment, and pain, but I must also apologize. If I do that and if you refuse to accept my apology, I must try again and again, but after three times you are the sinner, not I (M. B.K. 8:1, 7). Mai-monides specifically says that if the offender asks forgiveness "once and a second time," the injured party must forgive him. Otherwise the offender is, as the Mishnah calls him, "cruel," and as Maimonides says, "it is forbidden for the injured party to be cruel and refuse to forgive" ("Laws of Injury and Damage" 5:10; see also his "Laws of Ethics [De'ot]" 6:6 and "Laws of Repentance" 2:10). God, then, is the paradigm for our own behavior in situations of wrongdoing and the power that enables us to overcome the many obstacles to forgiveness.

———◆———

KUSHNER & POLEN (CHASIDISM)

Employing *gematria,* the tradition of assigning numerical equivalents to each Hebrew letter according to its sequence in the alphabet, Yakov Yosef goes on to suggest that the word for "sin," *chayt* (spelled *chet* [the eighth letter], *tet* [the ninth], *alef* [the first]), חטא, may hint at the same insight. Together, the two names of God —*yod, heh, vav, heh,* and *alef, dalet, nun, yod*— have a total of eight letters, corresponding to the first letter of "sin," the *chet* ח, which is 8. The second letter of "sin" is *tet* ט, which is also the first letter of word for "good," or *tov* טוב, and has a numerical value of 9. Sub-tracting the *chet* (8), which is the first letter of "sin," from *tet* (9), which is the first let-ter of "good" and the second letter of "sin," we are left with the last letter of "sin," *alef,* which has the numerical value of 1, representing God.

Thus Yakov Yosef concludes that even within each sin is a hint of the divine unity! And in a traditional Jewish universe, wherein letters are the building blocks of reality, his conclusions are compelling. While the logic of *gematria* may strike moderns as arcane, the conclusion is not only valid but even elegant: God is within everything, even sin!

When a person is aroused by *chemdah,* "yearning," he or she also arouses something in God. But if the yearning leads to the commission of a sin, there is a *k'lipah,* a "shard," which effectively serves as a screen or barrier, preventing us from discerning the presence of God. Once one makes repentance *(t'shuvah),* however, the screen falls away, enabling the penitent to see now the divine holiness "trapped" even in what was once a sin! In this way, through the process of *t'shuvah,* or return, one offers up all of oneself back to God.

◆ ◆ ◆

BRETTLER (BIBLE)

"Forgive us" The petition for forgiveness follows from the preceding blessing for repentance, especially from its third clause, "Turn us back, in perfect repentance before you." Blessings 4 through 6 thus constitute a logical cluster, asking for knowledge to follow Torah (#4) and to repent (#5) and then be forgiven (#6).

As elsewhere, even the style of writing has a story to tell, if we keep in mind the biblical models that the writer of this blessing used. It opens with a couplet, each half of which mirrors the other in meaning and form ("Forgive us . . . ; Pardon us . . ."); the couplet is followed by a third phrase (a "motive clause") that explains the reason why God should forgive: "For you, Adonai, are good and forgiving, abounding in steadfast love *(chesed)* to all who call on You." The opening imperative "Forgive us" followed by a motive clause, explaining why, is typical of biblical style — for example, Psalm 86, where the first four verses open with imperatives and then are followed by motive clauses, saying "because . . ." just like our benediction. Indeed, the fifth verse of that psalm is a long motive clause similar in content to *(p. 111)*

(p. 111)

L. HOFFMAN (HISTORY)

AS KNOWLEDGE (BLESSING 4) LED TO REPENTANCE (BLESSING 5), SO REPENTANCE LEADS TO FORGIVENESS, THE OBJECT OF BLESSING 6.

---

6. *S'LICHAH* ("FORGIVENESS")   סְלִיחָה

¹ Forgive us, our father, for we have sinned. ² Pardon us, our king, for we have transgressed, for You forgive and pardon. ³ Blessed are You, Adonai, who is gracious and quick to forgive.

¹ סְלַח־לָנוּ אָבִינוּ כִּי חָטָאנוּ. ² מְחַל־לָנוּ מַלְכֵּנוּ כִּי פָשָׁעְנוּ כִּי מוֹחֵל וְסוֹלֵחַ אָתָּה. ³ בָּרוּךְ אַתָּה יְיָ חַנּוּן הַמַּרְבֶּה לִסְלוֹחַ.

LANDES (HALAKHAH)

"Forgive us" Forgiving others is considered to be an attribute of God and, therefore, of us potentially as well. Halakhah therefore forbids unwillingness to forgive as being cruel and immoral (B.K. 92a; Maimonides, "Laws of Repentance" 2:10].

BRETTLER (BIBLE)

our benediction: "For you, Adonai, are good and forgiving, abounding in stead-fast love *(chesed)* to all who call on You."

In both the psalm and our benediction, the reason (or motive) behind forgiveness is not human repentance but God's fundamental forgiving nature. Elsewhere in Psalms, also, we see that God is "the one who forgives all my sins" (Ps. 103:3); our benediction therefore calls God *chanun,* "gracious" (one of God's positive attributes according to Exod. 34:5), adding *hamarbeh lislo'ach,* "the one who forgives time and time again." This last attribute is based on Isa. 55:7, part of the *Haftarah* for public fast days: "Let the wicked give up his ways, the sinful man his plans; let him turn back to Adonai, and He will pardon him, to our God, for He forgives abundantly." The point of Isaiah and our prayer is that unlike humans, who get tired of forgiving over and over, God is by nature willing to forgive again and again.

◆ ◆ ◆

BRETTLER (BIBLE)

"See our affliction" A new theme is introduced: the restoration of the people of Israel to the land of Israel. Its two opening parallel clauses ("See our affliction and fight our fight") paraphrase Psalm 119:153–154 but change the first-person singular reference there ("See my affliction . . . fight my fight") to the plural, since the *Amidah* is a corporate prayer.

As in previous benedictions, God's beneficence rather than the community's need or deservedness is invoked: restoration can be expected "for the sake of your name, for You are a mighty redeemer." The Bible often suggests that God cares about his reputation, which might become sullied if He harms Israel, even if they are deserving of punishment (see esp. Ezek. 20:9, 14, 22, 44; cf. Isa. 48:9; Jer. 14:7; Ps. 23:3).

The phrase "mighty redeemer" may echo Jer. 50:34, "Their redeemer is mighty. . . . He will certainly fight their battle." Jeremiah had in mind Israel's eventual redemption from Babylon, and the verb he chose, *ga'al*, "to redeem," is used in Isaiah 40–65 as well, to describe liberation from Babylon. From Jeremiah and Isaiah, it entered later literature, such as the prayer in the second-century B.C.E. work Ben Sirah (52:12), which has many parallels to the *Amidah*, including, "Acknowledge the redeemer of *(p. 114)*

ELLENSON (MODERN LITURGIES)

"See our affliction, and fight our fight; redeem us" The conditions of Jewish oppression that had motivated this prayer were, in the opinion of Isaac Mayer Wise, no longer extant in America, so that its sentiments seemed inappropriate for Jews living here. On the other hand, Jews elsewhere still confronted enmity, so he adapted the line to refer only to them: "O behold the oppression of our brethren, and redeem them speedily." With an even greater penchant for universalism, the *Union Prayer Book* went beyond Wise and omitted this theme altogether. In keeping with the renewed emphasis upon particularism that has marked recent years, however, a whole host of contemporary liberal prayer books (from *Gates of Prayer* to *Siddur Lev Chadash*) have restored the traditional text to their pages.

Interestingly, Israel's *Ha'avodah Shebalev* has replaced "for the sake of Your name" with *g'ullah sh'lemah,* "a complete redemption," so as to affirm a theology that sees the State of Israel as *at'chalta d'geulta,* "the *beginning* of redemption." Israel is seen as embodying a messianic hope that will one day come to full flowering for all Jews.

"Answer us, Adonai . . ." As most liberal Jews rarely observe *(p. 115)*

7. *G'ULAH* ("REDEMPTION")   גְּאוּלָה

¹ See our affliction, and fight our fight; redeem us quickly for the sake of your name, for You are a mighty redeemer. ² Blessed are You, Adonai, who redeems Israel.

[On fast days, add:

³ Answer us, Adonai, answer us on our fast day, for we are greatly distressed. ⁴ Do not regard our

DORFF (THEOLOGY)

"Who redeems Israel" After recognizing our ability to know, our penchant for sin, our ability to repent, and God's willingness to forgive, the slate is wiped clean, so to speak, and we can turn to our various needs. The ultimate need is redemption. In Christianity, Jesus redeems the *individual* from sin, but Judaism rejects that as impossible if we are to retain our distinctly human character as beings with free will and its attendant responsibility. Judaism therefore envisions redemption of the *community*, not from sin, but from the limitations and frustrations of life.

We therefore speak of God as "redeemer of Israel," after which *all the subsequent blessings of the middle section of the* Amidah *articulate what redemption is.* Following the order of the *Amidah,* redemption would be a state in which there is health, *(p. 115)*

J. HOFFMAN (TRANSLATION)

"Our fast day [tsom ta'aniteinu]" Two words appear for fast, *tsom* and *ta'anit*. The second carries with it associations of self-affliction.

"Do not regard" Literally, "turn to(ward)." Almost certainly an idiom (cf., e.g., Deut. 9:27).

L. HOFFMAN (HISTORY)

DIVINE PARDON (BLESSING 6) RENDERS US ALL WORTHY OF REDEMPTION. THE JEWISH CONCEPT OF REDEMPTION IS CORPORATE, NOT INDIVIDUAL—ALL THE WORLD WILL BE REDEEMED IN A PROCESS THAT BEGINS WITH THE INDIVIDUAL BUT CULMINATES IN A COSMIC CHANGE OF HISTORY, THE DETAILS OF WHICH ARE SPELLED OUT IN THE NEXT EIGHT BLESSINGS.

A SPECIAL INSERTION IS PROVIDED FOR ORDINARY FAST DAYS, WHICH EVOKE A REALISTIC EVALUATION OF THE HUMAN CONDITION AND THE NEED FOR REDEMPTION IN A WORLD STILL FILLED WITH SUFFERING.

———

¹רְאֵה בְעָנְיֵנוּ וְרִיבָה רִיבֵנוּ וּגְאָלֵנוּ מְהֵרָה לְמַעַן שְׁמֶךָ כִּי גוֹאֵל חָזָק אָתָּה. ²בָּרוּךְ אַתָּה יְיָ גּוֹאֵל יִשְׂרָאֵל.

[On fast days, add:

³עֲנֵנוּ יְיָ עֲנֵנוּ. בְּיוֹם צוֹם תַּעֲנִיתֵנוּ. כִּי בְצָרָה גְדוֹלָה אֲנָחְנוּ. ⁴אַל־תֵּפֶן

LANDES (HALAKHAH)

"Who redeems Israel" This blessing has three dimensions. It is usually interpreted as a plea for individual deliverance from personal travail and hardships (Abudarham, quoting Riva). Nonetheless, as the seventh blessing in the list, it has a cosmic significance in that it is connected also to the desire for universal salvation, which will occur at the end of time when (according to some) Israel will find itself at the end of a cycle of seven years *(sh'mitot)* of war (Meg. 17b; Rashi, ad loc.; *Tur* 116). Interpersonally, redemption is related to the halakhic responsibility for a relative to redeem property that *(p. 115)*

wickedness, do not hide your face from us, and do not hide from our supplication. [5]May You be near to our cry; may your kindness be a comfort to us. [6]Before we call to You, answer us, as it is written, "Before they call, I will answer. While they are still speaking, I will hear." [7]For You, Adonai, who answers in time of distress, redeems and delivers in every time of distress and woe. [8]Blessed are You, Adonai, who answers in time of distress.]

אֶל־רִשְׁעֵנוּ. וְאַל־תַּסְתֵּר פָּנֶיךָ מִמֶּנּוּ. וְאַל־תִּתְעַלַּם מִתְּחִנָּתֵנוּ. [5]הֱיֵה נָא קָרוֹב לְשַׁוְעָתֵנוּ. יְהִי נָא חַסְדְּךָ לְנַחֲמֵנוּ. [6]טֶרֶם נִקְרָא אֵלֶיךָ עֲנֵנוּ. כַּדָּבָר שֶׁנֶּאֱמַר וְהָיָה טֶרֶם יִקְרָאוּ וַאֲנִי אֶעֱנֶה. עוֹד הֵם מְדַבְּרִים וַאֲנִי אֶשְׁמָע. [7]כִּי אַתָּה יְיָ הָעוֹנֶה בְּעֵת צָרָה. פּוֹדֶה וּמַצִּיל בְּכָל־ עֵת צָרָה וְצוּקָה. [8]בָּרוּךְ אַתָּה יְיָ הָעוֹנֶה בְּעֵת צָרָה.]

BRETTLER (BIBLE)

Israel" (here) and "Acknowledge the shield of Abraham," as in Blessing 1 (see above, "Abraham's protector").

"Answer us, Adonai, answer us" Since most of the public fast days are connected to the destruction of Jerusalem, this addition for fast days follows the blessing of God the redeemer, which implicitly asks God to restore Jerusalem to its former glory. The basic idea is that God hears penitential prayer when Israel fasts — as in the story of Jonah, where the inhabitants of Nineveh fast, wear sackcloth, and "cry out forcefully to Adonai" (Jonah 3:5–8; see in addition, e.g., 1 Sam. 7:6; Jer. 14:12; Joel 2:12; Ps. 35:13; Dan. 9:3; Ezra 8:23; Neh. 1:4; 2 Chron. 20:3).

The hope is especially strong that God will not "hide his face" — a common biblical depiction of God not answering Israel's prayer, sometimes because God is appropriately angry with Israel, who has sinned; but other times, especially in the Psalms, for no apparent reason at all, in that the supplicant who is ignored can locate no sin deserving of God's anger.

This prayer is rich in biblical allusions. For example, its final words "You, Adonai, who answers in a time of distress" are likely based on Neh. 9:27, "In their time of distress they will cry out to You, and You will hear from the heavens." It focuses also on Isa. 65:24: "Before they call, I will answer. While they are still speaking, I will hear." This is part of a beautiful passage describing the complete restoration of Jerusalem, with such memorable phrases as "I will rejoice in Jerusalem" (v. 19) and "They shall do nothing evil or vile in all of my sacred mount" (v. 25). This context provides an appropriate antidote to the fast-day commemoration of the destruction.

——◆——

ELLENSON (MODERN LITURGIES)

communal fast days except for Yom Kippur and (on occasion) Tisha B'av, Reform and Reconstructionist liturgies have omitted this paragraph from their daily services. It remains in Conservative liturgy.

——◆——

DORFF (THEOLOGY)

food, gathering of the exiles, justice, defeat of Israel's enemies, reward for the righteous, a rebuilt Jerusalem, and the messianic rule of the scion of David. This blessing, then, acts as a heading for the blessings that follow, culminating in the last prayer of the middle section, asking God to listen to our prayer.

——◆——

LANDES (HALAKHAH)

a family member has lost or sold in a moment of distress (see the Book of Ruth and traditional commentaries on it).

———————— ◆ ◆ ◆ ————————

BRETTLER (BIBLE)

"Heal us" A reworking of Jer. 17:14: "Heal me, Adonai, so I shall be healed, save me so I shall be saved, for You are the One I praise." It is not clear whether Jeremiah was really ill or if he was using "heal" metaphorically to imply help or restoration in general. In the *Amidah,* however, the non-metaphorical sense of "heal" is certainly intended, though it is still not certain what "save" means here, since biblically "save" has a military rather than a health-related sense. Like the previous two benedictions, this one too has a motive clause: "For You are the one we praise." The implication is that God will miss the praise that will no longer be forthcoming if the supplicant dies. Though theologically surprising to us, this is a common biblical idea, especially in Psalms (see, e.g., Ps. 6:6, where the supplicant asks for mercy and healing: "For there is no memory of You in death; in the underworld, who shall praise You?").

Calling God *el* here may hark back to the name used by Moses when he prayed for Miriam's recovery (Num. 12:13): "God *[el]*, heal her!" In the ancient near east, the Canaanite god El was also a god of healing.

———◆———

DORFF (THEOLOGY)

"Heal us, Adonai, that we shall be healed" We are likely to be impressed with God's role in healing only in cases where human efforts to heal usually fail. We call such recoveries "miraculous," meaning that they were unexpected, not normally attainable by human means. Our prayer holds, however, that even when doctors effect cure fairly easily, God has a hand in the healing process. Doctors are God's agents, partners with God in healing. They are successful only because God created the world such that healing can occur in the first place.

This prayer does *not* assert that everyone stricken with illness is cured, but only that when cure does occur, we must acknowledge God's role in it. The prayer book thus bespeaks a viewpoint very different from what most of us believe. Nowadays we are likely to start with the assumption of health, so that when sickness occurs, we blame God and question why God does not heal. In times past, people began with the assumption that a person might become sick at any time, so that God was to be praised for moments of healing.

This disparity exists largely because prior to modern medicine, disease was common and often irreversible. *(p. 118)*

8. R'FU'AH ("HEALING")

רְפוּאָה

[1] Heal us, Adonai, that we shall be healed. [2] Save us that we shall be saved, for You are our praise. [3] Bring complete healing to all of our wounds.

[If praying for a specific individual, add:

[4] May it find favor before You, my God and my ancestors' God, that You speedily send complete

ELLENSON (MODERN LITURGIES)

"Bring complete healing to all of our wounds" The Hebrew *makoteinu,* "wounds," can also mean "plagues," which Wise saw as a vestigial medievalism. Taking his cue from the Spanish-Portuguese rite, he substituted *tachalu'einu ul'khol makho'veinu,* "our diseases and our wounds."

"May it find favor before You . . ." While most classical non-Orthodox liturgies removed this personal petition from their prayer books, the growing interest in the spiritual dimensions of healing has led to its reintroduction (in *Kol Hane-shamah, Siddur Lev Chadash, Siddur Sim Shalom,* and *Ha'avodah Shebalev).*

(p. 119)

KUSHNER & POLEN (CHASIDISM)

"Heal us, Adonai, that we shall be healed" According to *Divrei Shmuel* (Sha'arei T'fillah, Y'sod Ha'avodah, p. 37, bottom of column 1), the mother lode of all healing is *s'lichah,* "forgiveness." The business of prayer is not cure — that is for the physicians — but forgiving oneself, discovering acceptance, and thereby finding healing. When the blessing begins "Heal us, Adonai, that we shall be healed," it is actually a request for a permanent change in the worshiper, that he or she not fall back into old patterns and habits. Each of our limbs, (p. 119)

L. HOFFMAN (HISTORY)

THE FIRST SIGN OF REDEMPTION WILL BE THE ABSENCE OF PAIN AND ILLNESS. BLESSING 8 THEREFORE TURNS IMMEDIATELY TO A PLEA FOR HEALING.

LANDES (HALAKHAH)

"Heal us" The Talmud recognizes the human impulse to heal, but recognizes God as the only true healer (based on Exod. 21:18, *rapo y'rapei,* "He shall surely heal"). It therefore describes human healing as flowing from divine permission. But the Rabbis eventually go further and make healing a halakhic imperative.

It is an old and honored tradition for people saying this blessing silently to insert a personal prayer for specific people who are ill. Indeed, before *any* of (p. 119)

רְפָאֵנוּ יְיָ וְנֵרָפֵא. ²הוֹשִׁיעֵנוּ וְנִוָּשֵׁעָה כִּי
תְהִלָּתֵנוּ אָתָּה. ³וְהַעֲלֵה רְפוּאָה שְׁלֵמָה
לְכָל־מַכּוֹתֵינוּ.

[If praying for a specific individual, add:

⁴יְהִי רָצוֹן מִלְּפָנֶיךָ יְיָ אֱלֹהַי וֵאלֹהֵי אֲבוֹתַי
שֶׁתִּשְׁלַח מְהֵרָה רְפוּאָה שְׁלֵמָה

J. HOFFMAN (TRANSLATION)

"You are our praise" So reads the Hebrew, but it is not clear what this means.

"May it find favor before You" Others, "May it be Your will."

"Spiritual healing and physical healing" Following Artscroll (Orthodox). Others, "healing of soul and healing of body."

healing from the heavens, spiritual healing and physical healing to _____ who is sick, along with others who are sick among Israel.]

מִן הַשָּׁמַיִם רְפוּאַת הַנֶּפֶשׁ וּרְפוּאַת הַגּוּף לַחוֹלֶה/לַחוֹלָה _____ בְּתוֹךְ שְׁאָר חוֹלֵי יִשְׂרָאֵל.]

[5] For You are our sovereign, stead-fast, merciful healing God. [6] Praised are You, Adonai, who heals the sick among his People Israel.

[5] כִּי אֵל מֶלֶךְ רוֹפֵא נֶאֱמָן וְרַחֲמָן אָתָּה. [6] בָּרוּךְ אַתָּה יְיָ רוֹפֵא חוֹלֵי עַמּוֹ יִשְׂרָאֵל.

DORFF (THEOLOGY)

Healing, then, was appreciated as a gift of God. Nowadays, by contrast, we become almost indignant when doctors with advanced medical techniques cannot cure us.

But the difference in viewpoint exemplifies a more general phenomenon, namely, people in times past appreciated the gap between God and humans more than we do. Our increased expertise in all technologies, not just medicine, leads us to feel that "my strength and the power of my hands accomplished these things" (Deut. 8:17) — an atti-tude that the Torah defines as the essence of hubris. It is this false pride that makes us diminish God's role in healing — if we even acknowledge it at all.

Finally, in the ancient world, people assumed that sickness was the result of sin. The Torah (e.g., Deut. 7:15; 28:22, 59–60) links health to abiding by God's command-ments, and a variety of punishments, including illness, to disobeying them. When people like the biblical Job were convinced that they had not sinned, but suffered any-way, they complained bitterly to God about the injustice of it all. Most people, though, less self-confident of their goodness, saw healing not as deserved but as a gift of God's mercy. In our day, when we question the linkage between sickness and sin, we begin with the default assumption of health and question God's justice, power, and very exis-tence when we encounter suffering.

We may have good reasons to deny the Rabbis' tie between sickness and sin, but we need nonetheless to recapture their respect for God's role in healing. One medical pro-fessor tells his first-year medical school class, "You are embarking on a program to teach you how to treat disease. Let me tell you now that 90 percent of all diseases will cure themselves. Your job is not to botch that up!" According to the Jewish tradition, we def-initely do have the duty to imitate God in trying to prevent, cure, or at least ameliorate disease, but we also have the duty to recognize God's important role in these efforts.

—◆—

ELLENSON (MODERN LITURGIES)

"Who heals the sick among his people Israel" From Abraham Geiger and Isaac Mayer Wise in the nineteenth century to *Gates of Prayer* and *Siddur Lev Chadash* today, liberal liturgies have expanded the particularism of this declaration to include all sick people, by replacing "among his people Israel" with *rofei cholim,* "who heals the sick," a phrase that they found in the Talmud Yerushalmi (Ber. 4:3).

Interesting enough, despite Mordecai Kaplan's overwhelming commitment to universalism, Reconstructionist liturgists have all retained the particularistic Hebrew here, though with altered translation. Reconstructionist prayer books before *Kol Haneshamah* said, "who healest the sick." The Conservative *Weekday Prayer Book* also retains the traditional Hebrew, along with a more open-ended "Healer of His people," in English. Once more, translation is employed as a vehicle for presenting viewpoints at odds with the Hebrew text but more congenial to a modern temperament. But the more recent *Kol Haneshamah* and *Siddur Sim Shalom* reverse this trend. The former translates literally, "who heals the sick among the people Israel," and the latter says, "Healer of His people Israel." Again we see the rise of particularity in our time.

———◆———

KUSHNER & POLEN (CHASIDISM)

traditionally numbered at 248, will thus be increasingly nourished and draw its life force from the soul until there is no place devoid of holiness. Healing then, is a psycho-spiritual state wherein we forgive ourselves and realize that holiness is everywhere, perhaps even in our own infirmity! Indeed, such forgiving acceptance may be a necessary prerequisite for all healing.

———◆———

LANDES (HALAKHAH)

the blessings, not just this one, a short personal petition relevant to the blessing in question may be introduced *(Shulchan Arukh,* O. Ch. 119).

———◆ ◆ ◆———

BRETTLER (BIBLE)

"Bless this year" The blessing focuses on agricultural productivity in Eretz Yisrael, providing alternative petitions — for "blessing" or, specifically, for "dew and rain for blessing" — depending on the season. God is held to control agricultural productivity, which therefore figures significantly in the Bible's blessings and curses (e.g., Lev. 26:4–5, 10, 16, 19–20; Deut. 28:3–5, 8, 11–12, 16–18, 22–24, 33, 38–41, 43, 48). According to Amos 4:7, God may even manage it that rain falls on one city, but not another, or even on a particular field, but not the adjacent one.

———◆———

ELLENSON (MODERN LITURGIES)

"And grant (blessing / dew and rain for blessing)" Here too (see above, "You cause the wind . . ."), liberal Jews of the nineteenth century objected to tying God's mastery of nature to the specific seasonal cycle of Israel and Babylonia. Geiger and Wise "remedied" the problem by inserting "dew and rain for blessing" as a permanent part of the service, irrespective of the time of year; others (*Siddur Lev Chadash, Gates of Prayer,* and Reconstructionist *Daily Prayer Book*) followed suit but selected "blessing." *Siddur Lev Chadash* adds also an *(p. 122)*

9. *SHANIM* ("YEARS")

שָׁנִים

[1] Bless this year for us along with all its various produce for goodness, Adonai our God,

[From Passover to December 4, say:

and grant blessing]

[From December 4 to Passover, say:

and grant dew and rain for blessing]

LANDES (HALAKHAH)

"Bless this year" Understood traditionally in the broader sense of a prayer for *parnasah,* an adequate livelihood, this blessing obliges us to provide others with the ability to provide for themselves. We are to help them find employment, arrange funding for them to establish businesses, provide them with loans or gifts, and welcome them into partnerships in our own enterprises. Such activity is the highest form of righteousness (Maimonides, "Laws of Gifts to the Poor" 10:7).

"Grant blessing/dew and rain for blessing" As a prayer for the precipitation that is necessary for prosperity in the Land of Israel, the insertion "Grant dew and rain" is recited during the rainy season there. It is an express prayer for rain and goes beyond "You cause the wind to blow and . . . rain to fall" of the *G'vurot* (see above, Blessing 2), which is not a prayer of petition, but only of praise for God's power in causing rain to fall.

There are two customs as to when the insertion occurs. In the Land of Israel itself, it is said first just after the end of the Tishrei holiday season (Rosh Hashanah, Yom Kippur, Sukkot, Sh'mini Atseret), at *Ma'ariv* of the 7th of Cheshvan. This is right after the beginning of the period when *(p. 122)*

J. HOFFMAN (TRANSLATION)

"Bless this year for us . . . for goodness" "For us" is *benefactive*, as in the translation by Artscroll (Orthodox), "For our benefit." "Bless us with this year" has nearly the same meaning. It is not clear exactly how "for goodness" relates to the blessing. The idea is that the year is to be blessed, good, and that its being good and blessed will benefit us.

"Dew and rain" There are several words for "rain" in Hebrew, some of them referring to specifically seasonal rainfalls, and two for rain in general. *Geshem* is the more common of the two; the other, *matar*, is used here.

"With its goodness [mituvah]" Other versions of the Hebrew say *mituvekha*, meaning "your [God's] goodness." Both are ancient, and it is hard to say which is correct. Most prayer books (e.g., Birnbaum and Artscroll [both Orthodox], *Kol Haneshamah* [Reconstructionist], *Gates of Prayer* [Reform], *Forms of Prayer* [Liberal, England]) follow general usage in preferring "your blessing." Our authoritative Hebrew version, however, selects "its [the earth's] goodness," as does *Siddur Sim Shalom* (Conservative) and *Ha'avodah Shebalev* (Reform, Israel). *(p. 123)*

L. HOFFMAN (HISTORY)

AS THE INDIVIDUAL NEEDS HEALING, SO TOO DOES THE LAND ON WHICH WE LIVE AND FROM WHICH WE RECEIVE OUR NOURISHMENT. BLESSING 9 PRAYS FOR AGRICULTURAL SUSTENANCE, FOCUSING ON THE LAND OF ISRAEL, WHICH THE RABBIS SAW AS THE CENTER OF THE UNIVERSE AND THE PLACE WHERE MESSIANIC REDEMPTION WOULD OCCUR.

"Bless this year for us" The old Spanish-Portuguese custom is much richer than the Ashkenazi version. It reads as follows:

[From Passover to December 4, say:]

Bless us, our Father, with all the works of our hands, and bless our year with the dew of favor, blessing, and offering to God; and let it close with life, bounty, and peace, like the best of years for blessing, for you are the God who is good and who does good and who blesses our years. Blessed are You, Adonai, who blesses our years.

בָּרֵךְ עָלֵינוּ יְיָ אֱלֹהֵינוּ אֶת־הַשָּׁנָה הַזֹּאת וְאֶת־כָּל־מִינֵי תְבוּאָתָהּ לְטוֹבָה וְתֵן

[From Passover to December 4, say:

בְּרָכָה]

[From December 4 to Passover, say:

טַל וּמָטָר לִבְרָכָה]

בָּרְכֵנוּ אָבִינוּ בְּכָל־מַעֲשֵׂה יָדֵינוּ, וּבָרֵךְ שְׁנָתֵנוּ בְּטַלְלֵי רָצוֹן בְּרָכָה וּנְדָבָה וּתְהִי אַחֲרִיתָהּ חַיִּים וְשָׂבָע וְשָׁלוֹם כַּשָּׁנִים הַטּוֹבוֹת לִבְרָכָה כִּי אֵל טוֹב וּמֵטִיב אַתָּה וּמְבָרֵךְ הַשָּׁנִים בָּרוּךְ אַתָּה יְיָ מְבָרֵךְ הַשָּׁנִים. *(p. 123)*

upon the surface of the earth, and satisfy us with its goodness, and bless our year like the best of years. [2] Blessed are You, Adonai, who blesses our years.

עַל פְּנֵי הָאֲדָמָה וְשַׂבְּעֵנוּ מִטּוּבָהּ וּבָרֵךְ שְׁנָתֵנוּ כַּשָּׁנִים הַטּוֹבוֹת. [2] בָּרוּךְ אַתָּה יְיָ מְבָרֵךְ הַשָּׁנִים.

ELLENSON (MODERN LITURGIES)

ecological wish: "Bestow blessing on the earth, that it may have a future and a hope."

Unsurprisingly, the traditional language linked still to the particularity of the climate in nature in Eretz Yisrael is included in *Ha'avodah Shebalev*, the prayer book of Israeli Reform. It is also in the current Reconstructionist volume, *Kol Haneshamah*, which explains that a conscious decision was made to "demonstrate our concern for life in our ancestral home."

—◆—

LANDES (HALAKHAH)

rain can be expected in Israel. We delay the petition until after Sukkot to give pilgrims to Jerusalem *(olim laregel)* time to leave the country before being engulfed in rain.

The second custom is that of the diaspora *(Minhag Bavel)*. The date is later because Babylonian agriculture needed rain much later. Since Babylonia was the major center for the diaspora for a number of centuries, its date became the universal custom outside of Eretz Yisrael.

Mathematically speaking, the date was established as sixty days after the autumn equinox, known as *t'kufat Tishrei* and corresponding to September 23, as calculated by the talmudic Amora Samuel (c. 177–257). On that day, the sun crosses the equator, autumn begins, and day and night are of equal duration.

Since we use the solar calendar ourselves, we can fix the interval of sixty days thereafter as falling always on *Ma'ariv* of December 4 (except for a civil leap year, when it occurs one day later, December 5).

Both traditions insert "Grant dew and rain" until the first day of Passover. After that point, it is replaced with a general phrase, "Grant blessing." Sefardi versions of the Siddur include an extensive poetical and heartfelt insertion at "Grant dew and rain," expressing concern for the earth, crops, and rain, while the version of the spring and summer ("Grant blessing") accents a prayer for *parnasah* (livelihood) in general.

—◆—

J. Hoffman (Translation)

"Like the best of years" Birnbaum (Orthodox): "like other good years."

———◆———

L. Hoffman (History)

[From December 4 to Passover, say:]

Bless this year for us along with all its various produce for goodness, Adonai our God, and grant dew and rain for blessing upon the entire surface of the earth, and soak the surface of our world, and satisfy the world entire with your goodness, and fill our hands with your blessings and with the richness of the gifts of your hands. Guard and save this year from any bad thing and from any sort of destruction and from any sort of punishment, and grant it hope and goodness and a peaceful conclusion. Be kind and gracious to it and to all its produce and fruit, and bless it with the rain of favor, blessing, and offering to God; and let it close with life, bounty, and peace, like the best of years for blessing, for you are the God who is good and who does good and who blesses our years. Blessed are You, Adonai, who blesses our years.

בָּרֵךְ עָלֵינוּ יְיָ אֱלֹהֵינוּ אֶת־הַשָּׁנָה הַזֹּאת וְאֶת־כָּל־מִינֵי תְבוּאָתָהּ לְטוֹבָה וְתֵן טַל וּמָטָר לִבְרָכָה עַל כָּל־פְּנֵי הָאֲדָמָה וְרַוֵּה פְּנֵי תֵבֵל וְשַׂבַּע אֶת־הָעוֹלָם כֻּלּוֹ מִטּוּבֶךָ וּמַלֵּא יָדֵינוּ מִבִּרְכוֹתֶיךָ וּמֵעֹשֶׁר מַתְּנוֹת יָדֶיךָ שָׁמְרָה וְהַצִּילָה שָׁנָה זוֹ מִכָּל־דָּבָר רָע וּמִכָּל־מִינֵי מַשְׁחִית וּמִכָּל־מִינֵי פּוּרְעָנוּת וַעֲשֵׂה לָהּ תִּקְוָה טוֹבָה וְאַחֲרִית שָׁלוֹם חוּס וְרַחֵם עָלֶיהָ וְעַל כָּל־תְּבוּאָתָהּ וּפֵרוֹתֶיהָ וּבָרְכָהּ בְּגִשְׁמֵי רָצוֹן בְּרָכָה וּנְדָבָה וּתְהִי אַחֲרִיתָהּ חַיִּים וְשָׂבָע וְשָׁלוֹם כַּשָּׁנִים הַטּוֹבוֹת לִבְרָכָה כִּי אֵל טוֹב וּמֵיטִיב אָתָּה וּמְבָרֵךְ הַשָּׁנִים בָּרוּךְ אַתָּה יְיָ מְבָרֵךְ הַשָּׁנִים.

The words "offering to God" (above) are our translation of *n'davah*, usually translated (in the Torah) as the "free-will offering" to God. If, indeed, the intent here too is that we offer something of our produce back to God, we have a description of blessing that entails not just receiving but giving also.

———◆ ◆ ◆———

"Who gathers the dispersed among his people Israel" Modern Jews have generally rejected the concept of "exile," believing instead that the Diaspora countries where they enjoyed equality were their home. They therefore found the nationalistic orientation of this prayer offensive and worked at reworking it in a variety of ways.

One approach was to universalize the benediction into a prayer of freedom for all. Isaac Mayer Wise, for instance, prayed, "Let resound the great trumpet for the liberty of all nations; lift up the banner to unite them in the covenant of peace, and bring them nigh unto Thee, to worship Thee in truth." *Gates of Prayer* says, "Sound the great horn to proclaim freedom, inspire us to strive for the liberation of the oppressed, and let the song of liberty be heard in the four corners of the earth"; and the Conservative *Weekday Prayer Book* reads, "Sound the great shofar to herald man's freedom."

Most Conservative prayer books, however, and Reconstructionist ones too, amend the line to reflect a benign American vision of Zionism, one that promotes the centrality and importance of Israel as a land of refuge for the Jewish dispossessed while simultaneously affirming the right of American Jews to remain in a Diaspora that is regarded as "home" and not as "exile." Hence, the Reconstructionist

Daily Prayer Book changes Hebrew and English to read, "Bring the homeless of our People in peace from the four corners of the earth, and enable them to march erect into our Land." The Conservative *Weekday Prayer Book* substitutes *v'kabeitz nidacheinu,* "Gather the dispersed," for the traditional *v'kabetzeinu yachad,* "gather us together."

Interestingly, heightened ethnic consciousness in *Kol Haneshamah* and *Siddur Sim Shalom* reverses this trend and restores the original Ashkenazi Hebrew text in its entirety. *Kol Haneshamah* even provides a lyrical translation that is faithful to the literal meaning of the Hebrew. *Siddur Sim Shalom,* however, still mutes the particularity of the prayer in English, by universalizing "our exiles" as "all exiles," and translating "Gather *us* from the four corners of the Earth" as "Gather *the dispersed* from the ends of the earth." It therefore continues the American Jewish rejection of the doctrine known as *sh'lilat hagolah,* "The Negation of the Diaspora," a central concept in the ideology of Theodor Herzl's Zionism. At the same time, it reveals the affinity almost all American Jews feel for the more universalistic visions of a spiritual-cultural Zionism, usually associated with Ahad Ha'am.

Even the Israeli *Ha'avodah Shebalev* has amended this prayer to specify that God is to "gather *our* (p. 126)

10. *KIBBUTZ G'LUYOT* ("GATHERING OF THE EXILES") קִבּוּץ גָּלֻיּוֹת

¹ Sound a great shofar for our freedom, and lift up a banner to gather our exiles, and gather us together from the four corners of the earth. ² Blessed are You, Adonai, who gathers the dispersed among his People Israel.

BRETTLER (BIBLE)

"Sound a great shofar" The agricultural productivity of Israel (the theme of the last blessing) leads now to a prayer for the exiles to be gathered. Its style is elegant: a set of three parallel imperative requests to God (known as a "tricolon") based on biblical prototypes from Isaiah. "On that day, a great shofar (shofar gadol) will be sounded, and those who have strayed into the land of Assyria or been expelled in the land of Egypt will come to worship Adonai on the holy mount, in Jerusalem" (27:13); "He will hold up a banner (v'nasa nes) to the nations, and will assemble the dispersed of Israel, and will gather (y'kabets) the dispersed of Judah from the four corners of the earth (me'arba kanfot ha'arets)" (11:12).

The verses *(p. 126)*

LANDES (HALAKHAH)

"Gather us together" This blessing for communal redemption reflects the halakhic principle of Jewish unity and co-responsibility, best expressed by the principle *Kol yisra'el arevim zeh vazeh* ("All of Israel is responsible one for another"). One consequence is that Jews may perform certain ritual acts (e.g., *Kiddush* on Friday night) for each other. On a historical plane, we are obliged to rescue each other, as, for instance, Jews in the free world did for Jews in the former Soviet Union. Morally speaking, we must chastise each other when we see wrongs committed within the Jewish com- *(p. 126)*

L. HOFFMAN (HISTORY)

AFTER THE DESTRUCTION OF THE SECOND TEMPLE, JEWS WERE DISPERSED THROUGHOUT THE WORLD IN WHAT THE RABBIS DESCRIBED AS "EXILE," A STATE OF HOMELESSNESS THAT BECAME ETCHED INTO JEWISH MEMORY AS THE PARADIGMATIC CURSE OF HISTORY. WITH HEALING ACCOMPLISHED FOR PEOPLE AND FOR LAND, BLESSING 10 ADDRESSES THE HOPE FOR A RETURN FROM EXILE, THE PIVOTAL NEXT STAGE IN THE RABBINIC DRAMA OF REDEMPTION.

———◆———

J. HOFFMAN (TRANSLATION)

"A great shofar [b'shofar gadol]" Others, "*the* great shofar," but the Hebrew (both here and in Isa. 27:13, whence it is borrowed) is clearly "a great shofar."

¹ תְּקַע בְּשׁוֹפָר גָּדוֹל לְחֵרוּתֵנוּ וְשָׂא נֵס לְקַבֵּץ גָּלֻיּוֹתֵינוּ וְקַבְּצֵנוּ יַחַד מֵאַרְבַּע כַּנְפוֹת הָאָרֶץ. ² בָּרוּךְ אַתָּה יְיָ מְקַבֵּץ נִדְחֵי עַמּוֹ יִשְׂרָאֵל.

The other possibility is "a great horn," as JPS renders the Isaiah phrase. The transition from "horn" to "shofar" is typical of borrowed words, which, once borrowed, tend to become narrower in meaning (as in *sombrero,* which in Spanish means "hat" but in English means "Spanish hat," or *tof,* which means "drum" in Hebrew but "Israeli drum" in English).

"Lift up a banner [nes]" Most likely, the idea is "heralding our freedom," as in *Siddur Sim Shalom* (Conservative). The Hebrew, *nes,* is the word for "miracle" but is used here to mean *(p. 126)*

ELLENSON (MODERN LITURGIES)

dispossessed" (v'kabetz nidacheinu) rather than "gather *us" (v'kabetzeinu yachad).* Israeli Reform too has been touched by Ahad Ha'am's cultural Zionism.

———◆———

BRETTLER (BIBLE)

have been changed somewhat, especially with the addition of *galuyotenu,* "our exiles," a word that exists only in the singular in the Bible. Here, however, it is plural, reflecting the new reality of a vastly dispersed Jewish People. God appears as "the One who gathers the dispersed of his People Israel" (from Isa. 56:8, possibly written in the Babylonian exile itself and predicting that God would "gather the dispersed" back home in Jerusalem).

"The One who gathers the dispersed of his People Israel" occurs already as an epithet for God in the second-century B.C.E. work Ben Sirah (51:12).

———◆———

LANDES (HALAKHAH)

munity, because Jewish destiny is tied up in all of us acting in concert, not in just the course of individual Jewish lives.

———◆———

J. HOFFMAN (TRANSLATION)

"symbol," "sign," or "banner." Perhaps miracles were signs *par excellence;* leading to the dual meaning of *nes.*

"The dispersed" Or "the banished."

———————◆ ◆ ◆———————

BRETTLER (BIBLE)

"Restore our judges" According to the Bible, Joshua was succeeded by a series of local military chieftains known as judges *(shoftim)*, who were followed in turn by Saul, David, Solomon, and the other kings. (After the last of the five books of Torah, our Bible devotes separate books to Joshua, Judges, and, eventually, Kings; between Judges and Kings is Samuel, referring to a transitional era, when the prophet-judge Samuel dominated Israel's history and in whose time the first of the kings, Saul and David, were chosen.) Our benediction looks back nostalgically at the period of the judges as ideal, not because the judges are themselves so positively viewed, but because (following 1 Sam. 10:18–19) the subsequent election of earthly kings implied a rejection of God's kingship. Thus, the real focus is not the judges, but the absence of any king other than God. As the blessing says, God should "reign over us . . . alone." God is the only monarch who can be counted on to reign "in kindness and mercy" and "who loves righteousness and justice."

There is thus implicit tension between this blessing and the blessing later on (#15) for the offspring of David to arise as the messianic ruler. But the Bible itself (Ezek. 34:24) *(p. 130)*

11. *MISHPAT* ("JUSTICE") מִשְׁפָּט

[1] Restore our judges as in days of old and our counselors as in former times. [2] And remove sorrow and complaint from among us, and reign over us, You alone, Adonai, in kindness and mercy, and acquit us in trial. *[3] Blessed are You, Adonai, our king who loves righteousness and justice.

ELLENSON (MODERN LITURGIES)

"Restore our judges . . . remove sorrow and complaint . . ." Several aspects of this prayer have proved troublesome to moderns. It was Jewishly nationalistic and assumed that all Jews were living in a sorrow-filled exile. Isaac Mayer Wise universalized the petition to ask God simply to remove "injustice and violence," not just Jewish "sorrow and complaint." He also subtly altered the first verb, from *hashivah* (an imperative form of the Hebrew word *shuv,* meaning "Return our judges") to *hoshevah* (an imperative from the root *yashav,* meaning "Seat our judges"). He thereby avoided casting aspersion on America's courts and legal system. Instead of praying for the return of an all-Jewish Sanhedrin, his prayer could be understood as referring to the judges already in place in his own time.

Siddur Lev Chadash has emulated Wise, asking God to "let righteous judges sit among Your people," but it universalizes the hope even more than Wise did, by praying that "counsellors of peace [sit] throughout the world." *Gates of Prayer* strips away particularism altogether by omitting any reference to Israel at all: "Pour Your spirit upon the rulers of all lands; guide them that they may govern justly."

———◆———

L. HOFFMAN (HISTORY)

A JUST SOCIETY IS THE HALLMARK OF THE AGE OF REDEMPTION. HAVING PRAYED FOR AN END TO EXILE, WE TURN TO A PETITION FOR JUSTICE, A THEME THAT WILL BE ELABORATED IN BLESSINGS 12 AND 13.

"Restore our judges" The blessing for justice is said to follow the blessing for the redemptive return to Eretz Yisrael because (as one commentator called Etz Yosef puts it) it is well known that we will be redeemed only on account of justice.

———◆———

הָשִׁיבָה שׁוֹפְטֵינוּ כְּבָרִאשׁוֹנָה וְיוֹעֲצֵינוּ¹ כְּבַתְּחִלָּה. ²וְהָסֵר מִמֶּנּוּ יָגוֹן וַאֲנָחָה וּמְלוֹךְ עָלֵינוּ אַתָּה יְיָ לְבַדְּךָ בְּחֶסֶד וּבְרַחֲמִים וְצַדְּקֵנוּ בַּמִּשְׁפָּט. ³*בָּרוּךְ אַתָּה יְיָ מֶלֶךְ אוֹהֵב צְדָקָה וּמִשְׁפָּט.

LANDES (HALAKHAH)

"Return our judges as in days of old" It is a positive commandment of the Torah to appoint a judiciary and a police force throughout the Land of Israel (Maimonides, "Laws of Sanhedrin" 1:1, based on Deut. 16:18).

———◆———

J. HOFFMAN (TRANSLATION)

"In days of old [k'varishonah] . . . *as in former times* [k'vat'chilah]" Literally, "as at first . . . as at the beginning" presumably idioms in Hebrew and therefore translated idiomatically also, following *Siddur Sim Shalom* (Conservative). The idioms appear in Isa. 1:26, on which the opening of this prayer is based.

"Complaint" Literally, "groaning." But surely "remove sorrow and complaint/groaning" refers to the prayer's theme of justice. We guess that the groaning refers to complaints about unfair judges. On the other hand, this middle line may be a late addition to the prayer and, in fact, appears in a different blessing altogether in the Genizah fragments.

"Acquit us in trial [tsadkeinu bamishpat]" Birnbaum (Orthodox) agrees, translating "clear us in judgment." Artscroll (Orthodox) suggests "justify us through judgment." *Siddur Sim Shalom* (Conservative), probably paraphrasing, offers "sustain our cause." Either way, two alternative understandings present themselves: either God should acquit us when we have to appear before the false judges (the Romans) in power, or God should vindicate us when those judges are finally tried for exercising false judgment upon us.

"King of justice" The Hebrew, *hamelekh hamishpat,* is (p. 130)

AMIDAH: BLESSINGS OF PETITION

[*From Rosh Hashanah to Yom Kippur,
say instead:

⁴ Blessed are you, Adonai, the king of justice.]

[*From Rosh Hashanah to Yom Kippur,
say instead:

בָּרוּךְ אַתָּה יְיָ הַמֶּלֶךְ 4
הַמִּשְׁפָּט.]

BRETTLER (BIBLE)

resolves the conflict by positing an ideal world of the future where a messianic figure and God will rule together: "I, the Lord, will be their God, and my servant David will be a ruler among them."

——◆—

J. HOFFMAN (TRANSLATION)

ungrammatical, as Rashi already recognized (Ber. 12b). Considerable effort has been made to justify it, since it is cited in the Talmud, but in all probability, it is an error and ought to read *melekh hamishpat.*

——◆ ◆ ◆——

BRETTLER (BIBLE)

"May there be no hope for slanderers"
Blessings 11, 12, and 13 all focus on specific groups or types of people: judges (the prior blessing, #11), slanderers (here, #12), and the righteous (the next blessing, #13). This one is curious, since there is no biblical precedent for cursing *malshinim* ("slanderers") or, for that matter, whatever alternative reading might be suggested (e.g., *minim,* some form of "heretics"). Yet, the idea that God's enemies should be destroyed can be found, for example, in Mal. 3:19, which shares some vocabulary with some of the versions of this prayer: "Look! That day is coming, burning like an oven! All the arrogant, and all the doers of evil shall be like straw, and the following day shall set them
(p. 134)

ELLENSON (MODERN LITURGIES)

"May there be no hope for slanderers . . . who smashes his enemies and humbles the insolent" The imprecatory tone and content of this prayer has disturbed countless prayer book editors during the last two centuries. Rather than ask for divine vengeance on actual people ("the *insolent"),* Abraham Geiger prayed, "May those who stray from You return, and may all wickedness be lost, and may You humble *arrogance* in our time. Blessed are You, O God, who smashes evil and humbles arrogance." Israel's *Ha'avodah Shebalev* adopts Geiger's rendition word for word, and Great Britain's *Siddur Lev Chadash* follows Geiger's wording and tone very closely. Isaac Mayer Wise, however, considered the prayer unredeemable and omitted it altogether from his service — a tactic followed by *Gates of Prayer* and the old Reconstructionist *Daily Prayer Book. Kol Haneshamah,* the current Reconstructionist volume, restores the prayer's first line and concludes by praising God, "who subdues the evildoers." Conservative prayer books have usually retained the Hebrew text, but both its *Weekday Prayer Book* and *Siddur Sim Shalom* mitigate the severity of the prayer by removing "who smashes his enemies" from the translation.

---

12. *MINIM* ("HERETICS") מִינִים

[1] May there be no hope for slanderers, and may all wickedness instantly perish, and may all your enemies quickly be destroyed. [2] May You quickly uproot, smash, destroy, and humble the insolent quickly in our day.

LANDES (HALAKHAH)

"May all wickedness instantly perish" This harsh blessing, added during times of betrayal of the Jewish People by apostates, was composed by Shmuel Hakatan (Samuel the Younger), whom tradition remembers for being noble, humble, and devoid of personal enmity (Rabbi Joseph B. Soloveitchik, "In Aloneness, In Togetherness: A Selection of Hebrew Writings," *P'lilat Sofreihem).* Note the wording: "Wickedness" should "instantly vanish," not "those who act wickedly" *(Anaf Yosef,* referring to Ber. 10a).

L. HOFFMAN (HISTORY)

BLESSING 12 CONTINUES THE THEME OF BLESSING 11 (JUSTICE) BY CONSIDERING THE PUNISHMENT THAT A JUST SOCIETY WILL METE OUT IN ITS ATTEMPT TO ERADICATE EVIL.

"Slanderers" Through the years, no prayer has received more attention than this one, said to have been framed by Shmuel Hakatan (Samuel the Younger) at the behest of Rabban Gamaliel II in Yavneh, about 90 C.E. (see "How the *Amidah* Began," p. 21). Though known as *Birkat Minim,* "Blessing of the Heretics," it is actually a malediction, not a benediction. Some scholars think earlier forms of it existed, and Samuel's version is just one of many from the first century or so. Others see it as an innovation, occasioned by animosity against Rome (for the war just past) and against Christians (or Jewish-Christians specifically) who had left the Jewish fold and were writing their own scriptures in the form of Gospels that maligned the Pharisees and heaped animus on the Jews.

Whatever its origin, the list of those specified as deserving God's wrath has not always been as benign as our current version would suggest. By comparison, the Genizah version (which I have divided arbitrarily to facilitate analysis) says: *(p. 134)*

וְלַמַּלְשִׁינִים אַל־תְּהִי תִקְוָה וְכָל־
הָרִשְׁעָה כְּרֶגַע תֹּאבֵד וְכָל־אוֹיְבֶיךָ
מְהֵרָה יִכָּרֵתוּ. ²וְהַזֵּדִים מְהֵרָה תְעַקֵּר
וּתְשַׁבֵּר וּתְמַגֵּר וְתַכְנִיעַ בִּמְהֵרָה בְיָמֵינוּ.

J. HOFFMAN (TRANSLATION)

"May there be no hope for slanderers" Or "May slanderers have no hope." Our translation suggests that the issue is not whether slanderers do or do not personally feel hope, but whether, regardless of how they feel, there is any hope for them. The Hebrew is ambiguous.

"May all wickedness [harishah] . . . *perish"* Other versions read, "May all who act wickedly *[kol osei rishah]* . . . perish."

"Be destroyed" Or "cut off." The same root also means "tree trunk," which is significant perhaps because the next sentence asks that the insolent be "uprooted." Probably a coincidence, however.

"The insolent [zedim]*"* The Hebrew puts "insolent" at the beginning of the sentence, to continue the pattern begun with "slanderers" and "wickedness." English does not offer us this option. Some versions (the Genizah fragments, Maimonides) read, "[the] insolent kingdom" *(malkhut zadon),* not simply "insolent."

"Quickly . . . quickly" Curiously, "quickly" appears twice in the same sentence in the Hebrew and so, likewise, in English.

"Smashes" Hebrew, *shover,* not exactly the same as "smash" *(m'shaber)* in the former sentence, but from the same root and clearly related.

———◆———

³ Blessed are You, Adonai, who smashes his enemies and humbles the insolent.

בָּרוּךְ³ אַתָּה יְיָ שׁוֹבֵר
אוֹיְבִים וּמַכְנִיעַ זֵדִים.

BRETTLER (BIBLE)

ablaze. . . ." The slanderers of Israel are called God's enemies here, and that too is biblical; Israel's enemies are God's enemies, since God is Israel's ultimate protector (see, e.g., Ps. 83:3).

◆

L. HOFFMAN (HISTORY)

1. May there be no hope for apostates,
2. And may You quickly uproot the insolent reign in our day,
3. And may the Christians and heretics instantly perish.
4. "May they be erased from the book of life, and may they not be written with the righteous."
5. Blessed are You, Adonai, who humbles the insolent.

Lines 1 to 3 list the enemies in question. Line 5 (the conclusion, or *chatimah*) sums up what they have in common: insolence. The apostates (line 1), an unnamed reign (or kingdom) (line 2), and Christians and heretics (line 3) are all "insolent" and deserve destruction. Line 4 (in quotation marks) is a citation of Ps. 69:29, a proof text to support the validity of the petition. We can only guess that the heretics (line 3), who figure elsewhere in rabbinic writings, are nonspecific troublemakers who deny rabbinic beliefs (see Volume 1, *The Sh'ma and Its Blessings*, L. Hoffman commentary, p. 69). But the "insolent reign" (line 2) must be Rome, and the Christians (line 3) and "apostates" (line 1) may be twin attacks on long-term members of the Church and on new Jewish converts to it.

In the Middle Ages, Jews were frequently summoned to defend themselves in disputations, often with apostates who had left the Jewish community and joined the Church hierarchy. Some time shortly after 1389, for instance, Rabbi Yom Tov Lipmann Muelhausen of Prague debated Peter (Pesach) the apostate, who charged the Jews with damning Christians in general and priests in particular. Since the word "Christians" does not arise in the debate, we must imagine that it had already been removed by Jewish self-censorship, for obvious reasons. The rabbi still had to justify the other terms, however. He expected that Jews and Christians could alike agree that "insolent reigns" should be damned but had a harder time with "no hope for apostates." Jewishly speaking, he argued, "hope" means living a Jewish life, so that requesting no hope for apostates must mean that apostates be prohibited from returning to Judaism, precisely what the Church taught anyway, since rejoining Judaism after baptism was considered a capital crime. Why, he asked, should Christians object to a Jewish prayer that echoes the teaching of the Church? His most interesting claim was the meaning of "heretics" *(minim)*, which he linked etymologically to a similar word meaning "kinds" or "varieties." *Minim,* he said, are those who vacillate between Christianity and Judaism, following two different kinds of religion simultaneously: like Jews for Jesus, or "messianic Jews" today, whom, he thought, Christians would despise as much as Jews did.

Increasing anti-Jewish sentiment brought further emendations, so that today we have "slanderers" and "enemies" — mild epithets with no specific identifying power at all. This nonspecificity allowed modern Orthodox leaders (like Samson Raphael Hirsch, nineteenth-century Germany) to excuse the blessing as having been directed only at other Jews ("pernicious elements within our People . . . who had become estranged from true Judaism"), by which he probably meant to impugn secularists and perhaps even the Reformers of his day. For their part, Reformers, by and large, just dispensed with the troublesome blessing, as an anachronism that was best forgotten (see Ellenson, p. 132, for details).

◆ ◆ ◆

BRETTLER (BIBLE)

"Show compassion to the righteous" This blessing is the counterpoint of the previous one, focusing on the positive, not the negative. Of the six groups mentioned, the Bible knows some (e.g., the leaders of your People), but righteous converts play no part in biblical literature, since conversion did not then exist as an institution. The focus, however, is not on the various categories of righteous people, but on "us," who want to be blessed as they are: "Let our lot be among them." The theology is quite remarkable, in that the worshiper asks to ride the coattails of these righteous groups, as if God will exercise corporate judgment, rewarding the average Israelites for the good deeds of the specially righteous, or — the opposite — punishing them for the sins of society at large (cf., e.g., Lam. 4:13).

The Bible is not consistent in its theory of retribution. The corporate view expressed here is the basis of Abraham's "bargaining" with God over the fate of Sodom and Gomorrah (Genesis 18), the assumption being that just a few righteous individuals can save a whole city. This perspective was rejected by some prophets, most especially Ezekiel, who says explicitly (14:12, 20) that if Noah, Daniel, and Job inhabited an evil city, they *(p. 138)*

ELLENSON (MODERN LITURGIES)

"Show compassion to the righteous . . . to the House of Israel . . . to righteous converts . . . ." Many modern liturgies (Abraham Geiger, *Ha'avodah Shebalev, Kol Haneshamah)* have found nothing problematic about this prayer. Others, like Isaac Mayer Wise (in his 1857 edition of *Minhag America),* affirmed the content of the prayer but, for some reason, omitted the phrase "to righteous converts." By 1872, Wise had gone further, deleting all particularistic references to the People Israel and transforming the prayer into a universal benediction for the righteous of all people. Other liberal liturgies have followed his example. The Reconstructionist *Daily Prayer Book,* for example, deleted the first sentence and began with the phrase "Give a good reward." *Gates of Prayer* says, "Have mercy, O Lord our God, upon the righteous and faithful of all peoples." *Siddur Lev Chadash* blends particularism and universalism, with "For the righteous and faithful, for all who choose to join our people, and for all men and women of good will, we ask Your favour, Eternal God."

---

13. *TSADIKIM* ("THE RIGHTEOUS") צַדִּיקִים

[1] Show compassion to the righteous, to the pious, to the leaders of your People, the House of Israel, to the remnants of their sages, to righteous converts, and to us, Adonai our God. [2] And give a good reward to all who truly trust in your name, and let our lot be among them forever that we will not be shamed, for we put our trust in You.

LANDES (HALAKHAH)

"The leaders of your people [ziknei amkha] *. . . the remnants of their sages . . . righteous converts"* Ziknei amkha can better be translated as "elders of your people" and then classified along with the "sages," giving us the combined category of "elders and Torah scholars." We would then have a broad reference to two groups of people to whom we have halakhic responsibilities: the elders and scholars, who are grouped together, for halakhic purposes; and righteous converts. Our obligation to elders and Torah scholars derives from Lev. 19:32, "Rise in front of the aged, and adore the presence of the elder," which the Talmud (Kid. 32b) applies directly to Torah scholars). Of righteous converts, Maimonides writes, "Greater is the obligation that the Torah lays down regarding converts than our obligation to [our own] father and mother, for whom [only] respect and honor [are required] . . . but with converts, we are commanded to love them greatly in our hearts" *(Letter to Ovadiah The Proselyte [Hager]).*

L. HOFFMAN (HISTORY)

THE LAST OF THE THREE BLESSINGS ON THE THEME OF JUSTICE CONSIDERS THE REWARD THAT IS DUE THE RIGHTEOUS.

"To the righteous, to the pious, to the leaders of your People, the house of Israel, to the remnants of their sages, to righteous converts, and to us" Originally, this prayer must have referred to specific groups of identifiable classes, but over time, it has come to denote universal types deserving of divine reward. Abudarham (Spain, fourteenth century), for instance, identifies "the righteous" as a purely ideal class in which there may be no actual members at all: people who never sin! "The pious," by contrast, are those who (like us) do sin, but who repent and reform. The point of the

(p. 138)

עַל־הַצַּדִּיקִים וְעַל־הַחֲסִידִים וְעַל־ 1
זִקְנֵי עַמְּךָ בֵּית יִשְׂרָאֵל וְעַל פְּלֵיטַת
סוֹפְרֵיהֶם וְעַל גֵּרֵי הַצֶּדֶק וְעָלֵינוּ יֶהֱמוּ
רַחֲמֶיךָ יְיָ אֱלֹהֵינוּ. וְתֵן שָׂכָר טוֹב לְכֹל 2
הַבּוֹטְחִים בְּשִׁמְךָ בֶּאֱמֶת וְשִׂים חֶלְקֵנוּ
עִמָּהֶם לְעוֹלָם וְלֹא נֵבוֹשׁ כִּי־בְךָ בָּטָחְנוּ.

J. HOFFMAN (TRANSLATION)

"Show [yehemu] *compassion"* The meaning of the Hebrew verb is uncertain, but clear from context.

"Trust of the righteous" That is, one in which the righteous can trust.

³ Blessed are You, Adonai, who is the support and trust of the righteous.

‎³ בָּרוּךְ אַתָּה יי מִשְׁעָן וּמִבְטָח לַצַּדִּיקִים.

BRETTLER (BIBLE)

could save only themselves, not the evildoers there. Yet, Ezekiel did not totally eradicate the earlier corporate notion, which resurfaces here.

L. HOFFMAN (HISTORY)

prayer is therefore to rank repentance alongside perfection: if we cannot be perfect, we can at least repent!

"The leaders of your People" become identified by many as communal leaders in every age who work for the welfare of the community — but only out of a sense of a religious calling *(l'shem shamayim)*. "The remnants of their sages" is often taken to mean schoolteachers.

Righteous converts is an identifiable group within Jewish law even today. Every convert is such a person — by definition. Jewish law contrasts such a full convert to Judaism with the "resident convert," a *ger toshav,* meaning someone who agrees to follow certain aspects of Judaism in return for the right to live as a citizen within the Jewish community. A *ger toshav* is akin to resident aliens in American law, holders of green cards who become assimilated into American society, pay taxes, and follow American law — but who never fully commit to American citizenship. The full convert — known as a *ger tsedek,* a "righteous convert" — is like a full citizen: someone who joins the Jewish People out of complete and unquestioned commitment. Our prayer identifies such a Jew by choice as fully the equal of the paradigmatic perfect person who never ever sins.

But why add, "and to us"? Clearly, the assumption is that we real-life human beings never fully attain any of these statuses. We may repent — somewhat. We may teach children — but out of the pure sense of a divine calling? And we may convert to Judaism — but with never any struggle or second thoughts? Yes, some of us may fulfill these conditions, but most of us will not; so we add, "and to us." May we who become penitents, leaders, teachers, and converts in the real world be likened to the idealized version of what we strive to be.

BRETTLER (BIBLE)

"Return to Jerusalem" A new theme emerges, "eschatology," that is, concern for the end of time. It will be crucial for three of the next four blessings: Jerusalem as God's city (#14, here), the place for Davidic kingship (#15), and the site of the restored Temple (#17).

Jerusalem as God's city is a predominant biblical notion, seen, for example, in Isa. 60:14, which says of the restored Jerusalem: "You shall be called the City of Adonai." That God should dwell there is derived from an idea common to the ancient near east, whereby deities actually inhabit their temples, though they may be present elsewhere also. Some biblical texts moderate this idea, insisting that only God's name dwells in the Temple (e.g., Deut. 12:11), while others insist that God really resides there. Solomon, for instance, says (1 Kings 8:13), "I have certainly built an exalted house for You, a place where you may dwell forever."

It is likely that the opening of this prayer, with its verbs *tashuv* ("you will return") and *tishkon* ("dwell"), reflects the prophecy of consolation from Zech. 8:3: "Thus says the Lord of Hosts: 'I have returned *(shavti)* to Zion, and I will dwell *(v'shakhanti)* in Jerusalem." Our prayer says also, "As You promised," possibly referring to this very verse, but also to others that guarantee God's return to Jerusalem (Ezek. 43:9; Zech. 2:14; 8:8). This return is envisioned in tandem with a restoration of the Davidic monarchy, here expressed through "David's throne," a term especially popular in Jeremiah for describing the kingship of David's descendants (e.g., Jer. 17:25).

———◆———

ELLENSON (MODERN LITURGIES)

Return to Jerusalem. . . . Cause the progeny of David, your servant, to blossom" (Blessings 14 and 15) The manifest content and themes of these two benedictions have been regarded as untenable by many. The love for Zion and call for the restoration of the Davidic monarchy were anathema to nineteenth-century Reform editors, and the faith in a personal messiah remains problematic even today. Of all the ways the problem was attacked (see comments below), Abraham Geiger's solution deserves special commentary here. He collapsed the two benedictions into one, so as to combine particularism and universalism: "Remember Jerusalem in compassion, and may You cause the sprout of salvation to blossom quickly *(Vi'rushalayim b'rachamim tizkor, v'tzemach y'shu'ah m'herah tatzmiach)*.

14. *Y'RUSHALAYIM* ("JERUSALEM") יְרוּשָׁלַיִם

[1] Return to Jerusalem your city in compassion, and dwell in its midst as You promised You would, and rebuild it soon in our day into an eternal structure, and quickly establish David's throne within it. [2] Blessed are You, Adonai, who rebuilds Jerusalem.

(p. 141)

"And quickly establish David's throne within it" This prayer for a David reborn has been omitted from most Reform prayer books. The 1857 *Minhag America* replaced the phrase with Isa. 2:3, "For from Zion shall go forth Torah, and the word of God from Jerusalem," though the 1872 *Minhag America* was not content with such a minor change and completely transformed the prayer by asking God to cause the spirit of holiness to dwell among the People Israel so that Israel could serve as "a light to the nations." Later Reform liturgies, including *Gates of Prayer* and *Siddur Lev Chadash*, followed the 1857 pattern. *Ha'avodah Shebalev* and Reconstructionist liturgies (both *Daily Prayer Book* and *Kol Haneshamah*) delete this line from their service and offer no substitute in its stead.

LANDES (HALAKHAH)
"Return to Jerusalem" The settling of the Land is Israel is not a *mitzvah* given for one particular time only, but an eternal commandment, a *mitzvah* and a boon for all of Israel (*Responsa* of the Rivash, 101).

———

L. HOFFMAN (HISTORY)
WITH THE EXILES RETURNED, AND A COMPLETE SYSTEM OF JUSTICE IN PLACE, WE TURN TO THE IMAGE OF JERUSALEM REBUILT, THE ESTABLISHMENT OF A MODEL COMMUNITY DEVOTED SOLELY TO GOD AND GOD'S WAYS.

———

¹וְלִירוּשָׁלַֽיִם עִירְךָ בְּרַחֲמִים תָּשׁוּב וְתִשְׁכֹּן בְּתוֹכָהּ כַּאֲשֶׁר דִּבַּֽרְתָּ וּבְנֵה אוֹתָהּ בְּקָרוֹב בְּיָמֵֽינוּ בִּנְיַן עוֹלָם וְכִסֵּא דָוִד מְהֵרָה לְתוֹכָהּ תָּכִין. ²בָּרוּךְ אַתָּה יְיָ בּוֹנֵה יְרוּשָׁלָֽיִם.

J. HOFFMAN (TRANSLATION)
"Promised" Literally, "said."

"Rebuild" Literally, "build." But Hebrew has no word for "rebuild."

"Structure" The Hebrew for "build" and "structure" come from the same root, and so convey the same effect as "build it . . . into an eternal building," but while a city may be a structure, it is not a building.

"Throne" Literally, "chair," but used regularly for the chair of royalty, even the chair (or throne) on which God sits.

——— ◆ ◆ ◆ ———

"Cause the progeny of David" Most scholars consider this to be the "nineteenth" of the eighteen blessings, having developed from the previous one, which mentions "David's throne." The development of this into its own blessing indicates how significant messianic ideas were within segments of rabbinic culture. A more literal rendition of the blessing's opening is: "May You swiftly cause the sprout of David to flourish, and may his horn be raised through your deliverance." These idioms, so odd in English, are well anchored in biblical `rhetoric. The ideal Davidic king is frequently depicted in agricultural metaphor. The well-known Isa. 11:1 reads: "A shoot shall sprout out of the stump of Jesse [David's father], a twig shall sprout from its roots." Our blessing specifically recollects Jer. 33:15 (cf. 23:5), where the prophet predicts: "In those days and at that time I will cause to sprout *[atsmiach]* for David a righteous sprout *[tsemach]*. . . ." This prophecy is applied later by Zechariah (3:8, 6:12) to the post-exilic Davidic leader Zerubbabel, whose name (in Akkadian) means "seed of Babylon," making a prophecy that centers on agricultural renewal especially appropriate to him.

Ezek. 29:21 ("On that day I will cause a horn to grow for the house of Israel") is also evident here. The "raised horn" is animal imagery that supplements the agricultural metaphor of "a flourishing sprout." It denotes the raised horn of the victorious or proud ox, implying strength. It is widely used, appearing in Ps. 89:25 and Ezek. 29:21 specifically for the Davidic king.

Here, however (as in 1 Sam. 2:1, Hannah's prayer), the raised horn is specifically connected to divine deliverance, to demonstrate that the messiah is subservient to God. That idea is reinforced through the motive clause, "for we await your [God's] salvation." Similarly, David appears here as "your servant," a frequent biblical designation (e.g., 1 Kings 11:13), which emphasizes the king's subservience to God.

15. DAVID ("DAVID") דָּוִד

1 Cause the progeny of David, your servant, to blossom quickly. 2 Let him shine in your deliverance, for we await your salvation every day. 3 Blessed are You, Adonai, who causes the light of salvation to blossom.

The conclusion is atypical for the *Amidah*, in that it assembles a summary of key words from elsewhere in the blessing. It may be happenstance, however, for this concluding formula is found in the second-century B.C.E. work Ben Sirah (51:12) — "Give praise to the One who causes the light of salvation to blossom for the house of David" *(hodu l'matsmiach keren levet david),*— and is reflected also in Luke 1:68–69.

———◆———

ELLENSON (MODERN LITURGIES)

"Cause the progeny of David, your servant, to blossom. . . . Let him shine in your deliverance . . ." Reform and Reconstructionist thought has almost universally rejected the belief in a personal messiah descended from the house of David. *Minhag America* retained something of the prayer's particularity by substituting "your servants" *(avadekha)* for "David, your servant," thereby stressing the messianic potential of the Jewish People as a whole, consistent with Wise's belief in the mission of Israel as a light to the nations. *Gates of Prayer* and *Siddur Lev Chadash* universalize the prayer, asking that *ts'dakah* (righteousness and justice) flourish, while *Ha'avodah Shebalev* includes also *emet,* "truth."

Reconstructionist liturgies reword the blessing without reference to David. *Kol Haneshamah*   *(p. 144)*

LANDES (HALAKHAH)

"The progeny of David, your servant" Belief in the messiah who will spring from the house of David is one of the thirteen principles of faith by which Maimonides defines a Jew. Ultimately, the messiah is to rebuild the Temple in its place, gather the dispersed of Israel, and "repair the world so that it might together serve God" (Maimonides, "Laws of Kings" 11:4).

———◆———

L. HOFFMAN (HISTORY)

THE FINAL STEP IN REDEMPTION IS THE APPOINTMENT OF A MESSIAH, TRADITIONALLY VIEWED AS A DESCENDANT OF KING DAVID, WHO WILL REIGN OVER THE PERFECT SOCIETY OF PEACE AND UNIVERSAL HARMONY.

———◆———

J. HOFFMAN (TRANSLATION)

"Cause the progeny of David, your servant, to blossom quickly" There is no way to capture the beauty of the Hebrew, which combines agricultural imagery (from the Hebrew *tsemach,* "plant" or "progeny," and *tatsmi'ach,* "cause to blossom" or "cause to flourish") with the concepts of David's descendants and of flourishing. *Siddur Sim Shalom* (Conservative) gives us, "Bring to flower the shoot of your servant David."

¹אֶת־צֶמַח דָּוִד עַבְדְּךָ מְהֵרָה תַצְמִיחַ. ²וְקַרְנוֹ תָּרוּם בִּישׁוּעָתֶךָ כִּי לִישׁוּעָתְךָ קִוִּינוּ כָּל־הַיּוֹם. ³בָּרוּךְ אַתָּה יְיָ מַצְמִיחַ קֶרֶן יְשׁוּעָה.

"Let him shine [karno tarum] . . . the light of salvation to blossom [matsmi'ach keren y'shu'ah]"* The agricultural imagery of blossoming (see prior note) is enhanced, as it is wed to a further metaphor: David's *keren,* which has multiple meanings, including "horn" and "financial fund," but also "ray of light"—hence, "let him shine" and "light of salvation." Birnbaum (Orthodox) leaves *keren* untranslated; Artscroll (Orthodox) calls it "pride." It may actually refer to sexual prowess.   *(p. 144)*

AMIDAH: BLESSINGS OF PETITION

ELLENSON (MODERN LITURGIES)

asks, "May you speedily redeem your people Israel, and raise their stronghold with your help."

Conservative liturgy retains the traditional Hebrew but alters the English here and there. Instead of the personal "Let him shine in your deliverance," *Siddur Sim Shalom* and *Weekday Prayer Book* give us the more ambiguous and impersonal "Hasten the advent of the Messianic redemption."

———◆———

J. HOFFMAN (TRANSLATION)

"Every day" Artscroll (Orthodox) gives us "the whole day long."

————————◆ ◆ ◆————————

BRETTLER (BIBLE)

"Hear our voice" This general prayer interrupts the triad of blessings on the theme of restored Jerusalem. The next blessing is about sacrifice, however, so this one may be intended to remind us here that prayer replaces sacrifice. It is an extended plea to God to "hear" the people's prayers, since God is a prayer-hearing deity. The opening call for God to listen has several biblical parallels (e.g., Ps. 5:4), reflecting anxiety, common in the psalms, that God may not be listening to prayer that is about to be offered and must be asked explicitly to pay attention (Pss. 4:2; 54:4; 143:1). Not all the authors of our psalms share this anxiety; the writer of Ps. 65:3 makes a point of calling God *shome'a t'fillah,* "the one who hears prayer," a description that is borrowed here. Our prayer may open with anxious hope that God is listening, but it closes with certainty that God will do so.

———◆———

ELLENSON (MODERN LITURGIES)

"For You hear the prayer of your People Israel" The particularism of God's hearing only Israel's prayers disturbed Isaac Mayer Wise as well as the authors of *Ha'avodah Shebalev* and *Va'ani T'filati,* who universalized the phrase by substituting the Sefardi "every mouth" *(kol peh)* for "your People Israel" *(amkha yisrael). Ha'avodah Shebalev* and *Siddur Lev Chadash* adopt Wise's wording, and *Gates of Prayer* evokes the same universalistic sentiments by saying simply, "For You are a God who hears prayer and supplication." (See below, "Grant peace.")

———◆———

16. *T'FILLAH* ("PRAYER")

תְּפִלָּה

[1] Hear our voice, Adonai our God. [2] Have pity and mercy on us, and accept our prayer with favor, for You are the God who hears our prayers and supplications. [3] Do not turn us away from You, our ruler, empty-handed, for You hear the prayer of your People Israel in mercy. [4] Blessed are You, Adonai, who hears prayer.

LANDES (HALAKHAH)

"Hear our voice" This is the summary blessing of the *Amidah,* reminding us that we too must hear the cry of others if we are to emulate God. It comes at the end of all the middle blessings to teach us that before we move on, we are welcome to pour out our hearts to God in personal petition beyond what the individual words of the *Amidah* have to say. I commented above (see "Heal us") that personal insertions into the blessings are always in order but that they should be on the theme of the blessing in question, such as a prayer that someone we know be healed, added to the blessing on healing (#8). Here, however, we have a general benediction affirming God's readiness to hear prayer in general, so we may insert a prayer for anything we like and only then continue with the prescribed wording of the *Amidah.*

———◆———

L. HOFFMAN (HISTORY)

THE LAST OF THE MIDDLE BLESSINGS LOOKS BACK UPON ALL THE OTHERS, SEE-ING THEM AS A SINGLE EXTENDED PRAYER FOR HUMAN DELIVERANCE, BEGINNING WITH KNOWLEDGE AND REPENTANCE, AND ENDING WITH THE JUST SOCIAL ORDER THAT WE CALL MESSIANIC. OUR THEME HERE IS THE PETITION THAT GOD WILL HEAR OUR PRAYER.

"You hear the prayer of your People Israel in mercy" The Spanish-Portuguese version is more universalistic: "You hear the prayer of everyone" (literally, "of every mouth," *t'fillat kol peh*).

———◆———

¹שְׁמַע קוֹלֵנוּ יְיָ אֱלֹהֵינוּ. ²חוּס וְרַחֵם עָלֵינוּ וְקַבֵּל בְּרַחֲמִים וּבְרָצוֹן אֶת־תְּפִלָּתֵנוּ כִּי אֵל שׁוֹמֵעַ תְּפִלּוֹת וְתַחֲנוּנִים אָתָּה. ³וּמִלְּפָנֶיךָ מַלְכֵּנוּ רֵיקָם אַל תְּשִׁיבֵנוּ, כִּי אַתָּה שׁוֹמֵעַ תְּפִלַּת עַמְּךָ יִשְׂרָאֵל בְּרַחֲמִים. ⁴בָּרוּךְ אַתָּה יְיָ שׁוֹמֵעַ תְּפִלָּה.

J. HOFFMAN (TRANSLATION)

"You are the God" "You" is emphasized in Hebrew, conveying the same effect as if it were in italics or boldface.

"Empty-handed" Literally, "empty."

———◆ ◆ ◆———

C. Blessings of Thanksgiving

17. AVODAH ("SACRIFICIAL SERVICE")

עֲבוֹדָה

¹ Find favor, Adonai our God, in your People Israel and in their prayer. ² And return the sacrifice to the Holy of Holies. In favor accept the fire-offerings of Israel and their prayers in love. ³ And may the service of Israel your People always be favorable.

¹רְצֵה יְיָ אֱלֹהֵינוּ בְּעַמְּךָ יִשְׂרָאֵל וּבִתְפִלָּתָם. ²וְהָשֵׁב אֶת־הָעֲבוֹדָה לִדְבִיר בֵּיתֶךָ וְאִשֵּׁי יִשְׂרָאֵל וּתְפִלָּתָם בְּאַהֲבָה תְקַבֵּל בְּרָצוֹן. ³וּתְהִי לְרָצוֹן תָּמִיד עֲבוֹדַת יִשְׂרָאֵל עַמֶּךָ.

(On Rosh Chodesh—the New Month— and Chol Hamo'ed, the intermediary days of Passover and Sukkot, add:

(On Rosh Chodesh—the New Month— and Chol Hamo'ed, the intermediary days of Passover and Sukkot, add:

⁴ Our God and our ancestors' God, may these arise, come forth, reach up, be noted, be favored, be heard, be recorded, and be remembered before You for deliverance and goodness, for grace, kindness, and mercy, for life and peace: our memory; our record; our ancestors' memory; the memory of the messiah, son of David your servant; the memory of Jerusalem, your holy city; and the memory of the entire house of Israel, your People, on this

⁴אֱלֹהֵינוּ וֵאלֹהֵי אֲבוֹתֵינוּ. יַעֲלֶה וְיָבֹא וְיַגִּיעַ וְיֵרָאֶה וְיֵרָצֶה וְיִשָּׁמַע וְיִפָּקֵד וְיִזָּכֵר זִכְרוֹנֵנוּ וּפִקְדוֹנֵנוּ וְזִכְרוֹן אֲבוֹתֵינוּ. וְזִכְרוֹן מָשִׁיחַ בֶּן־דָּוִד עַבְדֶּךָ. וְזִכְרוֹן יְרוּשָׁלַיִם עִיר קָדְשֶׁךָ. וְזִכְרוֹן כָּל־עַמְּךָ בֵּית יִשְׂרָאֵל לְפָנֶיךָ. לִפְלֵיטָה וּלְטוֹבָה וּלְחֵן וּלְחֶסֶד וּלְרַחֲמִים וּלְחַיִּים וּלְשָׁלוֹם בְּיוֹם

[On Rosh Chodesh, the New Month, say:

[On Rosh Chodesh, the New Month, say:

start of this month.

רֹאשׁ הַחֹדֶשׁ הַזֶּה.

On Passover, say:

On Passover, say:

day of the holiday of Passover.

חַג הַמַּצוֹת הַזֶּה.

On Sukkot, say:

On Sukkot, say:

day of the holiday of Sukkot.]

חַג הַסֻּכּוֹת הַזֶּה.]

⁵ Remember us, Adonai our God, on this day for goodness. ⁶ Record us on this day for blessing. ⁷ And save us on this day for life.

⁵זָכְרֵנוּ יְיָ אֱלֹהֵינוּ בּוֹ לְטוֹבָה. ⁶וּפָקְדֵנוּ בּוֹ לִבְרָכָה. ⁷וְהוֹשִׁיעֵנוּ בוֹ לְחַיִּים.

8 In this matter of salvation and mercy, spare us and be gracious to us, have mercy upon us and bring salvation, for our eyes turn to You, for You are the sovereign God, gracious and merciful.)

9 May our eyes behold your return to Zion in mercy. 10 Blessed are You, Adonai, who restores his divine presence to Zion.

18. *HODA'AH* ("GRATEFUL ACKNOWLEDGMENT")

1 We gratefully acknowledge that You are Adonai our God and our ancestors' God for ever and ever. 2 You are the rock of our lives and the shield of our salvation from generation to generation. 3 We gratefully acknowledge You by rendering your praises, for our lives, which are in your hands, and for our souls, which are entrusted to You, and for your miracles that are with us on each day, and for the wonders and goodness at every time, evening, morning, and afternoon. 4 You are good, for your mercy never ceases. 5 You are merciful, for your kindness never ends. 6 You have always been our hope.

The *Modim D'rabbanan*—

[To be recited in an undertone, while the prayer leader repeats this blessing:

7 We gratefully acknowledge that You are Adonai our God and our ancestors' God, God of all flesh, our creator and creator of the universe. 8 We offer blessings and grateful acknowledgments to your great and holy name, for having given us life and having sustained us. 9 —So give us life and sustain us and gather our exiles

8 וּבִדְבַר יְשׁוּעָה וְרַחֲמִים חוּס וְחָנֵּנוּ. וְרַחֵם עָלֵינוּ וְהוֹשִׁיעֵנוּ. כִּי אֵלֶיךָ עֵינֵינוּ. כִּי אֵל מֶלֶךְ חַנּוּן וְרַחוּם אָתָּה.)

9 וְתֶחֱזֶינָה עֵינֵינוּ בְּשׁוּבְךָ לְצִיּוֹן בְּרַחֲמִים. 10 בָּרוּךְ אַתָּה יְיָ הַמַּחֲזִיר שְׁכִינָתוֹ לְצִיּוֹן.

הוֹדָאָה

1 מוֹדִים אֲנַחְנוּ לָךְ שָׁאַתָּה הוּא יְיָ אֱלֹהֵינוּ וֵאלֹהֵי אֲבוֹתֵינוּ לְעוֹלָם וָעֶד. 2 צוּר חַיֵּינוּ מָגֵן יִשְׁעֵנוּ אַתָּה הוּא לְדוֹר וָדוֹר. 3 נוֹדֶה לְּךָ וּנְסַפֵּר תְּהִלָּתֶךָ עַל חַיֵּינוּ הַמְּסוּרִים בְּיָדֶךָ וְעַל נִשְׁמוֹתֵינוּ הַפְּקוּדוֹת לָךְ וְעַל נִסֶּיךָ שֶׁבְּכָל־יוֹם עִמָּנוּ וְעַל נִפְלְאוֹתֶיךָ וְטוֹבוֹתֶיךָ שֶׁבְּכָל־עֵת עֶרֶב וָבֹקֶר וְצָהֳרָיִם. 4 הַטּוֹב כִּי לֹא־כָלוּ רַחֲמֶיךָ. 5 וְהַמְרַחֵם כִּי לֹא־תַמּוּ חֲסָדֶיךָ. 6 מֵעוֹלָם קִוִּינוּ לָךְ.

The *Modim D'rabbanan*—

[To be recited in an undertone, while the prayer leader repeats this blessing:

7 מוֹדִים אֲנַחְנוּ לָךְ שָׁאַתָּה הוּא יְיָ אֱלֹהֵינוּ וֵאלֹהֵי אֲבוֹתֵינוּ אֱלֹהֵי כָל בָּשָׂר יוֹצְרֵנוּ יוֹצֵר בְּרֵאשִׁית. 8 בְּרָכוֹת וְהוֹדָאוֹת לְשִׁמְךָ הַגָּדוֹל וְהַקָּדוֹשׁ עַל שֶׁהֶחֱיִיתָנוּ וְקִיַּמְתָּנוּ. 9 כֵּן תְּחַיֵּנוּ וּתְקַיְּמֵנוּ וְתֶאֱסֹף גָּלְיוֹתֵינוּ לְחַצְרוֹת קָדְשֶׁךָ לִשְׁמֹר חֻקֶּיךָ וְלַעֲשׂוֹת רְצוֹנֶךָ וּלְעָבְדְּךָ בְּלֵבָב שָׁלֵם עַל שֶׁאֲנַחְנוּ מוֹדִים לָךְ.

בָּרוּךְ אֵל הַהוֹדָאוֹת.] [10

to your holy courts to keep your laws and perform your will, to serve You whole-heartedly; and for our acknowledging You with gratitude. [10] Blessed is the God of grateful acknowledgment.]

[On Chanukah, add:

[11] For the miracles and for the redemption and for the mighty acts and for the triumphs and for the wars you brought about for our ancestors in those days at this time of year—[12] in the days of the Hasmonean, Mattathias ben Yohanan, the high priest, and his sons, when the evil government of Greece rose up against your People Israel to make them forget your Torah and to make them leave the laws of your will: [13] In your great mercy You rose up with them in their time of trouble and fought in their fight, judged their cause just, and avenged them with a vengeance. [14] You delivered the mighty into the hands of the weak, the many into the hands of the few, the unclean into the hands of the pure, the evil into the hands of the righteous, and the arrogant into the hands of those who engage in your Torah. [15] For You, You made a great and holy name in your world; and for your People Israel, You brought about a great triumph and redemption on that very day. [16] And then your children came to the Holy of Holies, and emptied your temple, and purified your holy place, and lit candles in your holy courts, and established these eight days of Chanukah gratefully to acknowledge, and to praise, your great name.]

[On Purim, add:

[17] For the miracles and for the redemption and for the mighty acts and for the triumphs and for the wars You brought

---

[On Chanukah, add:

[11] עַל הַנִּסִּים וְעַל הַפֻּרְקָן וְעַל הַגְּבוּרוֹת וְעַל הַתְּשׁוּעוֹת וְעַל הַמִּלְחָמוֹת שֶׁעָשִׂיתָ לַאֲבוֹתֵינוּ בַּיָּמִים הָהֵם בַּזְּמַן הַזֶּה. [12] בִּימֵי מַתִּתְיָהוּ בֶּן־יוֹחָנָן כֹּהֵן גָּדוֹל חַשְׁמוֹנַי וּבָנָיו. כְּשֶׁעָמְדָה מַלְכוּת יָוָן הָרְשָׁעָה עַל עַמְּךָ יִשְׂרָאֵל לְהַשְׁכִּיחָם תּוֹרָתֶךָ וּלְהַעֲבִירָם מֵחֻקֵּי רְצוֹנֶךָ: [13] וְאַתָּה בְּרַחֲמֶיךָ הָרַבִּים עָמַדְתָּ לָהֶם בְּעֵת צָרָתָם. רַבְתָּ אֶת־רִיבָם. דַּנְתָּ אֶת־דִּינָם. נָקַמְתָּ אֶת־נִקְמָתָם. [14] מָסַרְתָּ גִבּוֹרִים בְּיַד חַלָּשִׁים. וְרַבִּים בְּיַד מְעַטִּים. וּטְמֵאִים בְּיַד טְהוֹרִים. וּרְשָׁעִים בְּיַד צַדִּיקִים. וְזֵדִים בְּיַד עוֹסְקֵי תוֹרָתֶךָ. [15] וּלְךָ עָשִׂיתָ שֵׁם גָּדוֹל וְקָדוֹשׁ בְּעוֹלָמֶךָ. וּלְעַמְּךָ יִשְׂרָאֵל עָשִׂיתָ תְּשׁוּעָה גְדוֹלָה וּפֻרְקָן כְּהַיּוֹם הַזֶּה. [16] וְאַחַר כֵּן בָּאוּ בָנֶיךָ לִדְבִיר בֵּיתֶךָ. וּפִנּוּ אֶת־הֵיכָלֶךָ. וְטִהֲרוּ אֶת־מִקְדָּשֶׁךָ. וְהִדְלִיקוּ נֵרוֹת בְּחַצְרוֹת קָדְשֶׁךָ. וְקָבְעוּ שְׁמוֹנַת יְמֵי חֲנֻכָּה אֵלּוּ לְהוֹדוֹת וּלְהַלֵּל לְשִׁמְךָ הַגָּדוֹל.]

[On Purim, add:

[17] עַל הַנִּסִּים וְעַל הַפֻּרְקָן וְעַל הַגְּבוּרוֹת וְעַל הַתְּשׁוּעוֹת וְעַל הַמִּלְחָמוֹת שֶׁעָשִׂיתָ לַאֲבוֹתֵינוּ בַּיָּמִים הָהֵם בַּזְּמַן הַזֶּה. [18] בִּימֵי

about for our ancestors in those days at this time of year—18 in the days of Mordecai and Esther in the capital city of Shushan, when the evil Haman rose up against them and sought to destroy, to kill, and to wipe out all the Jews, young and old, women and children, in one day, on the thirteenth day of the twelfth month (which is Adar), and to plunder their wealth: 19 In your great mercy You brought his advice to naught and frustrated his plan. 20 You turned his scheme around on him, so that he and his sons were hanged from a tree.]

21 For all of these your name will be blessed and exalted, our king, forever to the ends of time.

[From Rosh Hashanah to Yom Kippur, add:

22 And write down all of the children of your covenant for good life.]

23 All that lives will gratefully acknowledge You forever and praise your name in truth, God, our salvation and our help, forever. 24 Blessed are You, Adonai, whose name is good and to whom grateful acknowledgment is befitting.

19. *Birkat Kohanim/Shalom* ("The Priestly Blessing/ Peace")

1 Our God and our ancestors' God, bless us with the threefold blessing in the Torah, written by Moses your servant, and said by Aaron and his sons the priests, your holy people:

2 "May Adonai bless you and keep you.

3 May Adonai shine his face toward you and treat you graciously.

מָרְדְּכַי וְאֶסְתֵּר בְּשׁוּשַׁן הַבִּירָה. כְּשֶׁעָמַד עֲלֵיהֶם הָמָן הָרָשָׁע. בִּקֵּשׁ לְהַשְׁמִיד לַהֲרֹג וּלְאַבֵּד אֶת־כָּל־הַיְּהוּדִים מִנַּעַר וְעַד־זָקֵן. טַף וְנָשִׁים. בְּיוֹם אֶחָד בִּשְׁלֹשָׁה עָשָׂר לְחֹדֶשׁ שְׁנֵים־עָשָׂר הוּא חֹדֶשׁ אֲדָר. וּשְׁלָלָם לָבֹז: 19וְאַתָּה בְּרַחֲמֶיךָ הָרַבִּים הֵפַרְתָּ אֶת־ עֲצָתוֹ. וְקִלְקַלְתָּ אֶת־מַחֲשַׁבְתּוֹ. 20וַהֲשֵׁבוֹתָ גְּמוּלוֹ בְּרֹאשׁוֹ. וְתָלוּ אֹתוֹ וְאֶת־בָּנָיו עַל־הָעֵץ.]

21וְעַל־כֻּלָּם יִתְבָּרַךְ וְיִתְרוֹמַם שִׁמְךָ מַלְכֵּנוּ תָּמִיד לְעוֹלָם וָעֶד.

[From Rosh Hashanah to Yom Kippur, add:

22וּכְתוֹב לְחַיִּים טוֹבִים כָּל־בְּנֵי בְרִיתֶךָ.]

23וְכֹל הַחַיִּים יוֹדוּךָ סֶּלָה וִיהַלְלוּ אֶת־ שִׁמְךָ בֶּאֱמֶת הָאֵל יְשׁוּעָתֵנוּ וְעֶזְרָתֵנוּ סֶלָה. 24בָּרוּךְ אַתָּה יְיָ הַטּוֹב שִׁמְךָ וּלְךָ נָאֶה לְהוֹדוֹת.

בִּרְכַּת כֹּהֲנִים/שָׁלוֹם

1אֱלֹהֵינוּ וֵאלֹהֵי אֲבוֹתֵינוּ בָּרְכֵנוּ בַבְּרָכָה הַמְשֻׁלֶּשֶׁת בַּתּוֹרָה. הַכְּתוּבָה עַל יְדֵי מֹשֶׁה עַבְדֶּךָ. הָאֲמוּרָה מִפִּי אַהֲרֹן וּבָנָיו כֹּהֲנִים עַם קְדוֹשֶׁךָ כָּאָמוּר:

2יְבָרֶכְךָ יְיָ וְיִשְׁמְרֶךָ.

3יָאֵר יְיָ פָּנָיו אֵלֶיךָ וִיחֻנֶּךָּ.

⁴ May Adonai lift his face toward you and grant you peace."

⁵ Grant peace, goodness, and blessing, grace, kindness, and mercy to us and to all of Israel, your People. ⁶ Bless us, our Father, all of us as one, in the light of your face, for in the light of your face, Adonai our God, You gave us a Torah of life, a love of grace, righteousness, blessing, mercy, life, and peace. ⁷ You see fit to bless your People Israel at all times, at every hour, with your peace. *⁸ Blessed are You, Adonai, who blesses his People Israel with peace.

[*From Rosh Hashanah to Yom Kippur, say instead:

⁹ May it be the book of life, blessing, peace, and prosperous goodness that we are remembered for and written in before You—we and all of your People, the House of Israel, for life, goodness, and peace. ¹⁰ Blessed are You, Adonai, who brings peace.]

⁴יִשָּׂא יְיָ פָּנָיו אֵלֶיךָ וְיָשֵׂם לְךָ שָׁלוֹם.

⁵שִׂים שָׁלוֹם טוֹבָה וּבְרָכָה חֵן וָחֶסֶד וְרַחֲמִים עָלֵינוּ וְעַל כָּל־יִשְׂרָאֵל עַמֶּךָ. ⁶בָּרְכֵנוּ אָבִינוּ כֻּלָּנוּ כְּאֶחָד בְּאוֹר פָּנֶיךָ. כִּי בְאוֹר פָּנֶיךָ נָתַתָּ לָּנוּ יְיָ אֱלֹהֵינוּ תּוֹרַת חַיִּים וְאַהֲבַת חֶסֶד וּצְדָקָה וּבְרָכָה וְרַחֲמִים וְחַיִּים וְשָׁלוֹם. ⁷וְטוֹב בְּעֵינֶיךָ לְבָרֵךְ אֶת־עַמְּךָ יִשְׂרָאֵל בְּכָל־עֵת וּבְכָל־שָׁעָה בִּשְׁלוֹמֶךָ. *⁸בָּרוּךְ אַתָּה יְיָ הַמְבָרֵךְ אֶת־עַמּוֹ יִשְׂרָאֵל בַּשָּׁלוֹם.

[*From Rosh Hashanah to Yom Kippur, say instead:

⁹בְּסֵפֶר חַיִּים בְּרָכָה וְשָׁלוֹם וּפַרְנָסָה טוֹבָה נִזָּכֵר וְנִכָּתֵב לְפָנֶיךָ אֲנַחְנוּ וְכָל־עַמְּךָ בֵּית יִשְׂרָאֵל לְחַיִּים טוֹבִים וּלְשָׁלוֹם. ¹⁰בָּרוּךְ אַתָּה יְיָ עוֹשֵׂה הַשָּׁלוֹם.]

BRETTLER (BIBLE)

"Find favor" One need not be a liturgical historian to see that the original focus of this blessing was likely the Temple service, as the rabbinic title, *Avodah* ("Sacrificial Service") implies. The festival addition *(Ya'aleh v'yavo,* "Our God . . . may these arise, come forth") is added because the festivals required additional offerings. Since sacrifices had once been fundamental to divine worship, the Rabbis assumed that they would some day be restored. Invoking the hope for their restoration is tempered, however, by the   *(p. 157)*

ELLENSON (MODERN LITURGIES)

"Return the sacrifice to the Holy of Holies . . . accept the fire-offerings of Israel" Pleas to restore the sacrificial cult have been altered or even deleted in virtually every non-Orthodox prayer book of the past two centuries. From Abraham Geiger's *Seder T'filah D'var Yom B'Yomo* through the liturgies of contemporary Reform and Reconstructionist Judaism in the United States, Israel, and the United Kingdom, these lines have been completely omitted. The 1974 edition of the Conservative *Weekday Prayer Book* also removes them, while *Siddur Sim Shalom* takes out only "the fire-offerings of Israel" and translates "sacrifice"   *(p. 158)*

DORFF (THEOLOGY)

The last three blessings of the *Amidah* ask God to "find favor in your People Israel and in their

17. AVODAH ("SACRIFICIAL SERVICE") עֲבוֹדָה

¹ Find favor, Adonai our God, in your People Israel and in their prayer. ² And return the sacrifice to the Holy of Holies. In favor accept the fire-offerings of Israel and their prayers in love. ³ And may the service of Israel your People always be favorable.

FALK (FEMINISM)

" W h o restores his [the divine] presence to Zion" The

prayer" so that God dwells again with us in Zion; we thank God for each day's miracles and beseech God for peace. Like the first three blessings, the last three too appear in every version of the *Amidah*. We should ask, therefore, as we did with the introductory benedictions, why those who composed the *Amidah* insisted on these paragraphs and this order.

The first three blessings identify the parties to the interaction of prayer, as if functioning effectively as a Jewish "Hello" to God. In a parallel way, these last three blessings say "Goodbye," making sure that both God   *(p. 157)*

seventeenth blessing is called *Avodah*, usually translated as "Worship." In context, though, it refers to the sacrificial cult that was practiced as the primary vehicle of Jewish devotion as long as the Temple stood. Probably the most ancient (and antiquated) part of the *Amidah*, this blessing asks that God restore the Temple service (i.e., the sacrifices) and concludes by praising God, who "restores his presence *[sh'khinato]* to Zion."

Despite its archaic nature, I believe this blessing contains promising potential for interpretation and re-creation into a meaningful   *(p. 159)*

KUSHNER & POLEN (CHASIDISM)

"Find favor . . . in your people Israel and in their prayer" Rabbi Kalynomos Kalmish Shapira of Piesetzna was a modern Chasidic master who perished in the Holocaust. In his *Derekh Hamelekh* (Tel Aviv: 1976, p. 93) he offers an extraordinary teaching about the nature of prayer. He begins by citing Berakhot 7a, which asks the question: "How do we know God prays?" The answer comes from Isa. 66:7, "I will bring them to my holy mountain. And I will gladden them in the house of my prayer": not "their prayer," but "my [God's] prayer."

We also have a tradition based on Gen. 28:11, normally rendered "And he [Jacob] came upon (*vayifga*) the place *(p. 160)*

L. HOFFMAN (HISTORY)

WE NOW INAUGURATE THE FINAL TRIAD OF BLESSINGS, WHICH ARE SAID TO BE ON THE THEME OF GRATITUDE. ACTUALLY, THEIR CONTENT IS MORE COMPLEX THAN THAT. THEY TOO ARE IN PART PETITIONARY. IN THEME AT LEAST, THEY ALL HARK BACK TO THE SACRIFICIAL CULT THAT ENDED IN THE YEAR 70 c.e. THE AMIDAH IS SAID TO REPLACE SACRIFICE, SO WE CONCLUDE IT JUST AS WE ONCE CONCLUDED THE DAILY OFFERINGS IN THE TEMPLE. ORIGINALLY, BLESSING 17 PRAISED GOD FOR ACCEPTING SACRIFICES. IT IS INTERPRETED MORE BROADLY NOW TO ENCOMPASS PRAYER AS WELL.

¹רְצֵה יְיָ אֱלֹהֵינוּ בְּעַמְּךָ יִשְׂרָאֵל וּבִתְפִלָּתָם. ²וְהָשֵׁב אֶת־הָעֲבוֹדָה לִדְבִיר בֵּיתֶךָ וְאִשֵּׁי יִשְׂרָאֵל וּתְפִלָּתָם בְּאַהֲבָה תְקַבֵּל בְּרָצוֹן. ³וּתְהִי לְרָצוֹן תָּמִיד עֲבוֹדַת יִשְׂרָאֵל עַמֶּךָ.

"Find favor" This blessing illustrates the way *(p. 161)*

J. HOFFMAN (TRANSLATION)

"Find favor" Others, "Be favorable" or "Be pleased," both of which, however, are odd as imperatives.

"The sacrifice" Hebrew, *avodah*, often translated as "worship." Prayer took the place of sacrifice, and both are subsumed under *avodah*, which might more generally be construed as holy "service." *Avodah* is related to *eved*, "servant," often mistranslated as "slave." Of the two (sacrifice and prayer), *avodah* must mean sacrifice here, because it is projected as eventually being restored to the innermost room of the Temple, where sacrifice was the norm. *(p. 163)*

LANDES (HALAKHAH)

"May the service . . . always be favorable" This blessing equates the Temple service, for whose return we pray, with our own service of prayer. As the etiquette of the Temple service was carried out with care for all the details that Torah stipulates, so too synagogue prayer should proceed with due concern for its proper performance.

Rabbi Joseph B. Soloveitchik points out that this central and crucial prayer was recited by the *kohanim* (the Temple priests of old) after the *(p. 160)*

(On Rosh Chodesh—the New Month—and Chol Hamo'ed, the intermediary days of Passover and Sukkot, add:

⁴ Our God and our ancestors' God, may these arise, come forth, reach up, be noted, be favored, be heard, be recorded, and be remembered before You for deliverance and goodness, for grace, kindness, and mercy, for life and peace: our memory; our record; our ancestors' memory; the memory of the messiah, son of David your servant; the memory of Jerusalem, your holy city; and the memory of the entire house of Israel, your People, on this

[On Rosh Chodesh, the New Month, say:

start of this month.

On Passover, say:

day of the holiday of Passover.

On Sukkot, say:

day of the holiday of Sukkot.]

⁵ Remember us, Adonai our God, on this day for goodness. ⁶ Record us on this day for blessing. ⁷ And save us on this day for life. ⁸ In this matter of salvation and mercy, spare us and be gracious to us, have mercy upon us and bring salvation, for our eyes turn to You, for You are the sovereign God, gracious and merciful.)

(On Rosh Chodesh—the New Month—and Chol Hamo'ed, the intermediary days of Passover and Sukkot, add:

⁴אֱלֹהֵינוּ וֵאלֹהֵי אֲבוֹתֵינוּ. יַעֲלֶה וְיָבֹא וְיַגִּיעַ וְיֵרָאֶה וְיֵרָצֶה וְיִשָּׁמַע וְיִפָּקֵד וְיִזָּכֵר זִכְרוֹנֵנוּ וּפִקְדּוֹנֵנוּ וְזִכְרוֹן אֲבוֹתֵינוּ. וְזִכְרוֹן מָשִׁיחַ בֶּן־ דָּוִד עַבְדֶּךָ. וְזִכְרוֹן יְרוּשָׁלַיִם עִיר קָדְשֶׁךָ. וְזִכְרוֹן כָּל־עַמְּךָ בֵּית יִשְׂרָאֵל לְפָנֶיךָ. לִפְלֵיטָה וּלְטוֹבָה וּלְחֵן וּלְחֶסֶד וּלְרַחֲמִים וּלְחַיִּים וּלְשָׁלוֹם בְּיוֹם

[On Rosh Chodesh, the New Month, say:

רֹאשׁ הַחֹדֶשׁ הַזֶּה.

On Passover, say:

חַג הַמַּצּוֹת הַזֶּה.

On Sukkot, say:

חַג הַסֻּכּוֹת הַזֶּה.]

⁵זָכְרֵנוּ יְיָ אֱלֹהֵינוּ בּוֹ לְטוֹבָה. ⁶וּפָקְדֵנוּ בוֹ לִבְרָכָה. ⁷וְהוֹשִׁיעֵנוּ בוֹ לְחַיִּים. ⁸וּבִדְבַר יְשׁוּעָה וְרַחֲמִים חוּס וְחָנֵּנוּ. וְרַחֵם עָלֵינוּ וְהוֹשִׁיעֵנוּ. כִּי אֵלֶיךָ עֵינֵינוּ. כִּי אֵל מֶלֶךְ חַנּוּן וְרַחוּם אָתָּה.)

9 May our eyes behold your return to Zion in mercy. 10 Blessed are You, Adonai, who restores his divine presence to Zion.

וְתֶחֱזֶינָה עֵינֵינוּ בְּשׁוּבְךָ 9
לְצִיּוֹן בְּרַחֲמִים. 10 בָּרוּךְ אַתָּה
יְיָ הַמַּחֲזִיר שְׁכִינָתוֹ לְצִיּוֹן.

BRETTLER (BIBLE)

double mention of prayer, which is assumed to be a valid substitute for sacrifices. Even the Bible shows some discomfort with the sacrificial system (cf., e.g., Pss. 40:7; 51:18–19), and the idea that prayer is at least the equivalent of sacrifice is found in Ps. 141:2, "Take my prayer as an offering of incense, my upraised hands as an evening sacrifice." However, there is no evidence of synagogue worship as a replacement for the missing sacrifices during the Babylonian exile. The usual ground for that faulty claim is a misunderstanding of Ezek. 11:16, where God promises the exiles a *mikdash m'at*. But *mikdash m'at* does not mean "a little sanctuary." The proper translation is "I have become for them *a diminished temple* in the countries where they have gone." The idea is that the divine presence rather than a building serves as a temple.

The closing formula, "who restores his divine presence to Zion," returns us to Blessing 14, "Return to Jerusalem . . . and dwell in its midst," furthering the argument that Blessings 14, 15, and 17 are a single group concerned with Jerusalem and its institutions.

———◆———

DORFF (THEOLOGY)

and we leave with the proper impression of each other and with the most important themes in our minds and hearts.

All three final benedictions request culminating blessings, the kind of things that make all other requests meaningful and all other blessings worthwhile. They move also from the least to the most comprehensive. First (Blessing 17), we ask that God dwell with us in Zion, a much hoped-for condition to be sure, but Jews have lived without that state for much too long to pin all their hopes on it. We do reiterate that longing before we take leave of God, and we ask God to be satisfied with our worship now even though He no longer dwells among us physically in the temple in Jerusalem. We then move on to a more fundamental matter of faith that can sustain us no matter when or where we live: God's inherent goodness (Blessing 18). God's goodness is a cardinal truth for Jews. God can therefore be counted on to continue the blessings we already have and to consider our requests for further blessings still. Finally (Blessing 19), we end with the most comprehensive wish of all — that God give us the context of peace, in which all other blessings can be enjoyed.

"May our eyes behold your return to Zion in mercy" The request for God's return to Zion is an expression of our own longing to return there. The *Amidah* was arranged after the destruction of the Second Temple in 70 C.E., when people could not possibly have known when a Third Jewish Commonwealth would finally arise. The prayer for God's return has reverberated throughout nineteen centuries of similar uncertainty. In each era, it reminded Jews of a time when they lived with dignity in their homeland and in the presence of God. More than a reminder of days long gone, this prayer has provided Jews with self-respect and with hope, even when little in their lives justified such feelings. The middle benedictions (14 and 15) of the *Amidah* articulate petitions for rebuilding Jerusalem and restoring the Davidic realm, but this aspiration was so important that it was placed here as well. That way, even on Shabbat and holidays (when the middle petitions are omitted), the hope for a return would be voiced.

The prayer requests not only that God return, but also that we dwell with God there. While God can be contacted anywhere in the universe, the Temple was "the place that God has chosen" (Deut. 17:8) as home and, hence, the symbol of God's abiding presence with Israel. God's refusal to occupy his home was a painful reminder that God had deserted both the Land and People of Israel; it was a direct slap in Israel's face, a punishment in itself, as almost every prophet clearly saw (see, e.g., Isa. 29:10; Jer. 7:1–15; Ezek. 7:23–27; Amos 8:11–12; Hos. 3:4 and 5:6; Micah 3:6–7; Lam. 2:9). More than a Zionist hope, this prayer is a theological aspiration that God again find us fit to dwell among us.

———◆———

ELLENSON (MODERN LITURGIES)

as "worship." Isaac Mayer Wise's 1857 edition of *Minhag America* proved similarly conservative. He replaced "Return the sacrifice to the Holy of Holies" with "Let the glory of Thy majesty return to the Hall of Thy House" and, like later Conservative prayer books, omitted the "fire-offerings of Israel."

The newest Conservative liturgy, the Israeli *Va'ani T'filati,* goes further still, by offering a Hebrew word play. It substitutes *avodah* (understood as "worship") for *ha'avodah* (translated here as "the sacrifice"), at this juncture in the service.

"Our ancestors' God" As elsewhere, *Kol Haneshamah,* displaying consistent fidelity to the principle of gender inclusivity, has added *v'imoteinu* ("and our mothers") to *avoteinu* ("our fathers") of the Hebrew text (see above, "Our ancestors' God").

"May these arise, come forth, reach up . . ." Reform and Reconstructionist liturgies tried to eliminate redundancy of verbiage. This lengthy word chain is therefore shortened in the English. The Conservative Movement too translates all these verbs as a single imperative (to God): "Remember."

"The memory of the messiah, son of David your servant" Typical of nineteenth-century thinkers who denied the notion of a personal messiah, David Einhorn believed

instead in the unique particularity of the Jewish People, chosen to be a messianic "light unto the nations." He therefore invoked not the memory of "the messiah," but of "Israel's messianic appointment" *(zikhron kol amkha bet yisrael m'shichekha)*. Most later Reform prayer books, however, just removed the passage.

The Reconstructionist *Kol Haneshamah* adopts another solution: history. It substitutes *zikhron y'mot ha'mashiach"* (literally, "the *memory* of messianic *days")*, which it translates "the *memory* of messianic *hopes."* Conservative editors cite history too. Sharing the discomfort of their Reform and Reconstructionist colleagues on the question of belief in a personal messiah, but, as usual, preferring to retain the traditional Hebrew without literal translation, *Siddur Sim Shalom* says, "Remember the People Israel standing before You praying for the days of Messiah and for Jerusalem."

"May our eyes behold your return to Zion" Distasteful of Jewish nationalism, most classical Reform liturgists at least altered this line, and both Abraham Geiger and David Einhorn omitted it completely. In his 1872 edition of *Minhag America,* Isaac Mayer Wise universalized it by amending Hebrew and English to say, "May all the Kingdoms of the earth behold Thy light and Thy truth, and may all flesh come to worship before Thee." *Gates of Prayer* restored the line to reflect the warm embrace that present-day Reform Judaism has extended to Zionism (see next comment).

"Who restores his divine presence to Zion." For the reasons cited immediately above ("May our eyes behold your return to Zion"), most nineteenth-century Reform editors (Geiger, Einhorn, and Wise) removed this line and substituted an alternative from the venerable Palestinian rite, "Whom alone we serve in reverence." While some modern Reform prayer books (e.g., *Gates of Prayer)* have restored the original, others (e.g., *Siddur Lev Chadash)* continue the Palestinian variant. Reconstructionist and Conservative liturgy — and certainly, the Israeli *Ha'avodah Shebalev*— affirm the centrality of Zion and pray without difficulty to a God "who restores his divine presence to Zion."

———◆———

FALK (FEMINISM)

contemporary analogue. We might begin by focusing on the word *sh'khinato,* "his [God's] presence," which is a possessive form of the word *sh'khinah,* "presence" or "indwelling." Over the course of Jewish history, *Sh'khinah* has been used as a name for the divine and, specifically, for divine immanence. The Hebrew word itself is grammatically feminine, and the figure of Shekhinah (now also a term in the English language) was explicitly portrayed as female in Kabbalah. One would be hard pressed to make the claim that the kabbalistic images of the divine were liberating for women, however, in that they were always defined in subordinate relationship to their male parallels. Nonetheless, today, the term *sh'khinah* has been revived in some Jewish feminist circles, where it is used as a symbol for women and as a name for the divine.

The mention of Zion in this blessing is also resonant, especially when taken as a name for the Jewish homeland rather than as a reference to the ancient Temple. Seeking the restoration of the Shekhinah to the Jewish homeland can mean several distinct but related things: that Israel be a place in which we live with reverence for all life; that divine immanence be sought out wherever we make our homes; and that women's experience be honored as part of the divine presence. I have tried to weave these ideas together in my new blessing (in *The Book of Blessings): Nachazir et hash'khinah limkomah / b'tziyon uvateiveil kulah.* The English version separates out the interwoven meanings of the Hebrew:

> *"Let us restore Shekhinah to her place*
> *in Israel and throughout the world,*
> *and let us infuse all places*
> *with her presence."*

———◆———

KUSHNER & POLEN (CHASIDISM)

(makom) and spent the night there because the sun had set." We know from the way the word "came upon" *(vayifga)* is used in Jer. 7:16 that it can also mean to pray (indeed, Ber. 26b cites this verse as proof that Jacob initiated the evening *Amidah).* And we further know that in rabbinic literature, the word "place" *(makom)* can also mean God.

These substitutions yield three additional ways to understand the verse: (1) Jacob prayed; (2) Jacob encountered God in his own act of prayer; and (3) Jacob encountered God in the midst of *God's* prayer! In this way, suggests the Piesetzner, God and Jew, as it were, pray together, finding one another in each other's prayers. The inner desire of the Jew is revealed as directed toward God, and the inner desire of God is revealed as being toward the worshiper. And in this way their mutual desire is united.

Prayer then is not so much an act of petition or a request for divine intercession as it is a gesture of uniting our will with God's. We say, in effect, I now want what God wants even as I discover that God wants what I want. The goal is not the granting of a petition but the moment of the encounter itself. In that moment, both our will and, as it were, God's will are united. We do not seek to nullify our will (simply nullifying your prayerful request or need would only be another way of reinforcing its importance), nor do we seek to alter God's will. We seek literally to unite our prayer and our will with God's. Thus the innermost desire of the worshiper is revealed as a yearning to be with God, just as the innermost desire of God is to be with us. And this is the meaning of prayer.

———◆———

LANDES (HALAKHAH)

sprinkling of the blood of the *tamid* sacrifice (the daily sacrifice that was offered mornings and afternoons). It was a prayer that the service be accepted with full grace by God. So too, we recite the *Avodah* in the hope that our own divine "offering" be accepted (*Ra'yanot Al Hat'fillah).*

But external etiquette and proper performance are insufficient, for the sacrifice required proper intention as well if it was to be acceptable to God. So too, the offerings of our lips must contain heartfelt intention *(Shulchan Arukh,* O. Ch. 98).

———◆———

L. HOFFMAN (HISTORY)

blessings grow with time. If we divide it into its parts, we can see how an editor has woven together various strands from before and after the Temple's destruction. We will have to render it literally, word for word, rather than try to make sense out of it, sentence by sentence, the way our official translation here does:

1. Find favor, Adonai our God, in your People Israel and in their prayer in love.
2. And return the sacrifice to the Holy of Holies.
3. And the fire-offerings of Israel, and their prayers in love, accept favorably.
4. And may you find favor always in the service of Israel, your People.
5. May our eyes behold your return to Zion in mercy.
6. Blessed are You, Adonai, who restores his divine presence to Zion.

Close study of the prayer reveals those parts of it that presuppose the Temple's destruction and must have been written after 70 C.E. We can write it again, bracketing those sections and leaving unbracketed those parts that predate the destruction:

1. Find favor, Adonai our God, in your People Israel and in their prayer in love.
2. [And return the sacrifice to the Holy of Holies.]
3. And the fire-offerings of Israel, and their prayers in love, accept favorably.
4. And may you find favor always in the service of Israel, your People.
5. [May our eyes behold your return to Zion in mercy.]
6. [Blessed are You, Adonai, who restores his divine presence to Zion.]

The pre-70 wording now presents a coherent request for the acceptance of sacrifice:

1. Find favor, Adonai our God, in your People Israel and in their prayer in love.
3. And the fire-offerings of Israel, and their prayers in love, accept favorably.
4. And may you find favor always in the service of Israel, your People.

But there is more. Lines 1 and 3 contain redundancies. They ask God to "find favor" *(r'tsei)* in our sacrifices and to accept "the fire offerings . . . favorably" *(b'ratson)*. However, the same lines ask God also to accept their prayers in love *(b'ahavah)*. The Hebrew word for "favorably" *(b'ratson)* implies "with love." Why do we need them both? I think the references to "prayers in love" were also added after 70. By then, the Temple had fallen, and there were no sacrifices. The old blessing was therefore amended to include a plea that until such time as the Temple was restored, God should accept our prayers on a par with the defunct sacrifices. The root word for "favorably" *(b'ratson* and *r'tsei)* is normally associated with sacrifice — we still say, *ken y'hi ratson,* "So may it be God's will," after the Priestly Blessing (see below, Blessing 19), a remnant of the sacrificial cult. But the Rabbis associated prayer with a different word: *ahavah,* God's love. We can therefore bracket also the references to prayer and love, and we will get even closer to the original blessing from before 70.

First, in bracketed form:

1. Find favor, Adonai our God, in your People Israel [and in their prayer in love].
3. And the fire-offerings of Israel, [and their prayers in love,] accept favorably.
4. And may you find favor always in the service of Israel, your People.

Also, before we take out the bracketed portions, consider the Hebrew words (in line 4) for "service" —*avodah;* and for "always" —*tamid. Avodah* definitely denotes the sacrificial service in general. And *tamid* need not mean "always." It was also the name given to the daily sacrifice because it was offered without fail, "always." In its original Hebrew syntax, then, line 4 can mean, "May You find favor in the *tamid,* the sacrificial service of Israel, your People.

Here, then is what we have left — the original prayer before 70:

1. Find favor, Adonai our God, in your People Israel.
3. And the fire-offerings of Israel, accept favorably.
4. And may you find favor in the *tamid,* the sacrificial service of Israel, your People.

This original prayer follows standard rules of ancient poetry. Each line begins with the closing thought of the line before it. "Your People Israel" (end of line 1) leads to "the fire-offerings of Israel" (beginning of line 2); and "accept favorably" (end of line 2) continues with "May you find favor" (beginning of line 3).

But blessings need concluding lines: the *chatimah,* as such a line is known, which summarizes the benediction's main point. Since we dispensed with the final line ("Blessed are You, Adonai, who restores his divine presence to Zion" [line 6, above]) as being an addition after 70, we ought to look for another *chatimah* somewhere that reflects the idea of sacrifice alone and may have been original here.

As it happens, the Genizah fragments contain such a line: "Blessed are You, Adonai, whom we will serve with awe." The Hebrew for "will serve with awe," *na'avod,* may equally mean (in the present) "we serve with awe." It is a verb from the noun *avodah,* our theme of the pre-70 blessing as a whole: our sacrificial service to God.

In sum, we have here one of many early blessings for the acceptance of sacrifice. When sacrifice ceased, Jews recast the blessing to ask also for the acceptance of prayer, which they saw as a substitute for animal offerings. They also added some lines beseeching God to return the sacrificial system to its place and, by extension, to return the divine presence to a restored Temple. A novel *chatimah* gave voice to the new petition: not that we might continue to serve God in sacrificial service (since that was patently impossible, the way things stood), but that God should "return the divine presence to Zion," allowing us to pick up where we had left off in 70.

Interestingly enough, early Reform Jews took exception to the idea of God's returning to Zion on the grounds that it sounded Zionistic. They therefore exchanged the new *chatimah* for the pre-70 one. They should have objected equally to it, since they opposed even more forcefully the idea of serving God through sacrifice. But they were able to reinterpret *avodah* ("sacrifice") as "service to God in general." The old *Union Prayer Book,* therefore, has the old pre-70 *chatimah,* but translated "Blessed art Thou, whom alone we serve in reverence."

———◆———

J. Hoffman (Translation)

"Holy of Holies" The Hebrew *(d'vir beitekha),* literally, "the innermost room of your house," refers technically to a freestanding structure within the Temple courtyard, only part of which was the Holy of Holies. The actual sacrifice was made outside the *d'vir,* in the courtyard itself. Our translation takes *d'vir* to be symbolic of the whole sacrificial procedure, for which the term "Holy of Holies" functions best in English.

"Fire-offerings" Literally, "fires."

"In favor . . . in love" Probably "in love" modifies "prayers" and "in favor" modifies "accept," though other interpretations are possible. Presumably the idea is that God should accept our prayers, offered in love as they are, in lieu of the sacrifice.

"Service" Translated above as "sacrifice." We have no word that subsumes sacrifice and prayer, and so we cannot capture the nuances of this prayer, which relates prayer to sacrifice.

"Be noted" In accord with Artscroll (Orthodox). More literally, "be seen."

"Goodness" Birnbaum (Orthodox), "happiness."

"Our memory [zikhroneinu]; *our record* [pikdoneinu]" Hebrew, *zikaron* from the root *z.kh.r,* "to remember" and usually translated here as "remembrance of us." But "remembrance of us" is barely English. The first question we face derives from the fact that, in all likelihood, *z.kh.r* originally meant to "point out," "demarcate," or "highlight" (it still means that in Arabic), and so, a *zikaron* might be a remembrance or a memory that highlights or points something out. It may also convey the sense of "souvenir," itself from the French for "remember," in that it brings to mind a prior event. Parallel to *zikaron,* here, we find *pikadon,* which usually means a "deposit" or something left in trust, but which here more likely means "numbering" or "enumeration," as in Artscroll's "consideration." Taken together, the two words represent a calling to mind and consideration.

Second, the Hebrew might equally mean that God remembers us or that we remember God. The later reference to "the memory of Jerusalem" makes it clear, however, that it must be God who is doing the remembering. We might, therefore, have said, "Your memory of us," but "our memory" retains the ambiguity of the Hebrew, and it provides a pattern that can be applied to the other nouns here, mirroring the parallelism of the Hebrew sentence as a whole.

"The memory of the messiah" Because of the awkwardness of "The messiah, son of your servant David's memory," we are forced to change the word order here.

———◆ ◆ ◆———

BRETTLER (BIBLE)

"We gratefully acknowledge" This paragraph breaks the stylistic continuity of the *Amidah,* which has been typified since Blessing 4 with opening petitions framed in the imperative — a pattern that will continue in the next and last blessing, "Grant peace." It is a reasonable conjecture that the *Amidah* may once have ended with this blessing.

Alternatively, it may have been a separate prayer altogether. Its introduction, *modim anachnu lakh,* "We gratefully acknowledge" (from 1 Chron. 29:13), is an appropriate beginning for a prayer that then might have been followed by a request. The Hebrew *(p. 169)*

DORFF
(THEOLOGY)
"Whose name is good and to whom grateful acknowledgment is befitting"

We owe God thanks for many things in our lives. On weekdays, "grateful acknowledgment" refers back to the intermediary petitions, as we thank God for the portion of those blessings that we already have. On holidays, we thank God for the gift of sacred time. On all days, we recognize and appreciate the daily miracles in our lives, which we should not take for granted, noticing them only when we feel their absence. We are dutybound to recognize the many boons we enjoy each day, even when we might wish for more. *(p. 170)*

ELLENSON (MODERN LITURGIES)

"For the miracles . . ." This insertion has proved problematic in many ways.

1. As a nineteenth-century rationalist and universalist, Isaac Mayer Wise expurgated the introductory lines as being both supernaturalistic and chauvinistic.
2. Though there seemed nothing wrong with saying, "in those days *(p. 170)*

FALK (FEMINISM)

"We gratefully acknowledge . . ." For me, the traditional blessing of "Grateful Acknowledgment" has always been the most satisfying portion of the *Amidah.* As a child praying in synagogue, I would say the opening three words, *(p. 171)*

18. HODA'AH   הוֹדָאָה
("GRATEFUL ACKNOWLEDGMENT")

¹We gratefully acknowledge that You are Adonai our God and our ancestors' God for ever and ever. ²You are the rock of our lives and the shield of our salvation from generation to generation. ³We gratefully acknowledge You by rendering your praises, for our lives, which are in your hands, and for our souls, which are entrusted to You, and for your miracles that are

HAUPTMAN (TALMUD)

"We gratefully acknowledge" Incredibly enough, this blessing expresses gratitude in advance for God's beneficence. A Jew is so sure that God will grant his or her requests that immediately upon articulating them the petitioner already acknowledges God for bestowing them. But what is it that we are being so grateful for?

This is the middle blessing of the last set of three, all of which are known collectively as *Hoda'ah,* the "Blessings of Thanksgiving." The previous blessing asks for a return of the *(p. 173)*

KUSHNER & POLEN (CHASIDISM)

"We gratefully acknowledge" Yakov Yitzchak, the *Chozeh* ("Seer") of Lublin (d. 1815), reminds us of how easy it is to forget that everything issues from God — whether apparently ordinary or miraculous; whether through other human beings or directly from God, everything issues from Heaven. And once we acknowledge this, once we understand how everything is therefore good, then it's ours forever. As we read in Psalm 136, "Give thanks to God, for it is good, for God's love is eternal." If you acknowledge how good it is, then you can have it all the time.

Commenting on Deut. 8:7, "For the Lord your God is bringing you into a good land, a land with streams and springs and *(p. 174)*

L. HOFFMAN (HISTORY)

FOLLOWING THE DAILY OFFERINGS IN THE TEMPLE, THOSE ON HAND WOULD PROSTRATE THEMSELVES AS A TOKEN OF THEIR GRATITUDE MIXED WITH ACKNOWLEDGMENT OF GOD'S REALITY. THAT ACT HAS BECOME A BLESSING IN ITS OWN RIGHT, BLESSING 18, WHICH VIRTUALLY CONCLUDES THE AMIDAH ON A NOTE OF GRATEFUL ACKNOWLEDGMENT.

———◆———

J. HOFFMAN (TRANSLATION)

"We gratefully acknowledge" The Hebrew *modim* implies both gratitude and acknowledgment. We have no such word in English and so are forced to use two words.

"Rock of our lives" Or "rock of our life." The Hebrew is ambiguous. The difference is subtle: God is either the rock of our lives individually or the rock of our collective life.

"Shield of our salvation" Or "saving shield," but we prefer to preserve the parallel structure found in the Hebrew.

"By rendering" Literally, "and render."

"Our lives, which are in your hands" The Hebrew idiom puts our lives in God's "hands" as well.

"The universe" Hebrew, *b'reishit*, literally, "in the beginning." The *(p. 174)*

¹מוֹדִים אֲנַחְנוּ לָךְ שָׁאַתָּה הוּא יְיָ אֱלֹהֵינוּ וֵאלֹהֵי אֲבוֹתֵינוּ לְעוֹלָם וָעֶד. ²צוּר חַיֵּינוּ מָגֵן יִשְׁעֵנוּ אַתָּה הוּא לְדוֹר וָדוֹר. ³נוֹדֶה לְךָ וּנְסַפֵּר תְּהִלָּתֶךָ עַל חַיֵּינוּ הַמְּסוּרִים בְּיָדֶךָ וְעַל נִשְׁמוֹתֵינוּ הַפְּקוּדוֹת לָךְ וְעַל נִסֶּיךָ שֶׁבְּכָל־יוֹם עִמָּנוּ וְעַל־נִפְלְאוֹתֶיךָ

LANDES (HALAKHAH)

"We gratefully acknowledge" As servants are obliged to thank their master, we too (who have made requests) are required to thank God (Ber. 34a). This is an essential element of prayer (Maimonides, "Laws of Prayer" 1:2).

At *Modim* (the first word), bow the back and head (but not the knees), in a motion described as bending "like a reed"; at the sixth word, *Ado-nai*, rise back up again.

In the prayer leader's repetition, the congregation *sotto voce* recites *(p. 174)* with us on each day, and for the wonders and goodness at every time, evening, morning, and afternoon. 4 You are good, for your mercy never ceases. 5 You are merciful, for your kindness never ends. 6 You have always been our hope.

The *Modim D'rabbanan*—

[*To be recited in an undertone, while the prayer leader repeats this blessing:*

7 We gratefully acknowledge that You are Adonai our God and our ancestors' God, God of all flesh, our creator and creator of the universe. 8 We offer blessings and grateful acknowledgments to your great and holy name, for having given us life and having sustained us. 9 —So give us life and sustain us and gather our exiles to your holy courts to keep your laws and perform your will, to serve You whole-heartedly; and for our acknowledging You with gratitude. 10 Blessed is the God of grateful acknowledgment.]

[*On Chanukah, add:*

11 For the miracles and for the redemption and for the mighty acts and for the triumphs and for the wars you brought about for our ancestors in those days at this time of year— 12 in the days of the Hasmonean, Mattathias ben Yohanan, the high

וְטוֹבוֹתֶיךָ שֶׁבְּכָל־עֵת. עֶרֶב וָבֹקֶר וְצָהֳרָיִם. 4 הַטּוֹב כִּי לֹא־כָלוּ רַחֲמֶיךָ. 5 וְהַמְרַחֵם כִּי לֹא־תַמּוּ חֲסָדֶיךָ. 6 מֵעוֹלָם קִוִּינוּ לָךְ.

The *Modim D'rabbanan*—

[*To be recited in an undertone, while the prayer leader repeats this blessing:*

7 מוֹדִים אֲנַחְנוּ לָךְ שָׁאַתָּה הוּא יְיָ אֱלֹהֵינוּ וֵאלֹהֵי אֲבוֹתֵינוּ אֱלֹהֵי כָל בָּשָׂר יוֹצְרֵנוּ יוֹצֵר בְּרֵאשִׁית. 8 בְּרָכוֹת וְהוֹדָאוֹת לְשִׁמְךָ הַגָּדוֹל וְהַקָּדוֹשׁ עַל שֶׁהֶחֱיִיתָנוּ וְקִיַּמְתָּנוּ. 9 כֵּן תְּחַיֵּנוּ וּתְקַיְּמֵנוּ וְתֶאֱסֹף גָּלֻיּוֹתֵינוּ לְחַצְרוֹת קָדְשֶׁךָ לִשְׁמֹר חֻקֶּיךָ וְלַעֲשׂוֹת רְצוֹנֶךָ וּלְעָבְדְּךָ בְּלֵבָב שָׁלֵם עַל שֶׁאֲנַחְנוּ מוֹדִים לָךְ. 10 בָּרוּךְ אֵל הַהוֹדָאוֹת.]

[*On Chanukah, add:*

11 עַל הַנִּסִּים וְעַל הַפֻּרְקָן וְעַל הַגְּבוּרוֹת וְעַל הַתְּשׁוּעוֹת וְעַל הַמִּלְחָמוֹת שֶׁעָשִׂיתָ לַאֲבוֹתֵינוּ בַּיָּמִים הָהֵם בַּזְּמַן הַזֶּה. 12 בִּימֵי מַתִּתְיָהוּ בֶּן־יוֹחָנָן

priest, and his sons, when the evil government of Greece rose up against your People Israel to make them forget your Torah and to make them leave the laws of your will: [13] In your great mercy You rose up with them in their time of trouble and fought in their fight, judged their cause just, and avenged them with a vengeance. [14] You delivered the mighty into the hands of the weak, the many into the hands of the few, the unclean into the hands of the pure, the evil into the hands of the righteous, and the arrogant into the hands of those who engage in your Torah. [15] For You, You made a great and holy name in your world; and for your People Israel, You brought about a great triumph and redemption on that very day. [16] And then your children came to the Holy of Holies, and emptied your temple, and purified your holy place, and lit candles in your holy courts, and established these eight days of Chanukah gratefully to acknowledge, and to praise, your great name.]

כֹּהֵן גָּדוֹל חַשְׁמוֹנַי וּבָנָיו. כְּשֶׁעָמְדָה מַלְכוּת יָוָן הָרְשָׁעָה עַל עַמְּךָ יִשְׂרָאֵל לְהַשְׁכִּיחָם תּוֹרָתֶךָ וּלְהַעֲבִירָם מֵחֻקֵּי רְצוֹנֶךָ. [13] וְאַתָּה בְּרַחֲמֶיךָ הָרַבִּים עָמַדְתָּ לָהֶם בְּעֵת צָרָתָם. רַבְתָּ אֶת־רִיבָם. דַּנְתָּ אֶת־דִּינָם. נָקַמְתָּ אֶת־נִקְמָתָם. [14] מָסַרְתָּ גִבּוֹרִים בְּיַד חַלָּשִׁים. וְרַבִּים בְּיַד מְעַטִּים. וּטְמֵאִים בְּיַד טְהוֹרִים. וּרְשָׁעִים בְּיַד צַדִּיקִים. וְזֵדִים בְּיַד עוֹסְקֵי תוֹרָתֶךָ. [15] וּלְךָ עָשִׂיתָ שֵׁם גָּדוֹל וְקָדוֹשׁ בְּעוֹלָמֶךָ. וּלְעַמְּךָ יִשְׂרָאֵל עָשִׂיתָ תְּשׁוּעָה גְדוֹלָה וּפֻרְקָן כְּהַיּוֹם הַזֶּה. [16] וְאַחַר כֵּן בָּאוּ בָנֶיךָ לִדְבִיר בֵּיתֶךָ. וּפִנּוּ אֶת־הֵיכָלֶךָ. וְטִהֲרוּ אֶת־מִקְדָּשֶׁךָ וְהִדְלִיקוּ נֵרוֹת בְּחַצְרוֹת קָדְשֶׁךָ. וְקָבְעוּ שְׁמוֹנַת יְמֵי חֲנֻכָּה אֵלּוּ לְהוֹדוֹת וּלְהַלֵּל לְשִׁמְךָ הַגָּדוֹל.]

[On Purim, add:

17 For the miracles and for the redemption and for the mighty acts and for the triumphs and for the wars You brought about for our ancestors in those days at this time of year— 18 in the days of Mordecai and Esther in the capital city of Shushan, when the evil Haman rose up against them and sought to destroy, to kill, and to wipe out all the Jews, young and old, women and children, in one day, on the thirteenth day of the twelfth month (which is Adar), and to plunder their wealth: 19 In your great mercy You brought his advice to naught and frustrated his plan. 20 You turned his scheme around on him, so that he and his sons were hanged from a tree.]

21 For all of these your name will be blessed and exalted, our king, forever to the ends of time.

[On Purim, add:

עַל הַנִּסִּים וְעַל הַפֻּרְקָן 17 וְעַל הַגְּבוּרוֹת וְעַל הַתְּשׁוּעוֹת וְעַל הַמִּלְחָמוֹת שֶׁעָשִׂיתָ לַאֲבוֹתֵינוּ בַּיָּמִים הָהֵם בַּזְּמַן הַזֶּה. 18 בִּימֵי מָרְדְּכַי וְאֶסְתֵּר בְּשׁוּשַׁן הַבִּירָה. כְּשֶׁעָמַד עֲלֵיהֶם הָמָן הָרָשָׁע. בִּקֵּשׁ לְהַשְׁמִיד לַהֲרֹג וּלְאַבֵּד אֶת־ כָּל־הַיְּהוּדִים מִנַּעַר וְעַד־זָקֵן. טַף וְנָשִׁים. בְּיוֹם אֶחָד בִּשְׁלֹשָׁה עָשָׂר לְחֹדֶשׁ שְׁנֵים־ עָשָׂר הוּא חֹדֶשׁ אֲדָר. וּשְׁלָלָם לָבֹז: 19 וְאַתָּה בְּרַחֲמֶיךָ הָרַבִּים הֵפַרְתָּ אֶת־ עֲצָתוֹ. וְקִלְקַלְתָּ אֶת־מַחֲשַׁבְתּוֹ. 20 וַהֲשֵׁבוֹתָ גְּמוּלוֹ בְּרֹאשׁוֹ. וְתָלוּ אֹתוֹ וְאֶת־בָּנָיו עַל־ הָעֵץ.]

21 וְעַל־כֻּלָּם יִתְבָּרַךְ וְיִתְרוֹמַם שִׁמְךָ מַלְכֵּנוּ תָּמִיד לְעוֹלָם וָעֶד.

[From Rosh Hashanah to Yom Kippur, add:

[From Rosh Hashanah to Yom Kippur, add:

22 And write down all of the children of your covenant for good life.]

23 All that lives will gratefully acknowledge You forever and praise your name in truth, God, our salvation and our help, forever. 24 Blessed are You, Adonai, whose name is good and to whom grateful acknowledgment is befitting.

22 וּכְתוֹב לְחַיִּים טוֹבִים כָּל־בְּנֵי בְרִיתֶךָ.]

23 וְכֹל הַחַיִּים יוֹדְוּךָ סֶּלָה וִיהַלְלוּ אֶת־שִׁמְךָ בֶּאֱמֶת הָאֵל יְשׁוּעָתֵנוּ וְעֶזְרָתֵנוּ סֶלָה. 24 בָּרוּךְ אַתָּה יְיָ הַטּוֹב שִׁמְךָ וּלְךָ נָאֶה לְהוֹדוֹת.

BRETTLER (BIBLE)

verb *modim*, meaning acknowledging or praising God, is a central idea of Psalms, which uses the word sixty-seven times, more than half of the times it is used in the whole Bible. Praising is fundamental to prayer, which should not be seen as predominantly petitionary — as we see from Ps. 92:2: "It is good to praise Adonai, and to sing hymns to Your name, O Most High."

Stylistically, the blessing is structured by what is called an *inclusio*, meaning that it opens and closes with a form of the same word: "We acknowledge" and "acknowledgment." As the second to last blessing, its content symmetrically balances the second blessing, which focused on God's power.

"For the miracles" The Chanukah section is based on events from 164 B.C.E., after the books of the Bible were written. The Purim story is biblical, however, and quite remarkable in the way it is retold here, since it focuses on God, who is addressed throughout as "You," whereas God is curiously missing from the entire biblical book of Esther. Greek-speaking Jews inserted God's presence in their Greek translations, and similar editorializing has occurred here.

"Our God and our ancestors' God" The well-known Priestly Blessing of Num. 6:24–26 is structurally compact, with each verse longer than the one before it, as if to suggest the growing outpouring of divine blessings. The context in Numbers does not indicate how, when, or where the blessing was used, but we know that it was popular in antiquity. There are several significant Mesopotamian parallels, and a version of the Bible's wording, from the seventh or sixth century B.C.E. and written on silver, was found in a burial trove in Jerusalem; it presumably functioned as an amulet. Biblical texts both before the exile (Psalms 4 and 6) and after the exile (Ps.

119:130–135 and Mal. 1:6–2:9) know of it. No wonder it was incorporated into the *Amidah* as well.

The blessing is strikingly anthropomorphic: Adonai shines and lifts his face on the recipient of the blessing. But biblical texts are quite comfortable with anthropomorphisms, and even rabbinic culture, which is often thought to reject them, very frequently views God in distinctly anthropomorphic form.

———◆———

DORFF (THEOLOGY)

Second, this blessing affirms Jewish tradition's insistence that God's primary characteristic is goodness. God is just and can punish us, sometimes even without apparent justification; but in the end we have the unshaken faith that God is good. Were that not so, it would make no sense whatsoever to ask God to respond to the needs we have. God's underlying goodness implies that however bad our circumstances, we can and should pray for manifestations of God's fundamental goodness.

———◆———

ELLENSON (MODERN LITURGIES)

at this time of year," *Ha'avodah Shebalev* and *Siddur Sim Shalom* adopted a variant text from the first known Jewish prayer book, *Seder Rav Amram Gaon* (c. 860), which read, "in other times, and in our day," so as to make the blessing reflect God's current miracles in history as well; they then composed a parallel prayer for Israeli Independence Day, to affirm that its founding ranks as an event equal to Chanukah and Purim.

3. Thanking God expressly "for the wars" has been difficult. Some (the Reconstructionist *Daily Prayer Book)* followed the convenient precedent of Sefardi tradition, which omits the phrase. Others *(Ha'avodah Shebalev* and *Kol Haneshamah)* substitute the euphemism *n'chamot* ("consolations") for *milchamot* ("wars"). *Gates of Prayer* and Conservative liturgies (both *Weekday Prayer Book* and *Siddur Sim Shalom)* preserve the Hebrew but, because they find its sentiment offensive, leave it untranslated.

4. Referring to Mattathias ben Yohanan as a "high priest" is historically inaccurate. Since he was just an ordinary priest, the old Reconstructionist *Daily Prayer Book* deleted the word for "high" *(gadol).* Its successor, *Kol Haneshamah,* however, joins the rest of the Jewish world in its unconcern for historical detail and restores the traditional text.

5. Liberal liturgies have shunned what they deem "invidious comparisons" such as those entailed in thanking God for delivering "the unclean into the hands of the pure, the evil into hands of the righteous, and the arrogant into the hands of those who engage in Torah." Isaac Mayer Wise and David Einhorn removed "the unclean into the hands of the pure," and the Reconstructionist *Daily Prayer Book* removed

the rest as well. *Gates of Prayer* and Conservative liturgy *(Weekday Prayer Book* and *Siddur Sim Shalom)* either preserve the Hebrew, but translate metaphorically (e.g., "You delivered the strong into the hands of the pure of heart" —*Siddur Sim Shalom),* or omit translation altogether.

6. Most of all, perhaps, liberal Jews have not taken kindly to the blatant vindictiveness that recollects the death of Haman, "You turned his scheme around on him, so that he and his sons were hanged from a tree" (Esther 9:25). Most editors removed the line, following the lead of Isaac Mayer Wise. Some, however, have replaced it with a more congenial passage from the Scroll of Esther.

———◆———

FALK (FEMINISM)

modim anachnu lakh, and then drift off, away from the text of the Siddur and into a silent reverie, in which I called to mind what I was grateful for. At the end of this period of reflection — which may have lasted several minutes or only a few seconds; it is hard to know, since time took on a different quality during it — I would feel renewed and (dare I say it?) uplifted. My heart would feel lighter, my head clearer, even if only a little bit. This experience of gratitude was the closest I came, as a child, to finding spirituality in the synagogue.

I would like to be able to say that my childhood experiences have been surpassed by other encounters with prayer in my adult life; but the truth is that, as an adult, I have hardly *ever* had what I would call a spiritual experience in synagogue, although I have certainly had spiritual moments in other settings. As a strongly self-identified Jew — someone passionately concerned with the survival of Jewish civilization, language, and Peoplehood — it saddens me that I cannot experience in the synagogue the depths of knowing and being that have come to me in a multitude of other places — at the edge of a pond or the middle of a forest, alone or in the midst of family or friends, even in the presence of strangers.

This inability to locate my true self in synagogue — or to encounter the divine presence there — would be of limited relevance to this discussion were it not for the fact that (as I have discovered repeatedly over the past two decades, while leading workshops and teaching classes on theology and prayer) I am not alone in this experience. I have heard some version of this lament so many times, in so many different voices, that I have come to believe there is a real problem with Jewish liturgical life — a problem that belongs to, and needs to be addressed by, the *community,* not by isolated individuals. The much spoken-about current crisis of "Jewish continuity" does not, finally, seem difficult to understand. If the liturgical realm is any indication, people are leaving Judaism because it doesn't give them what they deeply want and need, it doesn't address their spiritual yearnings, it is not meaningful to them.

At the risk of being presumptuous, I'd like to offer a brief explanation and an even briefer beginning of a solution to this problem. As a people, we have done a great deal with words; we are a lot less practiced in the art of silence. Despite — or perhaps because of — our emphasis on the verbal, words often aren't working the way we want them to. We want to be inclusive, yet our words often exclude; we want to empower, yet our words often suppress; we want to heal, but our words cause pain. The synagogue, in particular, is a place where words have failed — a place where many of us feel unheard and unseen, neither spoken to nor spoken for — so that, finally, the synagogue is a place where we are alienated, angered, and — most devastating — bored.

I think it is time to take another path. It is time we learn to listen — to the self and to the other, to the world and to the greater whole of being. It is time to learn the power of silence.

As a poet — that is, as someone who cannot imagine herself without language and, in particular, without Hebrew, the language of the Jewish soul — I know that words are meaningless without silence. Just as dark exists only in relation to light, black ink is given shape and sense by the white space surrounding it. And speech — which is black ink rendered into sound by the human voice — is incomprehensible without the silences indicated by the white page. I believe that, in our prayer, it is time we tip the balance away from where it has been — away from the black ink and toward the white page, away from the voice and deeper into the depths of the human heart.

On Shabbat and holy days, the morning liturgy leading up to the *Sh'ma* contains a prayer known as *Nishmat kol chai,* "The breath of all that lives," which states, "Even were our mouths filled with song as the sea [is filled with water] and our tongues [filled with] joyous praise as the multitude of waves," it would not be enough: we would still not be able to convey all we are grateful for. Hyperbolic and wordy — seeming to delight in its own verbal inventiveness — this poetic prayer might be seen as encouraging us to lavish praise on God's creation and to thank God ever more profusely. But it is equally possible to interpret it differently — not as a model of verbal devotion but as an acknowledgment of the ultimate inadequacy of words. Perhaps this prayer comes to teach us that when words cannot convey the fullness of our emotions — in particular, of our gratitude — they ought to be set aside.

Here in the penultimate benediction of the *Amidah,* we have an opportunity to reflect upon the state of gratitude itself and to enter into it personally. What better way to do so than with silence? If the *Amidah* was, for the Rabbis, the ultimate prayer, then this moment of silent gratitude might become the prayer within the prayer, the true *avodah shebalev,* "service of the heart."

———◆———

HAUPTMAN (TALMUD)

sacrificial cult to the Temple, and the following one for peace for God's People Israel. In contrast to these ultimate ideals, this blessing addresses life itself, the way the human body, in all of its complexity, needs miraculously to keep functioning smoothly from day to day.

"Gather our exiles to your holy courts" Our prayer occurs in two versions, one for recitation when praying the entire *Amidah* silently, and one for recitation by the congregation when the prayer leader repeats the *Amidah* aloud and reaches this point in the service. The text of this alternative paragraph is both similar to and different from the original one. It begins with a theological statement, acknowledging God as creator of the universe. It then thanks God for creating us in the past and requests continued existence in the future. But then it turns surprisingly to the topic of gathering in the exiles to God's holy precincts. The version that the individual says silently is all about life's daily needs; the version that is said during the public repetition begins with those needs but insists on viewing them against a backdrop of collective concerns: the ultimate fate of the Jewish People in the end of days.

The Talmud (Sotah 40a) informs us that there were several versions of this prayer extant, and the Rabbis had difficulty deciding which of them to accept and which to reject. In the end, it was decided to accept them all. What we have here, then, is a composite prayer, in which the competitive versions are all woven together.

Since this is the only time during the repetition of the *Amidah* that the passive listener is asked to recite a prayer, we might wonder why this blessing is singled out for special attention. The answer seems to be that this is the most personal and basic prayer of all: only if we are granted the ordinary gifts of daily living can we then go on to worship God, perform good deeds, and bring about peace in the world. The function of this blessing is to remind us that we are dependent for our very existence on someone outside ourselves. The world may revolve around us, and we may have an effect on it, but we do not sustain ourselves.

And we can make a somewhat similar statement about God: before gathering the People Israel from the four corners of the earth, and before restoring the worship service to Jerusalem, God needs to be certain that the individual can sustain his and her life systems.

We bow at the opening words *modim anachnu lakh*, "We gratefully acknowledge," just as we do in the *Alenu* when reciting the very same words, *va'anachnu . . . umodim*, "We . . . gratefully acknowledge." In both cases, acknowledgment entails a sense of humility for having received the largesse of a gracious benefactor.

"For the miracles" There are two prayers here, one for Purim and another for Chanukah, both very similar in style and in content. Both are about divine intervention in support of the Jewish People. The Chanukah version is recited on all eight days of Chanukah. It stands out because it portrays the miracle of Chanukah very differently from the way Chanukah is portrayed in the well-known "cruse of oil" story, even though both versions were composed at about the same period of time.

As it is presented here, the miracle is that God delivered the "many into the hands of the few" and "the mighty into the hands of the weak," unlikely occurrences but not ones that violate the laws of nature. This is precisely akin to the parallel prayer for Purim, which records the complete reversal of human plans by divine intervention. The lighting of oil lamps is mentioned in passing, but only as one of several activities that engaged

173

the Hasmoneans as they went about the task of rededicating the Temple. The military victory, achieved with the help of God, takes center stage in this synopsis of the events.

The more familiar story that we all like to tell about Chanukah comes from the Talmud (Shabbat 21b). That is where we find the story of a single cruse of oil that burned miraculously for eight days, as the main event of the story of Chanukah. The military victory is completely overlooked, as if it never occurred. Like the burning bush that continued aflame but was not consumed, so too the oil that burns for eight days without being depleted ranks as a miracle in the familiar sense of the laws of nature being contravened.

Apparently, as late as the talmudic period, there was still no single and standard interpretation of the real "miracle" of Chanukah. Both stories became canonized for Jewish use, one of them as the official talmudic tale of what Chanukah is all about, and the other as the Siddur's recollection of what happened. We therefore need not choose between the two. They are both part of our collective Jewish memory.

——◆——

KUSHNER & POLEN (CHASIDISM)

fountains issuing from both valleys and mountains," the *Chozeh* goes on to explain that the water of the streams and springs and fountains is a metaphor for God's love and favor. And thus when we recognize how everything issues from God, then that divine kindness will be ours, not only in the valleys, when times are easy, but also on the mountains, even when life is difficult — all the time. The experience then of gratitude — and subsequent expression of thanksgiving — transforms everything into an enduring gift.

——◆——

LANDES (HALAKHAH)

the parallel passage given in the margin, known as the *Modim D'rabbanan,* while the prayer leader in full voice recites the regular prayer that the congregation has said silently.

At the concluding line (the *chatimah), Barukh atah Ado-nai* ("Blessed are You, Ado-nai"), bow again, as at the beginning of the *Amidah,* from the knees (see above, "Blessed are You, Ado-nai").

——◆——

J. HOFFMAN (TRANSLATION)

word *b'reishit* begins the story of creation and is probably used here to represent all of creation, that is, "the universe."

"We offer blessing and grateful acknowledgment to your . . . name" The Hebrew is simply, "Blessing and praise to your name!" similar to the English "All praise to your name!" But this won't work with "grateful acknowledgment," so we reword the sentence.

"Your holy courts" Artscroll (Orthodox) takes this as a reference to the Temple courtyard, so translates it as "Courtyards of your Sanctuary."

"Whole-heartedly" Birnbaum (Orthodox), "with perfect heart." The ancient notion of "heart" differs from our modern-day understanding. For the Rabbis, "heart" encompassed both emotion and intellect; unfortunately, we have no term for that combination in English. See p. 100ff of Volume 1, *The Sh'ma and Its Blessings,* for more.

"For our acknowledging You with gratitude" This is most odd. It appears to be a continuation of the previous thought, that is, "we offer blessings . . . to your great and holy name for having given us life . . . ; for our acknowledging . . ." — a sort of "thank you for letting us thank you."

"Fought in their fight . . ." The Hebrew supplies an object for each verb, taken from the same root as the verb. We offer a similar repetition to mimic the emphatic nature of the original text.

"On that very day [k'hayom hazeh]" Literally "as on that day," but probably emphatic.

"Capital city" Birah, modern Hebrew for "capital," originally meant "fortified city" or "walled city." The point is the city's centrality, hence its extra fortification. We choose "capital" here, recognizing that the meaning of *birah* has changed, but that the concept to which it refers has likely remained more or less constant.

"In one day" Or, perhaps, "on one day, [that is, on the thirteenth . . .]."

"You brought his advice to naught" An odd way of phrasing this. The original idiom can be found in Isa. 8:10, "take council [together] and it shall be brought to naught." There, the idea is that in spite of the plans, nothing will happen. Here, it would seem, we have God causing nothing to happen. Other translations include "frustrate his council" (Birnbaum [Orthodox]), "frustrate his intention" (Artscroll [Orthodox]), and "thwart his designs" (*Siddur Sim Shalom* [Conservative]). Of these, "thwart" seems the most idiomatic, but the Hebrew itself is bizarre, and so probably the English ought to be, too.

"Turned his scheme around" An idiomatic interpretation of a likely idiom in Hebrew, literally, "You turned his reward on his head."

"Tree" Others, "gallows."

"Forever [tamid] *to the ends of time* [l'olam va'ed]" The Hebrew, too, uses two phrases for "forever."

"Write down" "Write down," not "inscribe," which carries connotations the Hebrew lacks. (See above, "Write.")

"Children of your covenant" As in Artscroll (Orthodox). *Siddur Sim Shalom* (Conservative) and Birnbaum (Orthodox) both use "people," perhaps to indicate that adults are to be included as well.

"Forever" See above, "Forever *[Selah]*".

"In truth" Others, "sincerely."

"Whose name is good" Artscroll (Orthodox) reads "good" as a proper noun, an actual name for God: "whose name is 'Good.'"

BRETTLER (BIBLE)

"Grant peace" In contrast to the modern reworkings of this blessings, some of which add *ba'olam*, "in the world," after the opening words of this blessing, its original focus is the Jewish community alone. This is obvious not only from its final line, "who blesses his people Israel with peace," and the introduction to it, "bless your people Israel at all times," but from the fact that this entire blessing is a reworking of the Priestly Blessing, which was directed toward Israel. In the words of Num. 6:27 (following the blessing), "They shall place my name on the Israelites, and I shall bless them."

The blessing really has two themes: blessing and peace, each of which is mentioned four times — "blessing" because it is an extension

(p. 179)

ELLENSON (MODERN LITURGIES)

"The threefold blessing in the Torah, written by Moses your servant, and said by Aaron and his sons the priests, your holy People" This prayer has posed two problems: first, contrary to the claims of liberal Jewish theology, it asserts Mosaic authorship of the Pentateuch; second, it affirms the prerogatives of the priesthood, which Reform Judaism replaced with the notion of the virtual priesthood of all Jews. The Reform Movement's 1885 Pittsburgh Platform resolved both difficulties formally by acknowledging the Bible as "the record of the consecration of the *(p. 179)*

19. *BIRKAT KOHANIM/SHALOM* ("THE PRIESTLY BLESSING/PEACE") בִּרְכַּת כֹּהֲנִים/שָׁלוֹם

¹ Our God and our ancestors' God, bless us with the threefold blessing in the Torah, written by Moses your servant, and said by Aaron and his sons the priests, your holy people:

² "May Adonai bless you and keep you.

³ May Adonai shine his face toward you and treat you graciously.

FALK (FEMINISM)

"Grant peace" The final blessing of the *Amidah* is the *Birkat Shalom*, literally, "The Blessing of Peace."

According to the talmudic overview of the *Amidah's* structure, in which the three concluding blessings all share the theme of thanksgiving, the Blessing of Peace should deal with our gratitude to God. But in fact, like the blessing of *Avodah* ("Sacrificial Service"), it begins with a petition and concludes with praise, once again raising the question of the place of petition in prayer. The issue is nowhere more poignant than here, for of all wishes and human needs, surely the desire for peace is as acute as any human desire — and as urgent today as it has ever been. At the *(p. 180)*

DORFF (THEOLOGY)

"Grace, righteousness, blessing, mercy, life, and peace" We ask not just for lack of conflict, but also for these things, as well as the favors requested previously in the intermediary benedictions. All of these blessings, though, mean much less to us if we are caught in conditions of war, so the beginning and end of this last benediction request God's ultimate blessing, the peace we need to experience all other blessings.

KUSHNER & POLEN (CHASIDISM)

"Bless us, our Father, all of us as one, in the light of your face" In his *Or Hame'ir* (volume 2, Jerusalem: 1995, p. 305), Zev Wolf of Zhitomir (d. 1800) is puzzled by how this blessing can ask God to bless all of us "as one." Surely the needs of the aggregate community are many and diverse. What one person lacks, for instance, another doesn't. How, therefore, could this prayer institute language apparently ignoring individual needs, lumping everyone together? The answer, suggests Zev Wolf, is that each soul yearns for God's beaming face, the *Or Hame'ir,* "the One who is the source of all light." This is the reason that the prayer states explicitly, "in the light of your face," denoting

(p. 180)

L. HOFFMAN (HISTORY)

WHEN THE SACRIFICIAL SERVICE ENDED, THE PEOPLE WERE DISMISSED WITH A PRIESTLY BLESSING, THE THEME OF WHICH IS PEACE. SO TOO, OUR AMIDAH ENDS WITH A PRAYER FOR PEACE, ENCOMPASSING BOTH THE WORDS OF THE PRIESTLY BLESSING ITSELF AND AN EXPANSION ON THE THEME OF PEACE.

"May Adonai bless you and keep you" This, the Priestly Blessing (as it is generally called), is the single benediction offered most often in Judaism and possibly in the western world. The late Nelson Glueck, then the president of the Hebrew Union College, offered it at the presidential inauguration of John F. Kennedy. It goes back to the

(p. 182)

אֱלֹהֵינוּ וֵאלֹהֵי אֲבוֹתֵינוּ בָּרְכֵנוּ¹
בַּבְּרָכָה הַמְשֻׁלֶּשֶׁת בַּתּוֹרָה הַכְּתוּבָה
עַל יְדֵי מֹשֶׁה עַבְדֶּךָ הָאֲמוּרָה מִפִּי
אַהֲרֹן וּבָנָיו כֹּהֲנִים עַם קְדוֹשֶׁךָ כָּאָמוּר:

יְבָרֶכְךָ יְיָ וְיִשְׁמְרֶךָ.²

יָאֵר יְיָ פָּנָיו אֵלֶיךָ וִיחֻנֶּךָ.³

LANDES (HALAKHAH)

"Bless us" The final blessing in the *Amidah* fulfills the positive commandment of *Birkat Kohanim,* "the Priestly Blessing" (*Sefer Charedim*). In the diaspora, it exists in two versions: this shorter form, where the prayer leader merely recollects the way the priests (the *kohanim*) bless Israel; and a longer form, the actual blessing itself, which is performed on holidays. In Israel, however, the actual benediction by the priests occurs daily as part of the ordinary service.

(p. 181)

J. HOFFMAN (TRANSLATION)

"Your holy people" Followed by *ka'amur,* in Hebrew, literally, "as it is said." The term functions as our modern-day quotation marks, and is best "translated" as appropriate punctuation, not as words.

"May Adonai shine his face. . . . May Adonai lift his face. . . ." It is difficult to capture the beauty of these three famous lines without sacrificing the content. Each line begins with a verb, followed by "Adonai," followed in turn by another verb. (Ps. 67:2 repeats part of the content of *(p. 183)*

4 May Adonai lift his face toward you and grant you peace."

5 Grant peace, goodness, and blessing, grace, kindness, and mercy to us and to all of Israel, your People. 6 Bless us, our Father, all of us as one, in the light of your face, for in the light of your face, Adonai our God, You gave us a Torah of life, a love of grace, righteousness, blessing, mercy, life, and peace. 7 You see fit to bless your People Israel at all times, at every hour, with your peace. *8 Blessed are You, Adonai, who blesses his People Israel with peace.

*[*From Rosh Hashanah to Yom Kippur, say instead:*

9 May it be the book of life, blessing, peace, and prosperous goodness that we are remembered for and written in before You—we and all of your People, the House of Israel, for life, goodness, and peace. 10 Blessed are You, Adonai, who brings peace.]

4 יִשָּׂא יְיָ פָּנָיו אֵלֶיךָ וְיָשֵׂם לְךָ שָׁלוֹם.

5 שִׂים שָׁלוֹם טוֹבָה וּבְרָכָה חֵן וָחֶסֶד וְרַחֲמִים עָלֵינוּ וְעַל כָּל־יִשְׂרָאֵל עַמֶּךָ. 6 בָּרְכֵנוּ אָבִינוּ כֻּלָּנוּ כְּאֶחָד בְּאוֹר פָּנֶיךָ. כִּי בְאוֹר פָּנֶיךָ נָתַתָּ לָּנוּ יְיָ אֱלֹהֵינוּ תּוֹרַת חַיִּים וְאַהֲבַת חֶסֶד וּצְדָקָה וּבְרָכָה וְרַחֲמִים וְחַיִּים וְשָׁלוֹם 7 וְטוֹב בְּעֵינֶיךָ לְבָרֵךְ אֶת־עַמְּךָ יִשְׂרָאֵל בְּכָל־עֵת וּבְכָל־שָׁעָה בִּשְׁלוֹמֶךָ. 8* בָּרוּךְ אַתָּה יְיָ הַמְבָרֵךְ אֶת־עַמּוֹ יִשְׂרָאֵל בַּשָּׁלוֹם.

*[*From Rosh Hashanah to Yom Kippur, say instead:*

9 בְּסֵפֶר חַיִּים בְּרָכָה וְשָׁלוֹם וּפַרְנָסָה טוֹבָה נִזָּכֵר וְנִכָּתֵב לְפָנֶיךָ אֲנַחְנוּ וְכָל־עַמְּךָ בֵּית יִשְׂרָאֵל לְחַיִּים טוֹבִים וּלְשָׁלוֹם. 10 בָּרוּךְ אַתָּה יְיָ עוֹשֶׂה הַשָּׁלוֹם.]

BRETTLER (BIBLE)

of the Priestly Blessing, and "peace" because "peace" is that blessing's concluding word. Other words from the blessing are interwoven here too; for example, "light of [or] your face" goes back to "shine [ya'er] his face." New here is the statement that "a Torah of life" is given from the light of God's face, a notion missing in the original Priestly Blessing, which predates the existence of the Torah in our sense, but is put here, reflecting the centrality of Torah to rabbinic culture.

It is unclear in what sense *shalom,* here translated as "peace," should be understood. Without any question, the word typically has that sense in rabbinic Hebrew, and it is one of the word's meanings in biblical Hebrew as well. But here it is used of people *(alenu,* "upon us") and perhaps is better translated as "well-being." That is probably what it means in Num. 6:26; and it fits the rest of the blessing better than "peace."

———◆———

ELLENSON (MODERN LITURGIES)

Jewish People to its mission as priest of the One God." But even before that, the issues had to be faced liturgically, especially in the Priestly Blessing which Jews knew well from their worship service and which could not easily be disregarded. Isaac Mayer Wise deleted the references to Moses and the priests by shortening the lines to "Bless us with the three-fold blessing written in the Torah." His contemporary, David Einhorn, addressed only the second issue, substituting, in Hebrew, "priests of Your holy People" for "the priests, your holy People," thereby avoiding the possible conclusion that of all the Jews, only the priests are sacred. In addition, he indicated, in translation, that the reference is purely a historical allusion to the priestly task once assigned to the sons of Aaron. Reconstructionists follow Einhorn but solve the first problem too by removing "written by Moses your servant."

"Grant peace, goodness, and blessing, grace, kindness, and mercy to us and to all of Israel Your people" The Conservative *Va'ani T'filati* adds the word *ba'olam* ("in the world") after "peace." Here, too, the particularism that asks peace and favor for Jews but not for others has been regarded as too narrow. Wise had added *al kol yirei sh'mecha,* "on all who fear Your name," as did the Reconstructionist *Daily Prayer Book.* Einhorn too expanded the prayer with *v'al kol b'nei adam banekha* (translated as "all the sons of men").

For similar reasons, liberal prayer books universalized "You see fit to bless your people Israel at all times, at every hour, with your peace." Most add *v'kol ha'amim,* "and all peoples," after "your people Israel." Wise borrowed the Sefardi wording, *b'rov oz v'shalom,* "with abundant peace and strength," which he added after "all peoples" — an innovation continued by Reconstructionists too. (See above, "For You hear the prayer of your People Israel.")

———◆———

179

FALK (FEMINISM)

same time, I cannot think of any single virtue or gift that depends more on our own actions, our own sustained and committed efforts — what some think of as our "partnership" with divinity — to bring it into being.

The connection between our longings and our actions suggests that there may be a role for commitment in prayer. As one who feels uncomfortable with prayer as petition (see p. 103), I find that prayer as promise — the assertion of personal or communal commitment — is a meaningful alternative. This is not to suggest that the uttering of a promise is a substitute for action; it is only a reminder, a beginning. But it is, I think, an important beginning. I believe, with Abraham Joshua Heschel, that "prayer is meaningless unless it is subversive," unless it seeks to overthrow injustice and oppression. As a liturgist, I am guided by the conviction that the purpose of prayer is to lead us, ultimately, to goodness — to the pursuit of justice and peace, and to acts of truth and loving-kindness.

We may wish and hope for redemption — we may even petition God for it, if we find this helpful — but we must also realize that redemption will not be ours unless we dedicate our lives to bringing it about, first through awareness and then through deeds. This need not be the result of a harsh self-discipline; it can arise out of gentle relations with others and with one's self. I believe that we help to bring about redemption when we assume the posture of giving ourselves over to our deepest desires — that is, to the yearnings that arise out of the wholeness of the self in connection to its source, connection to the greater whole of being. This prayer (from *The Book of Blessings)* is an example of what I have in mind when I suggest that we turn our petitionary posture into one of cooperation with the divine, which is to say, the commitment to be our best selves:

> "Eternal wellspring of peace —
> may we be drenched with the longing for peace
> that we may give ourselves over
> as the earth to the rain, to the dew,
> until peace overflows our lives
> as living waters overflow the seas."

———◆———

KUSHNER & POLEN (CHASIDISM)

God's presence. And in that pure, divine radiance there is, of course, no differentiation whatsoever. There, everything is One. All individuality, all divisions, all differences are absorbed.

It is only during the process of creation (Zev Wolf understands this in kabbalistic terms as the seven lower *s'firot* that construct the human personality) that the "light" becomes differentiated into the diversity of the world. Nevertheless, we intuit that the fulfillment of each one of our individual needs can only be found in our common, divine source. In this way, we understand that each one of us can all be blessed "as one," with one blessing, by the Source of all the colors of the rainbow, which is itself beyond all colors. And just this is the mystery of peace: all the differences ultimately issue from a single source. "Bless us, our Father, all of us as one, in the light of your face."

———◆———

LANDES (HALAKHAH)

The *kohanim* approach the front of the synagogue with their shoes off. When they recite the blessing, they make sure to stand on a rug or carpet, not on a bare floor, since bare floors may have originally had some connection to idolatry or idolatrous symbols. Then they cover their head and their hands with their *tallitot,* so that the fingers from which the blessings of the divine presence emanate are modestly covered, the idea being that neither the *kohanim* who invoke the blessing nor the worshipers who receive it should be able to see the blessing's source. The custom is first cited by Moses Isserles (the Rema), quoting the *Bet Yosef* of Joseph Caro, the author of the *Shulchan Arukh. Bet Yosef* is Caro's commentary to the *Tur.* Caro does not mention the practice in his *Shulchan Arukh,* but it has become the established custom by now. Clearly it is of late origin (Aryeh Strikowsky, contemporary scholar in Jerusalem).

A designated worshiper (not the prayer leader) in the synagogue calls out the cue, "*Kohanim,*" and they recite the benediction that fulfills their divinely given role to bless the people. The congregation (but again, not the prayer leader) answers, "Amen" (*Shulchan Arukh,* O. Ch. 125:19).

They then turn with their hands outstretched and their fingers spread in the prescribed manner to bless the congregation, whose members bow their heads reverently, so as not to look directly at the *kohanim* and thereby risk disturbing their concentration. But at the same time, they do not turn their bodies away from the *kohanim,* for they are to remain face to face with each other. The reader quietly prompts them, word for word, with the blessing as given in Numbers 6, and they repeat each word loudly. The congregation remains silent, saying only "Amen" after each line of the blessing.

After the blessing is over, the *kohanim* remain in place until the end of the *Amidah.* The prayer leader continues with *Sim Shalom.*

When the *kohanim* return to their seats after concluding the blessing, they are not allowed to respond to words of congratulation with the usual reply, *Barukh tihye* ("May you be blessed"), because this would constitute a violation of the negative commandment "You shall not add on" *(bal tosif)* to the *mitzvah* of the precise formulation of the Priestly Blessing; that is, only the verses from Num. 6:24–26 may be said as blessing by the priests *(Responsa Har Tzvi,* O. Ch. 62).

In the diaspora, the *Birkat Kohanim* is not said daily. Instead, at this point in the *Amidah,* the prayer leader says the stipulated verses from Numbers, on behalf of the priests, and the congregation responds, to each one, *Ken y'hi ratson,* "So may it be God's will" (Gra, *Ma'aseh Rav).* It does not say "Amen," because "Amen" is appropriate for the conclusion of blessings, whereas this is just a response to the evocation *(zekher)* of a blessing, not the actual blessing itself (Meir Schweiger, contemporary scholar in Israel).

At the concluding *Barukh atah Ado-nai,* bow again, as at the beginning of the *Amidah* (see p. 61, "Blessed are You, Ado-nai").

———◆———

L. HOFFMAN (HISTORY)

Bible (Num. 6:24–26), where God tells Aaron and his progeny ever after to bless Israel with it. In the Second Temple, the priests did so as part of the daily sacrifice, and from there it eventually entered the synagogue, as a recollection of the sacrifice that the *Amidah* was said to have replaced: as the priests ended the daily morning sacrifice with a blessing for God's peace, so too the daily morning *Amidah* ends that way.

For centuries (in Eretz Yisrael) only actual *kohanim* (men who traced their ancestry back to the priestly line) were allowed to utter this prayer. In Babylonia, however, any prayer leader was given the right to do so, and that is our custom today. On holidays, however (in all but Reform congregations), *kohanim* in the congregation are invited to rise before the congregation and engage in an elaborate expansion of the blessing, known as *dukh'n'n* (from the Hebrew word *dukhan,* meaning the dais where the *kohanim* stand). In Israel, the *dukh'n'n* occurs every Shabbat, and in Jerusalem, it is a daily occurrence, reminiscent of the Temple that once graced the holy city's sacred center.

Reform Jews did away with *dukh'n'n* because they objected to class distinctions within the Jewish People, preferring to see all Jews as equal members of a "holy people" and equally able to bless each other. Prerogatives once limited to those who actually sacrificed animals were to be viewed as the spiritual legacy of all Jews, who were seen as being charged with "the mission of Israel," to be "a light to the nations" by virtue of their living a model Jewish life. Reform Jews are therefore likely not to have seen *dukh'n'n,* but they will know the Priestly Blessing, not only as part of the *Amidah,* but also as the way the rabbi frequently concludes the service.

The midrash to the Book of Numbers identifies the distinction between "Bless you" and "Keep you."

"May God bless you" means "with physical possessions." Rabbi Nathan said, "Bless you" means "physical possessions," and "keep you" means "protect you from physical harm." Rabbi Isaac said, "Keep you" means "keep you from the evil inclination within you." Other interpretations are: "Keep you" means "from being dominated by others"; "Keep you" means "God will [keep] faithful to the covenant"; "Keep you" means "God will keep the messianic days reserved for you"; "Keep you" means "God will keep your soul when you die"; "Keep you" means "God will keep you in the world-to-come."

The midrash presents a logical progression. "Bless you" is mere mundane benefits: our physical possessions. "Keep you" refers to our person — physical harm from without, moral harm from within, or domination by others. But "our person" is not just who we are in this world. So ultimately, "Keep you" refers to covenantal faithfulness that stretches beyond our own earthly life, into messianic days, the eternal life of the soul, and the world-to-come (on which, see p. 73, "Giving life to the dead").

———◆———

J. HOFFMAN (TRANSLATION)

these lines, but without the poetic beauty.) An English version with the same poetic feel might read:

> "May you be blessed by Adonai and kept.
> May you be emblazened by Adonai's face and treated graciously.
> May you be witness to Adonai's face, and may He grant you peace."

But the passive is unacceptable here for other reasons.

In terms of content, the most serious question is whether "[May Adonai] shine his face" and "[May Adonai] lift his face" are idioms whose meanings we no longer know or poetic similes best translated word for word. Following Fox, the NSRV, and others, we assume the latter. JPS suggests, "deal kindly" and "bestow favor," respectively. Birnbaum (Orthodox) gives us "countenance" (a nice word play on "face") and "favor." *Siddur Sim Shalom* (Conservative) uses "favor" for "shine his face" and "show kindness" for "lift his face."

There is also a question whether the blessing is predictive ("Adonai will") or jussive ("May Adonai"), both of which are possible readings of the Hebrew.

"A Torah of life" Or "a living Torah." Context dictates "the Torah of life," but the Hebrew is clear in this regard.

"You see fit" Literally, "It is good in your eyes."

"Who brings peace" Literally, "makes," but "makes peace" is an idiom in English with a different meaning.

———◆ ◆ ◆———

3 | *Closing Meditation*

אֱלֹהַי נְצֹר לְשׁוֹנִי מֵרָע

¹ אֱלֹהַי, נְצֹר לְשׁוֹנִי מֵרָע וּשְׂפָתַי מִדַּבֵּר מִרְמָה. ²וְלִמְקַלְלַי נַפְשִׁי תִדּוֹם וְנַפְשִׁי כֶּעָפָר לַכֹּל תִּהְיֶה. ³פְּתַח לִבִּי בְּתוֹרָתֶךָ וּבְמִצְוֹתֶיךָ תִּרְדֹּף נַפְשִׁי. ⁴וְכָל הַחוֹשְׁבִים עָלַי רָעָה, מְהֵרָה הָפֵר עֲצָתָם וְקַלְקֵל מַחֲשַׁבְתָּם. ⁵עֲשֵׂה לְמַעַן שְׁמֶךָ עֲשֵׂה לְמַעַן יְמִינֶךָ עֲשֵׂה לְמַעַן קְדֻשָּׁתֶךָ עֲשֵׂה לְמַעַן תּוֹרָתֶךָ. ⁶לְמַעַן יֵחָלְצוּן יְדִידֶיךָ הוֹשִׁיעָה יְמִינְךָ וַעֲנֵנִי. ⁷יִהְיוּ לְרָצוֹן אִמְרֵי־פִי וְהֶגְיוֹן לִבִּי לְפָנֶיךָ יְיָ צוּרִי וְגֹאֲלִי. ⁸עֹשֶׂה שָׁלוֹם בִּמְרוֹמָיו הוּא יַעֲשֶׂה שָׁלוֹם עָלֵינוּ וְעַל כָּל־יִשְׂרָאֵל וְאִמְרוּ אָמֵן.

¹ My God, guard my tongue from evil and my lips from speaking deceit. ²To those who insult me, may my soul be silent; may my soul be like dust to everyone. ³Open my heart to your Torah, that my soul might pursue your commandments. ⁴As for all who think evil of me, quickly bring their advice to naught and frustrate their plan. ⁵Do this for the sake of your name, for the sake of your right hand, for the sake of your holiness, for the sake of your Torah. ⁶For the sake of delivering your beloved, save with your right hand and answer me. ⁷May the words of my mouth and the thoughts of my heart be favorable before You, Adonai, my rock and my redeemer. ⁸May the One who brings peace on high bring peace to us and to all Israel. Say: Amen.

⁹יְהִי רָצוֹן מִלְּפָנֶיךָ יְיָ אֱלֹהֵינוּ וֵאלֹהֵי אֲבוֹתֵינוּ שֶׁיִּבָּנֶה בֵּית הַמִּקְדָּשׁ בִּמְהֵרָה בְיָמֵינוּ וְתֵן חֶלְקֵנוּ בְּתוֹרָתֶךָ. ¹⁰וְשָׁם נַעֲבָדְךָ בְּיִרְאָה כִּימֵי עוֹלָם וּכְשָׁנִים קַדְמֹנִיּוֹת. ¹¹וְעָרְבָה לַיְיָ מִנְחַת יְהוּדָה וִירוּשָׁלַיִם כִּימֵי עוֹלָם וּכְשָׁנִים קַדְמֹנִיּוֹת.

⁹ May it be favorable before You, Adonai our God and our ancestors' God, that the Temple be speedily rebuilt in our day, and grant us a share in your Torah. ¹⁰There we will serve You in reverence, as in the ancient days and the earliest of years. ¹¹And the afternoon offering of Judah and Jerusalem will reach God, as in the ancient days and the earliest of years.

BRETTLER (BIBLE)

"My God" This additional prayer exactly follows the typical pattern of the biblical lament. It opens with an invocation of God, *elohai,* "My God," continues with requests ("guard . . . frustrate their plan"), and adds a set of motivations ("Do this for the sake . . ."). The biblical and rabbinic liturgical pattern may be natural to human discourse. Compare: "Boss [invocation], please give me tomorrow morning off [request] so I can go to my daughter's school play [motivation]." This section is concluded by two biblical verses. The first ("May the words of my mouth . . .") is the conclusion of Ps. 19:15 and an appropriate ending both there and here. The second verse is based on Job 25:2, which notes that God "makes peace in his heavens" *(oseh shalom bimromav).* This highly mythological verse about *shalom* concludes this prayer, echoing the final blessing's theme of *shalom,* "peace/well-being."

———◆———

ELLENSON (MODERN LITURGIES)

"That the Temple be speedily rebuilt in our day . . . and the afternoon offering of Judah and Jerusalem will reach God, as in the ancient days and the earliest of years." All non-Orthodox prayer books — Reform, Conservative, and Reconstructionist — have been of one mind in excising this paragraph. Conservative Jews are no more anxious for the restoration of the sacrificial cult than Reform Jews and Reconstructionists.

———◆———

J. HOFFMAN (TRANSLATION)

"May my soul be like dust" Birnbaum (Orthodox): "lowly as dust." *Siddur Sim Shalom* (Conservative): "humble."

"Your right hand" Birnbaum (Orthodox): "power."

"Say [v'imru]" The popular "and let us say" is more convenient, but wrong. Artscroll (Orthodox) suggests "respond."

"Rebuilt" Literally, "Built."

"Earliest of" Literally, "Early."   *(p. 191)*

CLOSING MEDITATION   אֱלֹהַי נְצֹר לְשׁוֹנִי מֵרָע

¹ My God, guard my tongue from evil and my lips from speaking deceit. ² To those who insult me, may my soul be silent; may my soul be like dust to everyone. ³ Open my heart to your Torah, that my soul might pursue your commandments.

LANDES (Halakhah)

"My God, guard my tongue from evil"
This personal meditation at the end of
the *Amidah* may be omitted in times of
emergency or even in just a pressing situation, even though, halakhically speaking, it is technically considered to be part
of the *Amidah*. This is a proper spot to
pray personally, in any language, for all
of one's needs, and especially for the spiritual welfare and Jewish continuity of
one's children and descendants *(Mishnah
B'rurah)*. At the words near the end,
Oseh shalom ("May the One who brings
peace"), as taking leave of a sovereign,
bow the back and head (but not the
knees), and take three steps backward.

Turn to the
left and say
*Oseh shalom
bimromav;*
then bow
f o r w a r d
while saying
the next
word, *hu,*
and con-
tinue to the
right for *ya'aseh shalom alenu*. Begin taking three steps forward now, still in the
bowed position, and say *v'al kol yisrael
v'imru amen*. If you can wait that long, it
is customary not to walk forward until
the prayer leader actually begins the repetition of the *Amidah,* or even (if possible) until he is about to begin the
K'dushah. Nonetheless, you can walk forward earlier if necessary.

—◆—

L. HOFFMAN (History)

THE AMIDAH *ENDS WITH AN OPPORTUNITY
FOR PRIVATE WORDS WITH GOD. TRADITION
PROVIDES A MEDITATION FOR THOSE WHO
WISH, BUT ANY WORDS ARE APPROPRIATE
HERE, AS WORSHIPERS ARE ENCOURAGED TO
ENGAGE GOD IN SILENT DIALOGUE.*

"My God, guard my tongue from evil"
Originally, private prayer was offered
after the *Sh'ma* and Its Blessings (the
rubric that now precedes the *Amidah*).
When Gamaliel II ordained the *Amidah,*
he wanted to be sure people said it, so he
banned private prayer there. People thus
moved their private prayer to the end of
the *Amidah*.

The Tal-
mud pro-
vides several
examples of
p r i v a t e
prayers by
the Rabbis
of old, and
this is one of
t h e m ,
attributed to
Mar bar Ravina, a late Babylonian master. Somehow, by the ninth century, it
had become popular in the academies
of Babylonia, and when Amram Gaon
codified our first known prayer book
(see Volume 1, *The Sh'ma and Its Blessings,* p. 8), he included this prayer as a
fitting meditation for people who had
nothing that they wanted to say on
their own.   *(p. 191)*

¹אֱלֹהַי, נְצֹר לְשׁוֹנִי מֵרָע וּשְׂפָתַי מִדַּבֵּר
מִרְמָה. ²וְלִמְקַלְלַי נַפְשִׁי תִדֹּם וְנַפְשִׁי
כֶּעָפָר לַכֹּל תִּהְיֶה. ³פְּתַח לִבִּי בְּתוֹרָתֶךָ
וּבְמִצְוֹתֶיךָ תִּרְדֹּף נַפְשִׁי.

⁴ As for all who think evil of me, quickly bring their advice to naught and frustrate their plan. ⁵ Do this for the sake of your name, for the sake of your right hand, for the sake of your holiness, for the sake of your Torah. ⁶ For the sake of delivering your beloved, save with your right hand and answer me. ⁷ May the words of my mouth and the thoughts of my heart be favorable before You, Adonai, my rock and my redeemer. ⁸ May the One who brings peace on high bring peace to us and to all Israel. Say: Amen.

⁹ May it be favorable before You, Adonai our God and our ancestors' God, that the Temple be speedily rebuilt in our day, and grant us a share in your Torah. ¹⁰ There we will serve You in reverence, as in the ancient days and the earliest of years. ¹¹ And the afternoon offering of Judah and Jerusalem will reach God, as in the ancient days and the earliest of years.

⁴וְכֹל הַחוֹשְׁבִים עָלַי רָעָה, מְהֵרָה הָפֵר עֲצָתָם וְקַלְקֵל מַחֲשַׁבְתָּם. ⁵עֲשֵׂה לְמַעַן שְׁמֶךָ. עֲשֵׂה לְמַעַן יְמִינֶךָ. עֲשֵׂה לְמַעַן קְדֻשָּׁתֶךָ. עֲשֵׂה לְמַעַן תּוֹרָתֶךָ. ⁶לְמַעַן יֵחָלְצוּן יְדִידֶיךָ הוֹשִׁיעָה יְמִינְךָ וַעֲנֵנִי. ⁷יִהְיוּ לְרָצוֹן אִמְרֵי־פִי וְהֶגְיוֹן לִבִּי לְפָנֶיךָ יְיָ צוּרִי וְגֹאֲלִי. ⁸עֹשֶׂה שָׁלוֹם בִּמְרוֹמָיו הוּא יַעֲשֶׂה שָׁלוֹם עָלֵינוּ וְעַל כָּל־יִשְׂרָאֵל וְאִמְרוּ אָמֵן.

⁹יְהִי רָצוֹן מִלְּפָנֶיךָ יְיָ אֱלֹהֵינוּ וֵאלֹהֵי אֲבוֹתֵינוּ שֶׁיִּבָּנֶה בֵּית הַמִּקְדָּשׁ בִּמְהֵרָה בְיָמֵינוּ וְתֵן חֶלְקֵנוּ בְּתוֹרָתֶךָ. ¹⁰וְשָׁם נַעֲבָדְךָ בְּיִרְאָה כִּימֵי עוֹלָם וּכְשָׁנִים קַדְמֹנִיּוֹת. ¹¹וְעָרְבָה לַיְיָ מִנְחַת יְהוּדָה וִירוּשָׁלָיִם כִּימֵי עוֹלָם וּכְשָׁנִים קַדְמֹנִיּוֹת.

J. HOFFMAN (TRANSLATION)

"Reach God" Sacrifice was apparently thought of as something earth-bound that could be converted by the flame into smoke that reaches God. The whole point was that only by consuming the offering on a fire could it find its way on high. By contrast, Birnbaum and Artscroll (both Orthodox) prefer "be pleasing to God," thereby emphasizing God's will in accepting it.

L. HOFFMAN (HISTORY)

The first prayer book in Europe came into being in eleventh-century France, a work called *Machzor Vitry* ("The book of annual prayers composed by [Rabbi Simchah from the town of] Vitry"). Holding Amram in high regard, the author of this book simply tells people to say whatever Amram advocated. No longer can readers make up their own prayer at all! And with that decision, Jewish prayer dropped the original idea of reserving a spot for private meditation in the midst of public worship.

From time to time, rabbis spoke out against the omission, but the printing press virtually ended the matter by printing Mar's prayer and making it normative for everyone who read the prayers from a book and did whatever it asked of them, but no more and no less. A century ago, Reform Judaism reinstated a period of "silent devotion" here, and nowadays, it is common in all movements for Jews to offer their own prayers, either in addition to Rav's masterpiece, or in place of it. *Siddur Sim Shalom* (Conservative), for instance, says, "At the conclusion of the *Amidah,* personal prayers may be added." The Reconstructionist *Kol Haneshamah* provides two guided meditations along with a kabbalistic diagram, as well as Mar's prayer, with the further instructions, "If this prayer does not speak to you, make up your own."

---

4 *The* Havineinu
הֲבִינֵנוּ

¹ Adonai our God, grant us wisdom to know your ways and open our minds to revere You; forgive us that we may be redeemed; keep us far from suffering; satisfy us with the goodness of your land; gather our dispersed People from the four corners of the earth. ² Let those who stray be judged by your disposition; wield your hand against the wicked; let the righteous rejoice in the rebuilding of your city, and in the reconstruction of your Temple, and in the blossoming of your servant David's progeny, and in the continuance of the light of your anointed, the son of Jesse. ³ You answer us before we even call. ⁴ Blessed are You, Adonai, who hears prayer.

¹הֲבִינֵנוּ יְיָ אֱלֹהֵינוּ לָדַעַת דְּרָכֶיךָ. וּמוֹל אֶת־לְבָבֵנוּ לְיִרְאָתֶךָ. וְתִסְלַח־לָנוּ לִהְיוֹת גְּאוּלִים. וְרַחֲקֵנוּ מִמַּכְאוֹב. וְדַשְּׁנֵנוּ בִּנְאוֹת אַרְצֶךָ. וּנְפוּצוֹתֵינוּ מֵאַרְבַּע כַּנְפוֹת הָאָרֶץ תְּקַבֵּץ. ²וְהַתּוֹעִים עַל־דַּעְתְּךָ יִשָּׁפֵטוּ. וְעַל־הָרְשָׁעִים תָּנִיף יָדֶךָ. וְיִשְׂמְחוּ צַדִּיקִים בְּבִנְיַן עִירֶךָ וּבְתִקּוּן הֵיכָלֶךָ וּבִצְמִיחַת קֶרֶן לְדָוִד עַבְדֶּךָ וּבַעֲרִיכַת נֵר לְבֶן־יִשַׁי מְשִׁיחֶךָ. ³טֶרֶם נִקְרָא אַתָּה תַעֲנֶה. ⁴בָּרוּךְ אַתָּה יְיָ שׁוֹמֵעַ תְּפִלָּה.

L. HOFFMAN (HISTORY)

L. HOFFMAN (HISTORY)

FROM THE FIRST CENTURY ON, TRADITION HAS PROVIDED A SHORTENED VERSION OF THE AMIDAH, *WHICH NOWADAYS IS RESERVED FOR OCCASIONS WHEN TIME DOES NOT ALLOW THE RECITATION OF ALL NINETEEN BENEDICTIONS.*

The *Amidah* was codified into eighteen separate blessings by Rabban Gamaliel II, around the end of the first century C.E. (see "How the *Amidah* Began, p. 17). Rabbi Eliezer dissented, saying, "A synopsis of the *Amidah* suffices." The Talmud wonders what synopsis he had in mind and cites this one as an illustration.

The word "synopsis," however, is misleading, since it implies that someone had the complete text of Gamaliel's entire *Amidah* in front of him and then synopsized it in a tighter and more compact paragraph. But the words here do not at all seem to be derived from the full versions of the *Amidah* that we have. It should be regarded, therefore, as an independent composition, composed for *(p. 195)*

J. HOFFMAN (TRANSLATION)

"Open our minds" Literally, "circumcise our hearts," an idiom from Deut. 10:16 and 30:6. Birnbaum (Orthodox) translates the phrase here as "subject our heart." The JPS Bible offers "open your hearts," while Fox and NSRV prefer the more literal "circumcise your heart." The heart was thought of as the seat of understanding, not just feeling, however, and circumcision was believed to be a means of correcting a malfunctioning organ. Hence our translation, "Open our minds" — make our minds function as they should.

"Satisfy us" From the Hebrew root *d.sh.n,* which also means "to fatten." The idea is that we will be satisfied from the produce of the earth, as opposed to going hungry.

"Wield your hand" That is, "punish," as in Birnbaum (Orthodox).

"Rebuilding" Literally, "Building."

"Reconstruction" Literally, "Construction." *(p. 195)*

THE *HAVINEINU*

[1] Adonai our God, grant us wisdom to know your ways and open our minds to revere You; forgive us that we may be redeemed; keep us far from suffering; satisfy us with the goodness of your land; gather our dispersed People from the four corners of the earth.

הֲבִינֵנוּ

הֲבִינֵנוּ יְיָ אֱלֹהֵינוּ לָדַעַת דְּרָכֶיךָ. וּמוֹל אֶת־לְבָבֵנוּ לְיִרְאָתֶךָ. וְתִסְלַח־לָנוּ לִהְיוֹת גְּאוּלִים. וְרַחֲקֵנוּ מִמַּכְאוֹב. וְדַשְּׁנֵנוּ בִּנְאוֹת אַרְצֶךָ. וּנְפוּצוֹתֵינוּ מֵאַרְבַּע כַּנְפוֹת הָאָרֶץ תְּקַבֵּץ.

²Let those who stray be judged by your disposition; wield your hand against the wicked; let the righteous rejoice in the rebuilding of your city, and in the reconstruction of your Temple, and in the blossoming of your servant David's progeny, and in the continuance of the light of your anointed, the son of Jesse. ³You answer us before we even call. ⁴Blessed are You, Adonai, who hears prayer.

²וְהַתּוֹעִים עַל־דַּעְתְּךָ יִשָּׁפֵטוּ. וְעַל־הָרְשָׁעִים תָּנִיף יָדֶךָ. וְיִשְׂ־מְחוּ צַדִּיקִים בְּבִנְיַן עִירֶךָ וּבְתִקּוּן הֵיכָלֶךָ וּבִצְמִיחַת קֶרֶן לְדָוִד עַבְדֶּךָ וּבַעֲרִיכַת נֵר לְבֶן־יִשַׁי מְשִׁיחֶךָ. ³טֶרֶם נִקְרָא אַתָּה תַעֲנֶה. ⁴בָּרוּךְ אַתָּה יְיָ שׁוֹמֵעַ תְּפִלָּה.

L. HOFFMAN (HISTORY)

people who followed Rabbi Eliezer and wanted to say the *Amidah* in a shorter format.

With the passage of time, Gamaliel's eighteen-blessing version triumphed, and the *Havineinu* was reserved for times of emergency. The rule is, therefore, that when time is lacking for the whole *Amidah,* the *Havineinu* can become its temporary replacement. One says the first and last three blessings and, in between, recites this one-paragraph summation of all the necessary themes.

J. HOFFMAN (TRANSLATION)

"Light" Birnbaum (Orthodox), "Offspring"; see "Let him shine" earlier.

About the Commentators

MARC BRETTLER
Marc Brettler, Ph.D., is Associate Professor of Hebrew Bible in the Department of Near Eastern and Judaic Studies at Brandeis University. His major areas of research are biblical historical texts, religious metaphors, and gender issues in the Bible. Brettler is author of *God Is King: Understanding an Israelite Metaphor* (Sheffield Academic Press) and *The Creation of History in Ancient Israel* (Routledge) as well as a variety of articles on the Hebrew Bible.

ELLIOT N. DORFF
Elliot N. Dorff, Ph.D., is Rector and Professor of Philosophy at the University of Judaism in Los Angeles. His book *Knowing God: Jewish Journeys to the Unknowable* (Jason Aronson) includes an extensive analysis of the nature of prayer. Ordained a rabbi by The Jewish Theological Seminary of America, Dorff is a member of the Conservative Movement's Committee on Jewish Law and Standards, its Commission on the Philosophy of the Conservative Movement, and its Commission to write a new Torah commentary for the Conservative Movement.

DAVID ELLENSON
David Ellenson, Ph.D., is the I.H. and Anna Grancell Professor of Jewish Religious Thought at Hebrew Union College–Jewish Institute of Religion in Los Angeles, as well as an adjunct faculty member at the Center for Jewish Studies at the University of California at Los Angeles. Ordained a rabbi by Hebrew Union College–Jewish Institute of Religion, he currently serves as the Lady Davis Visiting Professor in the Department of Jewish Thought at Hebrew University in Jerusalem. Ellenson has published and lectured extensively on diverse topics in modern Jewish thought, history, and ethics.

MARCIA FALK

Marcia Falk, Ph.D., is a poet, translator, and Judaic scholar whose recent books include *The Book of Blessings: New Jewish Prayers for Daily Life, the Sabbath, and the New Moon Festival* (HarperSanFrancisco, 1996), *With Teeth in the Earth: Selected Poems of Malka Heifetz Tussman* (Wayne State University, 1992), and *The Song of Songs: A New Translation and Interpretation* (HarperSanFrancisco, 1990). She is currently writing *The Book of Blessings for the Turning of the Year: New Prayers, Poems, and Reflections for the High Holiday Season.* A university professor for fifteen years, she now lectures widely on college campuses and in the Jewish community, on topics ranging from the love lyrics of the Bible to contemporary Jewish women writers.

JUDITH HAUPTMAN

Judith Hauptman, Ph.D., is the Rabbi Philip R. Alstat Professor of Talmud at The Jewish Theological Seminary in New York City. Her many publications focus on Talmud, Jewish feminism, and their points of intersection. The author of two books, *Development of the Talmudic Sugya: Relationship Between Tannaitic and Amoraic Sources* (University Press of America) and *Rereading the Rabbis, A Woman's Voice* (Westview/HarperCollins), she is currently researching religious pluralism in the Talmud.

JOEL M. HOFFMAN

Joel M. Hoffman, Ph.D., teaches advanced Hebrew and the history of Hebrew at Hebrew Union College–Jewish Institute of Religion in New York, and also coordinates Hebrew studies for its School of Education and Graduate Studies Program. Hoffman's doctorate is in theoretical linguistics, and he is particularly interested in understanding ancient Hebrew not merely as a dead language, but as a spoken language of antiquity. He has served as Hebrew consultant to HarperSanFrancisco and Jewish Lights Publishing.

LAWRENCE A. HOFFMAN

Lawrence A. Hoffman, Ph.D., has served for over two decades as Professor of Liturgy at Hebrew Union College–Jewish Institute of Religion in New York, where he was ordained a rabbi. Widely recognized for his liturgical scholarship, Hoffman has combined research in Jewish ritual, worship, and spirituality with a passion for the spiritual renewal of contemporary Judaism.

He has written and edited numerous books, including *The Art of Public Prayer, 2nd Edition: Not for Clergy Only* (Jewish Lights), now used nationally by Jews and Christians as a handbook for liturgical planners in church and synagogue, as well as a revision of *What Is a Jew?*, the best-selling classic that remains the most widely-read introduction to Judaism ever written in any language. He is also the author of *Israel — A Spiritual Travel Guide: A Companion for the Modern Jewish Pilgrim* (Jewish Lights). Hoffman is currently a developer of Synagogue 2000, a transdenominational project designed to envision and implement the ideal synagogue of the spirit for the 21st century.

LAWRENCE KUSHNER

Lawrence Kushner has served as spiritual leader of Congregation Beth El in Sudbury, Mass., for the past 25 years and is widely regarded as one of the most creative religious writers in America. Ordained a rabbi by Hebrew Union College–Jewish Institute of Religion, Kushner led his congregants in publishing their own prayer book, *V'taher Libenu (Purify Our Hearts)*, the first gender-neutral liturgy ever written. Through his lectures and nine books, including *Invisible Lines of Connection: Sacred Stories of the Ordinary; The Book of Letters: A Mystical Hebrew Alphabet; Honey from the Rock: An Easy Introduction to Jewish Mysticism; God Was in This Place and I, i Did Not Know: Finding Self, Spirituality, and Ultimate Meaning;* and *Eyes Remade for Wonder: A Lawrence Kushner Reader,* all published by Jewish Lights, he has helped shape the Jewish community's present focus on personal and institutional spiritual renewal.

NEHEMIA POLEN

Nehemia Polen, Ph.D., is Associate Professor of Jewish Thought and Associate Dean of Students at Hebrew College in Boston. Ordained a rabbi by Ner Israel Rabbinical College, Polen, a prolific writer whose academic and popular articles have appeared in many journals, is the author of *The Holy Fire: The Teachings of Rabbi Kalonymus Shapira, the Rebbe of the Warsaw Ghetto* (Jason Aronson).

DANIEL LANDES

Daniel Landes is Director of the Pardes Institute of Jewish Studies in Jerusalem and an adjunct Professor of Jewish Law at Loyola University Law School in Los Angeles. Ordained a rabbi by Rabbi Isaac Elchanan Theological Seminary, Landes was a founding faculty member of the Simon Wiesenthal Center and the Yeshiva of Los Angeles. He has lectured and written various popular and scholarly articles on the subjects of Jewish thought, social ethics, and spirituality.

List of Abbreviations

Artscroll	*Siddur Kol Ya'akov*, 1984.
Birnbaum	*Daily Prayer Book: Hasiddur Hashalem*, 1949.
FOP	*Forms of Prayer*, 1997.
Fox	Everett Fox, *The Five Books of Moses* (New York: Schocken Books, 1995).
GOP	*Gates of Prayer*, 1975.
SSS	*Siddur Sim Shulom*, 1985.
KH	*Kol Haneshamah*, 1994.
JPS	*Jewish Publication Society Bible* (Philadelphia: Jewish Publication Society, 1962).
NRSV	*New Revised Standard Bible*, 1989.
SLC	*Siddur Lev Chadash*, 1995.
SOH	*Service of the Heart*, 1967.
UPB	*Union Prayer Book*, 1894–1895.

Glossary

The following glossary defines Hebrew words used regularly throughout this volume, and provides the way the words are pronounced. Sometimes two pronunciations are common, in which case the first is the way the word is sounded in proper Hebrew, and the second is the way it is sometimes heard in common speech, under the influence of Yiddish, the folk language of Jews in northern and eastern Europe (it is a combination, mostly, of Hebrew and German). Our goal is to provide the way that many Jews actually use these words, not just the technically correct version.

- The pronunciations are divided into syllables by dashes.
- The accented syllable is written in capital letters.
- "Kh" represents a guttural sound, similar to the German (as in "sprach").
- The most common vowel is "a" as in "father," which appears here as "ah."
- The short "e" (as in "get") is written either "e" (when it is in the middle of a syllable) or "eh" (when it ends a syllable).
- Similarly, the short "i" (as in "tin") is written either "i" (when it is in the middle of a syllable) or "ih" (when it ends a syllable).
- A long "o" (as in "Moses") is written "oe" (as in the English word "toe") or "oh" (as in the English word "Oh!").

Acharonim (pronounced ah-khah-roe-NEEM, or, commonly, ah-chah-ROE-nim): The name given to Jewish legal authorities from roughly the sixteenth century on. The word means, literally, "later ones," as opposed to the "earlier ones," authorities prior to that time who are held in higher regard and are called *rishonim* (pronounced ree-shoh-NEEM, or, commonly, ree-SHOH-nim). Singular: *acharon* (pronounced ah-chah-RONE) and *rishon* (pronounced ree-SHONE).

Alenu (pronounced ah-LAY-noo): The first word and, therefore, the title of a major prayer compiled in the second or third century as part of the New Year *(Rosh Hashanah)* service, but from about the fourteenth century on, used also as part of the concluding section of every daily service. *Alenu* means "it is incumbent upon us . . ." and introduces the prayer's theme: our duty to praise God.

Amidah (pronounced either ah-mee-DAH or, commonly, ah-MEE-dah): One of three commonly used titles for the second of two central units in the worship service, the first being The *Sh'ma* and Its Blessings. It is composed of a series of blessings, many of which are petitionary, except on Sabbaths and holidays, when the petitions are removed out of deference to the holiness of the day. Also called *T'fillah* and *Sh'moneh Esreh*. *Amidah* means "standing," and refers to the fact that the prayer is said standing up.

Amora (pronounced ah-MOE-rah): A title for talmudic authorities and, therefore, living roughly from the third to the sixth centuries. Plural: *amoraim* (pronounced ah-moe-rah-EEM, or, commonly, ah-moe-RAH-yim). Often used in contrast to a *tanna* (pronounced TAH-nah), the title of authorities in the time of the Mishnah, that is, prior to the third century. Plural: *tannaim* (pronounced tah-nah-EEM, or, commonly, tah-NAH-yim).

Arvit (pronounced ahr-VEET, or, commonly, AHR-veet): From the Hebrew word *erev* (pronounced EH-rev) meaning "evening." One of two titles used for the evening worship service (also called *Ma'ariv*).

Ashkenazi (pronounced ahsh-k'-nah-ZEE, or, commonly, ahsh-k'-NAH-zee): From the Hebrew word *Ashkenaz,* meaning the geographic area of northern and eastern Europe; *Ashkenazi* is the adjective, describing the liturgical rituals and customs practiced there, as opposed to *Sefardi,* meaning the liturgical rituals and customs that are derived from *Sefarad,* Spain (see *Sefardi*).

Ashre (pronounced ahsh-RAY, or, commonly, AHSH-ray): The first word and, therefore, the title of a prayer said three times each day, composed primarily of Psalm 145. *Ashre* means "happy" and introduces the phrase "Happy are they who dwell in your [God's] house."

Avodah (pronounced ah-voe-DAH): Literally, "sacrificial service," a reference to the sacrificial cult practiced in the ancient temple until its destruction by the Romans in the year 70 C.E.; also the title of the third to last blessing in the *Amidah,* a petition for the restoration of the Temple in messianic times. Many liberal liturgies either omit the blessing or reframe it as a petition for divine acceptance of worship in general.

Avot (pronounced ah-VOTE): Literally, "fathers" or "ancestors," and the title of the first blessing in the *Amidah*. The traditional wording of the blessing recollects the covenantal relationship between God and the patriarchs: Abraham, Isaac, and Jacob. Most liberal liturgies include also explicit reference to the matriarchs: Sarah, Rebekah, Rachel, and Leah.

[The] **Bach** (pronounced BAHKH): An acronym for Rabbi Joel Sirkes (Poland, 1561–1640), formed by juxtaposing the two Hebrew initials of his major legal work, *Bayit Chadash* (BaCH).

Bar'khu (pronounced bah-r'-KHOO, or, commonly, BOH-r'khoo): The first word and, therefore, the title of the formal call to prayer with which the section called The *Sh'ma* and Its Blessings begins. *Bar'khu* means "praise," and introduces the invitation to the assembled congregation to praise God.

Barukh k'vod (pronounced bah-RUKH k'-VOD): The first two words of a response in the third blessing of the *Amidah* taken from Ezekiel 3:12, meaning "the glory of Adonai is blessed from his place."

Benediction (also called **Blessing**): One of two terms used for the Rabbis' favorite prose formula for composing prayers. The worship service is composed of many different literary genres, but most of it is benedictions. Long benedictions end with a summary line that begins *Barukh atah Adonai* . . . "Blessed are You, Adonai . . ." Short blessings have only the summary line alone.

Binah (pronounced bee-NAH, or, commonly, BEE-nah): Literally, "knowledge" or "understanding," and the title of the fourth blessing in the daily *Amidah*. It is a petition for human knowledge, particularly insight into the human condition, leading to repentance.

Birkat (pronounced beer-KAHT): Literally, "Blessing of . . ." The titles of many blessings are known as "Blessing of . . . ," for example, "Blessing of Torah" and "Blessing of Jerusalem." Some titles are commonly shortened so that only the qualifying last words are used (such as "Jerusalem" instead of "Blessing of Jerusalem"), and they are listed in the glossary by the last words, e.g., *Y'rushalayim* instead of *Birkat Y'rushalayim* ("Jerusalem" instead of "Blessing of Jerusalem"). Those blessings that are more generally cited with the full title appear under *Birkat*.

Birkat Hatorah (pronounced beer-KAHT hah-toe-RAH): Literally, "Blessing of Torah," the title for the second blessing in the liturgical section called The *Sh'ma* and Its Blessings; its theme is the revelation of the Torah to Israel on Mount Sinai.

Birkhot Hashachar (pronounced beer-KHOT hah-SHAH-khar): Literally, "Morning Blessings," the title of the first large section in the morning prayer regimen of Judaism; originally said privately upon arising in the morning, but now customarily recited immediately upon arriving at the synagogue. It is composed primarily of benedictions thanking God for the everyday gifts of health and wholeness, as well as study sections taken from the Bible and rabbinic literature.

Birkat Kohanim (pronounced beer-KAHT koe-hah-NEEM): Literally, "blessing of the priests," but usually referred to as "the priestly benediction," a reference to Numbers 6:24–25. Also the title of the final blessing of the *Amidah*. See also *Kohanim*.

B'rakhah (pronounced b'-rah-KHAH): The Hebrew word for "benediction" or "blessing." See *Benediction*. Plural ("benedictions") is *b'rakhot* (pronounced b'-rah-KHOTE).

Chanukah (pronounced KHAH-noo-kah): An eight-day festival beginning on the twenty-fifth day of the Hebrew month of Kislev, corresponding, usually, to some time in December. Chanukah celebrates the miraculous deliverance of the Jews as described in the books known as *Maccabees* (pronounced MA-kah-beez). Although not canonized in the Jewish Bible, Maccabees is carried in Catholic scripture and describes the heroic acts of a priestly family, known also as the Maccabees, or the Hasmoneans (pronounced has-moe-NEE-'ns), in 167 B.C.E.

Chasidism (pronounced KHAH-sih-dizm): The doctrine generally traced to an eighteenth-century Polish Jewish mystic and spiritual leader known as the Ba'al Shem Tov (called also the BeSHT, an acronym composed of the initials of his name B, SH, and T). Followers are called *Chasidim* (pronounced khah-see-DEEM or khah-SIH-dim; singular, *Chasid* pronounced khah-SEED, or, commonly, KHA-sid) from the Hebrew word *chesed* (pronounced KHEH-sed), meaning "loving-kindness" or "piety."

Chatimah (pronounced chah-tee-MAH): The final summary line of a benediction (see *Benediction*).

Cheshvan (pronounced KHESH-vahn): A Hebrew month corresponding to late October or November.

David (pronounced dah-VEED): Literally, "David," a reference to the biblical King David, and the title of the fifteenth blessing of the daily *Amidah*, a petition for the appearance of the messianic ruler said by tradition to be a descendent of King David. Some liberal liturgies omit the blessing or reframe it to refer to a messianic age of perfection, but without the arrival of a human messianic ruler.

Doxology: Technical term for a congregational response to an invitation to praise God; generally a single line of prayer affirming praise of God forever and ever. Examples in The *Sh'ma* and Its Blessings are the responses to the Call to Prayer and to the *Sh'ma* itself. From the Greek word *doxos,* meaning "glory."

Eretz Yisrael (pronounced EH-retz yis-rah-AYL): Hebrew for "the Land of Israel."

Gaon (pronounced gah-OHN; plural: *Geonim*, pronounced g'-oh-NEEM): Title for the leading rabbis in Babylon (present-day Iraq) from about 750 to 1038. From a biblical word meaning "glory," which is equivalent in the title to saying "Your Excellence."

Genizah (pronounced g'-NEE-zah): A cache of documents, in particular, the one discovered at the turn of the twentieth century in an old synagogue in Cairo; the source of our knowledge about how Jews prayed in the Land of Israel and vicinity prior to the twelfth century. From a word meaning "to store or hide away," "to archive."

G'ulah (pronounced g'-oo-LAH): Literally, "redemption" or "deliverance," and the title of the seventh blessing of the daily *Amidah,* as well as the third blessing in The *Sh'ma* and Its Blessings; its theme affirms God's redemptive act of delivering the Israelites from Egypt, and promises ultimate deliverance from suffering and want at the end of time.

G'vurot (pronounced g'voo-ROTE): Literally, "strength" or "power," and the title of the second blessing in the *Amidah.* It affirms the power of God to bring annual rain and new growth in nature and, by extension, to resurrect the dead. Some liberal liturgies omit the belief in resurrection or replace it with wording that suggests other concepts of eternal life.

Haftarah (pronounced hahf-tah-RAH, or, commonly, hahf-TOE-rah): The section of Scripture taken from the prophets and read publicly as part of Shabbat and holiday worship services. From a word meaning "to conclude," since it is the "concluding reading," that is, it follows a reading from the Torah (the five books of Moses).

Haggadah (pronounced hah-gah-DAH, or, commonly, hah-GAH-dah): The liturgical service for the Passover eve Seder meal. From a Hebrew word meaning "to tell," since the *Haggadah* is a telling of the Passover narrative.

Halakhah (pronounced hah-lah-KHAH, or, commonly, hah-LAH-khah): The Hebrew word for "Jewish law." Used as an anglicized adjective, *halakhic* (pronounced hah-LAH-khic), meaning "legal." From the Hebrew word meaning "to walk, to go," so denoting the way on which a person should walk through life.

Hallel (pronounced hah-LAYL, or, commonly, HAH-layl): A Hebrew word meaning "praise," and by extension, the name given to sets of psalms that are recited liturgically in praise of God. Psalms 145–150, the Daily *Hallel,* is recited each morning; Psalm 136, the Great *Hallel,* is recited on Shabbat and holidays and is part of the Passover Seder. Psalms 113–118, the best-known *Hallel,* known more fully as the Egyptian Hallel, is recited on holidays and gets its name from Psalm 114:1, which celebrates the moment "when Israel left Egypt."

Halleluyah (pronounced hah-l'-loo-YAH, but sometimes anglicized as hah-l'-LOO-yah): A common word in psalms, meaning "praise God," and the final word of a congregational response within the third blessing of the *Amidah* (from Psalms 146:10).

Hat'fillah (pronounced hah-t'-fee-LAH): Literally, "the *T'fillah,*" another name for the *Amidah.* See *T'fillah.*

Hoda'ah (pronounced hoe-dah-AH): Literally, a combination of the English words "gratitude" and "acknowledgment," so translated here as "grateful acknowledgment." The title of the second to last blessing in the *Amidah,* an expression of our grateful acknowledgment to God for the daily wonders that constitute human existence.

Hoeche K'dushah (pronounced HAY-kh' k'DOO-shah): A Yiddish term combining German and Hebrew and meaning, literally, "the High *Kedushah*." Refers to a way to shorten the time it takes to say the *Amidah* by avoiding the necessity of having the prayer leader repeat it all after it is said silently by the congregation.

Kabbalah (pronounced kah-bah-LAH, or, commonly, kah-BAH-lah): A general term for Jewish mysticism, but used properly for a specific mystical doctrine that began in western Europe in the eleventh or twelfth centuries; recorded in the *Zohar* (see *Zohar*) in the thirteenth century, and then was further elaborated, especially in the Land of Israel (in Safed), in the sixteenth century. From a Hebrew word meaning "to receive" or "to welcome," and secondarily, "tradition," implying the receiving of tradition from one's past.

Kabbalat Shabbat (pronounced kah-bah-LAHT shah-BAHT): Literally, "welcoming Sabbath," and therefore a term for the introductory synagogue prayers that lead up to the arrival of the Sabbath at sundown Friday night.

Kaddish (pronounced kah-DEESH, or, more commonly, KAH-dish): One of several prayers from a Hebrew word meaning "holy," and therefore the name given to a prayer affirming God's holiness. This prayer was composed in the first century but later found its way into the service in several forms, including one known as the Mourners' *Kaddish* and used as a mourning prayer.

Kavvanah (pronounced kah-vah-NAH): From a word meaning "to direct," and therefore used technically to denote the state of directing one's words and thoughts sincerely to God, as opposed to the rote recitation of prayer.

K'dushah (pronounced k'-doo-SHAH, or, commonly, k'-DOO-shah): From the Hebrew word meaning "holy," and therefore one of several prayers from the first or second century occurring in several places and versions, all of which have in common the citing of Isaiah 6:3: *kadosh, kadosh kadosh . . . ,* "Holy, holy, holy is the Lord of hosts. The whole earth is full of His glory."

K'dushat Hashem (pronounced k'-doo-SHAHT hah-SHEM): Literally, "sanctification of the name [of God]," and the full name for the prayer that is generally called *K'dushah* (See *K'dushah*). Best known as the third blessing in the *Amidah,* but found also prior to the morning *Sh'ma.* Used also in variant form *kiddush hashem* (pronounced kee-DOOSH hah-SHEM) as a term to describe dying for the sanctification of God's name, that is, martyrdom.

Keva (pronounced KEH-vah): A Hebrew word meaning "fixity, stability," and therefore the aspect of a service that is fixed and immutable: the words on the page, perhaps, or the time at which the prayer must be said. In the early years, when prayers were delivered orally and improvised on the spot, *keva* meant the fixed order in which the liturgical themes had to be expressed.

Kibbutz G'luyot (pronounced kee-BOOTS g'-loo-YOTE): Literally, "gathering the exiles," and the title of the tenth blessing of the daily *Amidah*, a petition for Jews outside the Land of Israel to return home to their land as a sign that messianic times are imminent. Some liberal liturgies omit the blessing or interpret it more broadly to imply universal messianic liberation, but without the literal belief that Jews outside the Land of Israel are in "exile," or that they need to or want to "return home."

Kiddush (pronounced kee-DOOSH, or, commonly, KIH-d'sh): Literally, "sanctification," the name given to the prayer recited over wine at the outset of Sabbaths and holy days, declaring the day in question sanctified. A shorter version is recited the next morning after services, at which time worshipers commonly share a meal or light refreshments together. By extension, *Kiddush* is sometimes used to designate that meal as well.

Kohanim (pronounced koe-hah-NEEM): Literally, "priests," plural of *kohen* (pronounced koe-HAYN), "priest," a reference to the priests who offered sacrifices in the ancient temple until its destruction by Rome in the year 70 C.E. Also the name of modern-day Jews who claim priestly descent, and who are customarily given symbolic recognition in various ritual ways — as, for instance, being called first to stand beside the Torah reader and to recite a blessing over the reading. It is also the title of the last blessing in the *Amidah*, which contains the priestly benediction from Numbers 6:24–25. Another more popular name for that blessing is *Shalom* (pronounced shah-LOME), "peace," because the priestly benediction requests peace. See also *Birkat Kohanim*.

Krivat Sh'ma (pronounced k'-ree-YAHT sh'-MAH): Literally, "reciting the *Sh'ma*," and therefore a technical term for the liturgical act of reading the prayer known as the *Sh'ma* (See *Sh'ma*).

Liturgy Public worship, from the Greek word *liturgia*, meaning "public works." Liturgy in ancient Greece was considered a public work, the act of sacrificing or praising the gods, from which benefit would flow to the body politic.

Ma'ariv (pronounced mah-ah-REEV, or, commonly, MAH-ah-reev): From the Hebrew word *erev* (pronounced EH-rev), meaning "evening": one of two titles used for the evening worship service (also called *Arvit*).

Midrash (pronounced meed-RAHSH, or, commonly, MID-rahsh): From a Hebrew word meaning "to ferret out the meaning of a text," and therefore a rabbinic interpretation of a biblical word or verse. By extension, a body of rabbinic literature that offers classical interpretations of the Bible.

Minchah (pronounced meen-CHAH, or, more commonly, MIN-chah): Originally the name of a type of sacrifice, then the word for a sacrifice offered during the afternoon, and now the name for the afternoon synagogue service usually scheduled just before nightfall. *Minchah* means "afternoon."

Minhag (pronounced meen-HAHG, or, commonly, MIN-hahg): The Hebrew word for custom and, therefore, used liturgically to describe the customary way that different groups of Jews pray. By extension, *minhag* means a "rite," as in *Minhag Ashkenaz*, meaning "the rite of prayer, or the customary way of prayer for Jews in *Ashkenaz*" — that is, northern and eastern Europe.

Minim (pronounced mee-NEEM): Literally, "heretics" or "sectarians," and the title of the twelfth blessing of the daily *Amidah*, a petition that heresy be eradicated, and heretics punished. Liberal liturgies frequently omit the blessing, considering it an inappropriate malediction, not a benediction at all, or reframe it as a petition against evil in general.

Minyan (pronounced meen-YAHN, or, commonly, MIN-y'n): A quorum, the minimum number of people required for certain prayers. *Minyan* comes from the word meaning "to count."

Mishnah (pronounced meesh-NAH, or, commonly, MISH-nah): The first written summary of Jewish law, compiled in the Land of Israel about the year 200 C.E., and therefore our first overall written evidence for the state of Jewish prayer in the early centuries.

Mishpat (pronounced meesh-PAHT): Literally, "justice," and the title of the eleventh blessing of the daily *Amidah;* a petition for just rulership, a condition associated with the messianic age.

Mitzvah (pronounced meetz-VAH, or, commonly, MITZ-vah; plural, *mitzvot,* pronounced meetz-VOTE): A Hebrew word used commonly to mean "good deed," but in the more technical sense, denoting any commandment from God, and therefore, by extension, what God wants us to do. Reciting the *Sh'ma* morning and evening, for instance, is a *mitzvah.*

Modim D'rabbanan (pronounced moe-DEEM d'-rah-bah-NAHN): *Modim* is the first word of the second to last blessing of the *Amidah,* and therefore a shorthand way of referring to that prayer. *Modim D'rabbanan* is the name given to the form of the prayer that is reserved for congregational recitation during the repetition of the *Amidah* by the prayer leader. Literally, it means "the *Modim* of our Rabbis," and refers to the fact that the prayer is composed of what were once several alternative responses, each of which was the custom of one of the Rabbis of the Talmud.

Musaf (pronounced moo-SAHF, or, commonly, MOO-sahf): The Hebrew word meaning "extra" or "added," and therefore the title of the additional sacrifice that was offered in the Temple on Shabbat and holy days. It is now the name given to an added service of worship appended to the morning service on those days.

M'zuzah (pronounced m'-zoo-ZAH, or, commonly, m'-ZOO-zah): The Hebrew word in the Bible meaning "doorpost," and by extension, the term now used for a small casement that contains the first two sections of the *Sh'ma* (Deut. 6:4–9, 11:13–21) and is affixed to the doorposts of Jewish homes.

N'kadesh (pronounced n'kah-DAYSH): The *Amidah* is first recited silently by each worshiper individually and then repeated aloud by the prayer leader, at which time its third blessing appears in extended form. *N'kadesh* (literally, "Let us sanctify . . .") is the first Hebrew word of that extended blessing and is thus, by extension, a common way to refer to it.

Orach Chayim (pronounced OH-rakh CHA-yim): Abbreviated as O. Ch. Literally, "The Way of Life," one of four sections in the *Tur* and the *Shulchan Arukh*, two of Judaism's major law codes; the section containing the rules of prayer.

Payy'tan (pronounced pah-y'-TAHN; plural *Payy'tanim,* pronounced pah-y'-tah-NEEM): A poet; the name given particularly to classical and medieval poets whose work is inserted into the standard prayers for special occasions.

Perek (pronounced PEH-rek; plural, *p'rakim,* pronounced p'-rah-KEEM): Literally, a "section" or "chapter" of a written work, and used liturgically to mean the sections of the *Sh'ma*. Each of its three biblical sections is a different *perek*.

Piyyut (pronounced pee-YOOT; plural: pee-yoo TEEM): Literally, "a poem," but used technically to mean liturgical poems composed in classical and medieval times, and inserted into the standard prayers on special occasions.

P'sukei D'zimrah (pronounced p'-soo-KAY d'-zeem-RAH, or, commonly, p'-SOO-kay d'-ZIM-rah): Literally, "verses of song," and therefore the title of a lengthy set of opening morning prayers that contain psalms and songs, and serve as spiritual preparation prior to the official call to prayer.

Purim (pronounced PU-rim, or, pu-REEM): A festival falling on the fourteenth day of the Hebrew month of Adar, generally corresponding to late February or early March. It celebrates the miraculous deliverance referred to in the biblical Book of Esther. Literally, *purim* means "lots," as in the phrase "drawing of lots," because the date on which the Jews were to have been killed was chosen by lot.

R'fuah (pronounced r'-foo-AH, or, commonly, r'-FOO-ah): Literally, "healing," and the title of the eighth blessing of the daily *Amidah,* a petition for healing.

Rosh Chodesh (pronounced rohsh CHOH-desh): Literally, "the head of the month," and therefore the Hebrew name for the one- or two-day new moon period with which lunar months begin. It is marked as a holiday in Jewish tradition, a period of new beginnings.

Rubric (pronounced ROO-brick): A technical term for any discrete section of liturgy, whether a prayer or a set of prayers. The *Sh'ma* and Its Blessings is one of several large rubrics in the service; within that large rubric, the *Sh'ma* or any one of its accompanying blessings may be called a rubric as well.

Seder (pronounced SEH-der, or, commonly, SAY-der): The Hebrew word meaning "order," and therefore 1) the name given to the ritualized meal eaten on Passover eve, and 2) an early alternative term for the order of prayers in a prayer book. The word *Siddur* (see *Siddur*) is now preferred for the latter.

Sefardi (pronounced s'-fahr-DEE, or, commonly s'-FAHR-dee): From the Hebrew word *Sefarad* (pronounced s'-fah-RAHD), meaning the geographic area of modern-day Spain and Portugal. *Sefardi* is the adjective, describing the liturgical rituals and customs that are derived from Sefarad prior to the expulsion of Jews from there at the end of the fifteenth century, as opposed to *Ashkenazi* (see *Ashkenazi*), meaning the liturgical rituals and customs common to northern and eastern Europe. Nowadays, *Sefardi* refers also to the customs of Jews from North Africa and Arab lands, whose ancestors came from Spain.

S'firot (pronounced s'-fee-ROTE; singular: *s'firah,* pronounced s'-fee-RAH): According to the Kabbalah (Jewish mysticism, see *Kabbalah*), the universe came into being by a process of divine emanation, whereby the divine light, as it were, expanded into empty space, eventually becoming physical matter. At various intervals, this light was frozen in time, as if captured by containers, each of which is called a *s'firah.* Literally, *s'firah* means "number," because early theory conceptualized the stages of creation as primordial numbers.

Shabbat (pronounced shah-BAHT): The Hebrew word for "Sabbath," from a word meaning "to rest."

Shacharit (pronounced shah-khah-REET, or, commonly, SHAH-khah-reet): The name given to the morning worship service; from the Hebrew word *shachar* (SHAH-khar), meaning "morning."

Shalom (pronounced shah-LOME): Literally, "peace," and a popular title for the final benediction of the *Amidah,* more properly entitled *Kohanim* (pronounced koe-hah-NEEM), "priests," or, more fully, *Birkat Kohanim* (pronounced beer-KAHT koe-hah-NEEM), "blessing of the priests," "priestly benediction." See also *Birkat Kohanim, Kohanim.*

Shanim (pronounced shah-NEEM): Literally, "years," and the title of the ninth blessing of the daily *Amidah;* a petition for a year of agricultural abundance, such as is associated with messianic days.

Sh'ma (pronounced sh'-MAH): The central prayer in the first of the two main units in the worship service, the second being the *Amidah* (See *Amidah*). The *Sh'ma* comprises three citations from the Bible, and the larger unit in which it is embedded (called The *Sh'ma* and Its Blessings) is composed of a formal call to prayer (see *Bar'khu*) and a series of blessings on the theological themes that, together with the *Sh'ma,* constitute a liturgical creed of faith. *Sh'ma,* meaning "hear," is the first word of the first line of the first biblical citation, "Hear O Israel: Adonai is our God; Adonai is One," which is the paradigmatic statement of Jewish faith, the Jews' absolute commitment to the presence of a single and unique God in time and space.

Sh'liakh Tsibbur (pronounced sh'-LEE-ahkh tsee-BOOR): Literally, the "agent of the congregation," and therefore the name given to the person who leads the prayer service.

Sh'mini Atseret (pronounced sh'-MEE-nee ah-TSEH-ret): Literally, "the eighth day of solemn assembly," and the name given to the eighth and final day of the Autumn festival of Sukkot.

Sh'moneh Esreh (pronounced sh'-MOE-neh ES-ray): A Hebrew word meaning "eighteen," and therefore a name given to the second of the two main units in the worship service that once had eighteen benedictions in it (it now has nineteen), known also as the *Amidah* (see *Amidah*).

Shulchan Arukh (pronounced shool-KHAN ah-ROOKH, or, commonly, SHOOL-khan AH-rookh): The name given to the best-known code of Jewish law, compiled by Joseph Caro in the Land of Israel and published in 1565. *Shulchan Arukh* means "The Set Table," and refers to the ease with which the various laws are set forth — like a table prepared with food ready for consumption.

Siddur (pronounced see-DOOR, or, commonly, SIH-d'r): From the Hebrew word *seder* (see *Seder*) meaning "order," and therefore, by extension, the name given to the "order of prayers," or prayer book.

S'lichah (pronounced s'lee-KHAH, or, commonly S'LEE-khah): Literally, "pardon" or "forgiveness," and the title of the sixth blessing of the daily *Amidah,* a petition for divine forgiveness of our sins.

Tachanun (pronounced TAH-khah-noon): A Hebrew word meaning "supplications," and therefore, by extension, the title of the large unit of prayer that follows the *Amidah,* and which is largely supplicatory in character.

Tallit (pronounced tah-LEET; plural: *talitot*, pronounced tah-lee-TOTE): The prayer shawl equipped with tassels (see *Tsitsit*) on each corner, and generally worn during the morning (*Shacharit*) and additional (*Musaf*) synagogue service.

Talmud (pronounced tahl-MOOD, or, more commonly, TAHL-m'd): The name given to each of two great compendia of Jewish law and lore compiled over several centuries, and ever since, the literary core of the rabbinic heritage. The *Talmud Yerushalmi* (pronounced y'-roo-SHAHL-mee), the "Jerusalem Talmud," is earlier, a product of the Land of Israel generally dated about 400 C.E. The better-known *Talmud Bavli* (pronounced BAHV-lee), or "Babylonian Talmud," took shape in Babylonia (present-day Iraq), and is traditionally dated about 550 C.E. When people say "the" Talmud without specifying which one they mean, they are referring to the Babylonian version. *Talmud* means "teaching."

Tetragrammaton: The technical term for the four-letter name of God that appears in the Bible. Treating it as sacred, Jews stopped pronouncing it centuries ago, so that the actual pronunciation has been lost; instead of reading it according to its letters, it is replaced in speech by the alternative name of God, Adonai.

T'fillah (pronounced t'-fee-LAH, or, commonly, t'-FEE-lah): A Hebrew word meaning "prayer," but used technically to mean a specific prayer, namely, the second of the two main units in the worship service. It is known also as the *Amidah* or the *Sh'moneh Esreh* (see *Amidah*). Also the title of the sixteenth blessing of the *Amidah*, a petition for God to accept our prayer.

T'fillin (pronounced t'-FIH-lin, or, sometimes, t'-fee-LEEN): Two cube-shaped black boxes containing biblical quotations (Ex. 13:1–10; 13:11–16; Deut. 6:4–9; Deut. 11:13–21) and affixed by means of attached leather straps to the forehead and left arm (right arm for left-handed people) during morning prayer.

Tsadikim (pronounced tsah-dee-KEEM): Literally, "the righteous," and the title of the thirteenth blessing of the daily *Amidah*, a petition that the righteous be rewarded.

Tsitsit (pronounced tsee-TSEET): A Hebrew word meaning "tassels" or "fringes" and used to refer to the tassels affixed to the four corners of the *tallit* (the prayer shawl, see *tallit*) as Numbers 15:38 instructs.

T'shuvah (pronounced t'shoo-VAH, or, commonly, t'SHOO-vah): Literally, "repentance," and the title of the fifth blessing in the daily *Amidah*, a petition by worshipers that they successfully turn to God in heartfelt repentance.

Tur (pronounced TOOR): The shorthand title applied to a fourteenth-century code of Jewish law, compiled by Jacob ben Asher in Spain, and the source for much of our knowledge about medieval liturgical practice. *Tur* means "row" or "column." The full name of the code is *Arba'ah Turim* (pronounced ahr-bah-AH too-REEM), "The Four Rows," with each row (or *Tur*) being a separate section of law on a given broad topic.

Yotser (pronounced yoe-TSAYR, or, commonly, YOE-tsayr): The Hebrew word meaning "creator," and by extension, the title of the first blessing in The *Sh'ma* and Its Blessings, which is on the theme of God's creation of the universe.

Y'rushalayim (pronounced y'roo-shah-LAH-yeem): Literally, "Jerusalem," and the title of the fourteenth blessing of the daily *Amidah;* a petition for the divine building up of Jerusalem, a condition associated with the imminence of the messianic age. Some liberal liturgies interpret it more broadly to include the restoration of modern-day Jerusalem, currently under way.

Zohar (pronounced ZOE-hahr): A shorthand title for *Sefer Hazohar* (pronounced SAY-fer hah-ZOE-hahr), literally, "The Book of Splendor," which is the primary compendium of mystical thought in Judaism; written mostly by Moses de Leon in Spain near the end of the thirteenth century, and ever since, the chief source for the study of Kabbalah (see **Kabbalah**).

A Note on the Border

The border decoration used in this book is from the Sarajevo Haggadah, one of the best-known Hebrew illuminated manuscripts; Barcelona (?), Spain, 14th century.

About JEWISH LIGHTS Publishing

People of all faiths and backgrounds yearn for books that attract, engage, educate and spiritually inspire.

Our principal goal is to stimulate thought and help all people learn about who the Jewish People are, where they come from, and what the future can be made to hold. While people of our diverse Jewish heritage are the primary audience, our books speak to people in the Christian world as well and will broaden their understanding of Judaism and the roots of their own faith.

We bring to you authors who are at the forefront of spiritual thought and experience. While each has something different to say, they all say it in a voice that you can hear.

Our books are designed to welcome you and then to engage, stimulate and inspire. We judge our success not only by whether or not our books are beautiful and commercially successful, but by whether or not they make a difference in your life.

We at Jewish Lights take great care to produce beautiful books that present meaningful spiritual content in a form that reflects the art of making high quality books. Therefore, we want to acknowledge those who contributed to the production of this book.

PRODUCTION
Bronwen Battaglia

EDITORIAL & PROOFREADING
Jennifer Goneau & Martha McKinney

COVER DESIGN
Glenn Suokko

COVER PRINTING
John P. Pow Company, Inc., South Boston, Massachusetts

PRINTING AND BINDING
Hamilton Printing Company, Rensselaer, New York

Spirituality

The Women's Torah Commentary: *New Insights from Women Rabbis on the 54 Weekly Torah Portions* Ed. by *Rabbi Elyse Goldstein*

For the first time, women rabbis provide a commentary on the entire Torah. More than 25 years after the first woman was ordained a rabbi in America, women have an impressive group of spiritual role models that they never had before. Here, in a week-by-week format, these inspiring teachers bring their rich perspectives to bear on the biblical text. A perfect gift for others, or for yourself. 6 x 9, 496 pp, HC, ISBN 1-58023-076-8 **$34.95**

Bringing the Psalms to Life
How to Understand and Use the Book of Psalms by *Rabbi Daniel F. Polish*

Here, the most beloved—and least understood—of the books in the Bible comes alive. This simultaneously insightful and practical guide shows how the psalms address a myriad of spiritual issues in our lives: feeling abandoned, overcoming illness, dealing with anger, and more. 6 x 9, 208 pp, HC, ISBN 1-58023-077-6 **$21.95**

Stepping Stones to Jewish Spiritual Living: *Walking the Path*
Morning, Noon, and Night by *Rabbi James L. Mirel* & *Karen Bonnell Werth*

Transforms our daily routine into sacred acts of mindfulness. Chapters are arranged according to the cycle of each day. "A wonderful, practical, and inspiring guidebook to gently bring the riches of Jewish practice into our busy, everyday lives. Highly recommended." —*Rabbi David A. Cooper.* 6 x 9, 240 pp, Quality PB, ISBN 1-58023-074-1 **$16.95**; HC, ISBN 1-58023-003-2 **$21.95**

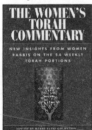 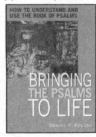 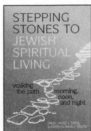  

Parenting As a Spiritual Journey:
Deepening Ordinary & Extraordinary Events into Sacred Occasions
by Rabbi Nancy Fuchs-Kreimer 6 x 9, 224 pp, Quality PB, ISBN 1-58023-016-4 **$16.95**

The Year Mom Got Religion: *One Woman's Midlife Journey into Judaism*
by Lee Meyerhoff Hendler 6 x 9, 208 pp, Quality PB, ISBN 1-58023-070-9 **$15.95**; HC, ISBN 1-58023-000-8 **$19.95**

Moses—The Prince, the Prophet: *His Life, Legend & Message for Our Lives*
by Rabbi Levi Meier, Ph.D. 6 x 9, 224 pp, Quality PB, ISBN 1-58023-069-5 **$16.95**; HC, ISBN 1-58023-013-X **$23.95**

Ancient Secrets: *Using the Stories of the Bible to Improve Our Everyday Lives*
by Rabbi Levi Meier, Ph.D. 5½ x 8½, 288 pp, Quality PB, ISBN 1-58023-064-4 **$16.95**

Spirituality & More

These Are the Words: *A Vocabulary of Jewish Spiritual Life*

by *Arthur Green*

What are the most essential ideas, concepts and terms that an educated person needs to know about Judaism? From *Adonai* (My Lord) to *zekhut* (merit), this enlightening and entertaining journey through Judaism teaches us the 149 core Hebrew words that constitute the basic vocabulary of Jewish spiritual life. 6 x 9, 304 pp, HC, ISBN 1-58023-024-5 **$21.95**

The Enneagram and Kabbalah: *Reading Your Soul*

by *Rabbi Howard A. Addison*

Combines two of the most powerful maps of consciousness known to humanity—The Tree of Life (the *Sefirot*) from the Jewish mystical tradition of *Kabbalah*, and the nine-pointed Enneagram—and shows how, together, they can provide a powerful tool for self-knowledge, critique, and transformation. 6 x 9, 176 pp, Quality PB, ISBN 1-58023-001-6 **$15.95**

Embracing the Covenant
Converts to Judaism Talk About Why & How

Ed. and with Intros. by *Rabbi Allan L. Berkowitz* and *Patti Moskovitz*

Through personal experiences of 20 converts to Judaism, this book illuminates reasons for converting, the quest for a satisfying spirituality, the appeal of the Jewish tradition and how conversion has changed lives—the convert's, and the lives of those close to them.
6 x 9, 192 pp, Quality PB, ISBN 1-879045-50-8 **$15.95**

Shared Dreams: *Martin Luther King, Jr. and the Jewish Community*
by Rabbi Marc Schneier; Preface by Martin Luther King III
6 x 9, 240 pp, HC, ISBN 1-58023-062-8 **$24.95**

Mystery Midrash: *An Anthology of Jewish Mystery & Detective Fiction*
Ed. by Lawrence W. Raphael; Preface by Joel Siegel, ABC's *Good Morning America*
6 x 9, 304 pp, Quality PB, ISBN 1-58023-055-5 **$16.95**

The Jewish Gardening Cookbook: *Growing Plants & Cooking for Holidays & Festivals*
by Michael Brown 6 x 9, 224 pp, HC, Illus., ISBN 1-58023-004-0 **$21.95**

Wandering Stars: *An Anthology of Jewish Fantasy & Science Fiction* Ed. by Jack
Dann; Intro. by Isaac Asimov 6 x 9, 272 pp, Quality PB, ISBN 1-58023-005-9 **$16.95**

More Wandering Stars
An Anthology of Outstanding Stories of Jewish Fantasy and Science Fiction
Ed. by Jack Dann; Intro. by Isaac Asimov 6 x 9, 192 pp, Quality PB, ISBN 1-58023-063-6 **$16.95**

A Heart of Wisdom: *Making the Jewish Journey from Midlife through the Elder Years*
Ed. by Susan Berrin; Foreword by Harold Kushner
6 x 9, 384 pp, Quality PB, ISBN 1-58023-051-2 **$18.95**; HC, ISBN 1-879045-73-7 **$24.95**

Sacred Intentions: *Daily Inspiration to Strengthen the Spirit, Based on Jewish Wisdom*
by Rabbi Kerry M. Olitzky and Rabbi Lori Forman
4½ x 6½, 448 pp, Quality PB, ISBN 1-58023-061-X **$15.95**

Spirituality

My People's Prayer Book: *Traditional Prayers, Modern Commentaries*

Ed. by *Dr. Lawrence A. Hoffman*

This momentous, critically-acclaimed series is truly a people's prayer book, one that provides a diverse and exciting commentary to the traditional liturgy. It will help modern men and women find new wisdom and guidance in Jewish prayer, and bring liturgy into their lives. Each book includes Hebrew text, modern translation, and commentaries *from all perspectives* of the Jewish world. Vol. 1—*The Sh'ma and Its Blessings,* 7 x 10, 168 pp, HC, ISBN 1-879045-79-6 **$23.95**
Vol. 2—*The Amidah,* 7 x 10, 240 pp, HC, ISBN 1-879045-80-X **$23.95**
Vol. 3—*P'sukei D'zimrah* (Morning Psalms), 7 x 10, 240 pp, HC, ISBN 1-879045-81-8 **$23.95**
Vol. 4—*Seder K'riyat Hatorah* (Shabbat Torah Service), 7 x 10, 240 pp, ISBN 1-879045-82-6 **$23.95**
(Avail. Nov. 2000)

Voices from Genesis: *Guiding Us through the Stages of Life*

by *Dr. Norman J. Cohen*

In a brilliant blending of modern *midrash* (finding contemporary meaning from biblical texts) and the life stages of Erik Erikson's developmental psychology, the characters of Genesis come alive to give us insights for our own journeys. 6 x 9, 192 pp, HC, ISBN 1-879045-75-3 **$21.95**

  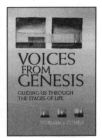 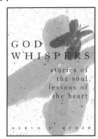 

God Whispers: *Stories of the Soul, Lessons of the Heart*
by Rabbi Karyn D. Kedar 6 x 9, 176 pp, Quality PB, ISBN 1-58023-088-1 **$15.95**;
HC, ISBN 1-58023-023-7 **$19.95**

Being God's Partner: *How to Find the Hidden Link Between Spirituality and Your Work*
by Rabbi Jeffrey K. Salkin; Intro. by Norman Lear **AWARD WINNER!**
6 x 9, 192 pp, Quality PB, ISBN 1-879045-65-6 **$16.95**; HC, ISBN 1-879045-37-0 **$19.95**

ReVisions: *Seeing Torah through a Feminist Lens* **AWARD WINNER!**
by Rabbi Elyse Goldstein 5½ x 8½, 208 pp, HC, ISBN 1-58023-047-4 **$19.95**

Soul Judaism: *Dancing with God into a New Era*
by Rabbi Wayne Dosick 5½ x 8½, 304 pp, Quality PB, ISBN 1-58023-053-9 **$16.95**

Finding Joy: *A Practical Spiritual Guide to Happiness* **AWARD WINNER!**
by Rabbi Dannel I. Schwartz with Mark Hass
6 x 9, 192 pp, Quality PB, ISBN 1-58023-009-1 **$14.95**; HC, ISBN 1-879045-53-2 **$19.95**

The Empty Chair: *Finding Hope and Joy—*
Timeless Wisdom from a Hasidic Master, Rebbe Nachman of Breslov **AWARD WINNER!**
Adapted by Moshe Mykoff and the Breslov Research Institute
4 x 6, 128 pp, Deluxe PB, 2-color text, ISBN 1-879045-67-2 **$9.95**

The Gentle Weapon: *Prayers for Everyday and Not-So-Everyday Moments*
Adapted from the Wisdom of Rebbe Nachman of Breslov by Moshe Mykoff and
S. C. Mizrahi, with the Breslov Research Institute
4 x 6, 144 pp, Deluxe PB, 2-color text, ISBN 1-58023-022-9 **$9.95**

"Who Is a Jew?" *Conversations, Not Conclusions* by Meryl Hyman
6 x 9, 272 pp, Quality PB, ISBN 1-58023-052-0 **$16.95**; HC, ISBN 1-879045-76-1 **$23.95**

Spirituality—The Kushner Series

Honey from the Rock, Special Anniversary Edition
An Introduction to Jewish Mysticism

by *Lawrence Kushner*

An insightful and absorbing introduction to the ten gates of Jewish mysticism and how it applies to daily life. "The easiest introduction to Jewish mysticism you can read."
6 x 9, 176 pp, Quality PB, ISBN 1-58023-073-3 **$15.95**

Eyes Remade for Wonder
The Way of Jewish Mysticism and Sacred Living
A Lawrence Kushner Reader

Intro. by *Thomas Moore*

Whether you are new to Kushner or a devoted fan, you'll find inspiration here. With samplings from each of Kushner's works, and a generous amount of new material, this book is to be read and reread, each time discovering deeper layers of meaning in our lives.
6 x 9, 240 pp, Quality PB, ISBN 1-58023-042-3 **$16.95**; HC, ISBN 1-58023-014-8 **$23.95**

Invisible Lines of Connection
Sacred Stories of the Ordinary

by *Lawrence Kushner* **AWARD WINNER!**

Through his everyday encounters with family, friends, colleagues and strangers, Kushner takes us deeply into our lives, finding flashes of spiritual insight in the process.
6 x 9, 160 pp, Quality PB, ISBN 1-879045-98-2 **$15.95**; HC, ISBN 1-879045-52-4 **$21.95**

The Book of Letters
A Mystical Hebrew Alphabet **AWARD WINNER!**
by Lawrence Kushner
Popular HC Edition, 6 x 9, 80 pp, 2-color text, ISBN 1-879045-00-1 **$24.95**; *Deluxe Gift Edition,* 9 x 12, 80 pp, HC, 2-color text, ornamentation, slipcase, ISBN 1-879045-01-X **$79.95**; *Collector's Limited Edition,* 9 x 12, 80 pp, HC, gold-embossed pages, hand-assembled slipcase. With silkscreened print. Limited to 500 signed and numbered copies, ISBN 1-879045-04-4 **$349.00**

The Book of Words
Talking Spiritual Life, Living Spiritual Talk **AWARD WINNER!**
by Lawrence Kushner   6 x 9, 160 pp, Quality PB, 2-color text, ISBN 1-58023-020-2 **$16.95**; 152 pp, HC, ISBN 1-879045-35-4 **$21.95**

God Was in This Place & I, i Did Not Know
Finding Self, Spirituality & Ultimate Meaning
by Lawrence Kushner   6 x 9, 192 pp, Quality PB, ISBN 1-879045-33-8 **$16.95**

The River of Light: *Jewish Mystical Awareness*
by Lawrence Kushner   6 x 9, 192 pp, Quality PB, ISBN 1-879045-03-6 **$14.95**

Children's Spirituality

A Prayer for the Earth
The Story of Naamah, Noah's Wife
by *Sandy Eisenberg Sasso*
Full-color illus. by *Bethanne Andersen*

For ages 4 & up

NONDENOMINATIONAL, NONSECTARIAN

This new story, based on an ancient text, opens readers' religious imaginations to new ideas about the well-known story of the Flood. When God tells Noah to bring the animals of the world onto the ark, God also calls on Naamah, Noah's wife, to save each plant on Earth.

"A lovely tale. . . . Children of all ages should be drawn to this parable for our times."
—*Tomie dePaola*, artist/author of books for children

9 x 12, 32 pp, HC, Full-color illus., ISBN 1-879045-60-5 **$16.95**

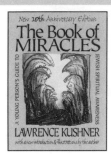

The 11th Commandment: Wisdom from Our Children
by The Children of America

For all ages

MULTICULTURAL, NONDENOMINATIONAL, NONSECTARIAN

"If there were an Eleventh Commandment, what would it be?" Children of many religious denominations across America answer this question—in their own drawings and words. "A rare book of spiritual celebration for all people, of all ages, for all time."—*Bookviews*
8 x 10, 48 pp, HC, Full-color illus., ISBN 1-879045-46-X **$16.95**

Sharing Blessings: Children's Stories for Exploring the Spirit of the Jewish Holidays
by *Rahel Musleah* and *Rabbi Michael Klayman*
Full-color illus. by *Mary O'Keefe Young*

For ages 6 & up

What is the spiritual message of each of the Jewish holidays? How do we teach it to our children? Many books tell children about the historical significance and customs of the holidays. Now, through engaging, creative stories about one family's preparation, *Sharing Blessings* explores ways to get into the *spirit* of 13 different holidays. "Lighthearted, and yet thorough—allows all Jewish parents (even those with very little Jewish education) to introduce the spirit of our cherished holiday traditions." —*Shari Lewis*, creator and star of PBS' *Lamb Chop's Play-Along*
8½ x 11, 64 pp, HC, Full-color illus., ISBN 1-879045-71-0 **$18.95**

The Book of Miracles
A Young Person's Guide to Jewish Spiritual Awareness
by *Lawrence Kushner*

For ages 9 & up

From the miracle at the Red Sea to the miracle of waking up this morning, this intriguing book introduces kids to a way of everyday spiritual thinking to last a lifetime. Kushner, whose award-winning books have brought spirituality to life for countless adults, now shows young people how to use Judaism as a foundation on which to build their lives. "A well-written, easy to understand, very lovely guide to Jewish spirituality. I recommend it to all teens as a good read." —*Kimberly Kirberger*, co-author, *Chicken Soup for the Teenage Soul* 6 x 9, 96 pp, HC, 2-color illus., ISBN 1-879045-78-8 **$16.95**

Children's Spirituality

In Our Image
God's First Creatures
by *Nancy Sohn Swartz*
Full-color illus. by *Melanie Hall*

For ages 4 & up

NONDENOMINATIONAL, NONSECTARIAN

A playful new twist on the Creation story—from the perspective of the animals. Celebrates the interconnectedness of nature and the harmony of all living things. "The vibrantly colored illustrations nearly leap off the page in this delightful interpretation." —*School Library Journal*

"A message all children should hear, presented in words and pictures that children will find irresistible." —*Rabbi Harold Kushner*, author of *When Bad Things Happen to Good People*

9 x 12, 32 pp, HC, Full-color illus., ISBN 1-879045-99-0 **$16.95**

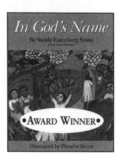

God's Paintbrush

For ages 4 & up

by *Sandy Eisenberg Sasso*; Full-color illus. by *Annette Compton*
MULTICULTURAL, NONDENOMINATIONAL, NONSECTARIAN

Invites children of all faiths and backgrounds to encounter God openly in their own lives. Wonderfully interactive; provides questions adult and child can explore together at the end of each episode. "An excellent way to honor the imaginative breadth and depth of the spiritual life of the young." —*Dr. Robert Coles*, Harvard University
11 x 8½, 32 pp, HC, Full-color illus., ISBN 1-879045-22-2 **$16.95**

Also available: A Teacher's Guide: **A Guide for Jewish & Christian Educators and Parents**
8½ x 11, 32 pp, PB, ISBN 1-879045-57-5 **$6.95**

God's Paintbrush Celebration Kit 9½ x 12, HC, Includes 5 sessions/40 full-color Activity Sheets and Teacher Folder with complete instructions, ISBN 1-58023-050-4 **$21.95**

In God's Name

For ages 4 & up

by *Sandy Eisenberg Sasso*; Full-color illus. by *Phoebe Stone*
MULTICULTURAL, NONDENOMINATIONAL, NONSECTARIAN

Like an ancient myth in its poetic text and vibrant illustrations, this award-winning modern fable about the search for God's name celebrates the diversity and, at the same time, the unity of all the people of the world. "What a lovely, healing book!" —*Madeleine L'Engle*
9 x 12, 32 pp, HC, Full-color illus., ISBN 1-879045-26-5 **$16.95**

What Is God's Name? (A Board Book)

For ages 0–4

An abridged board book version of the award-winning *In God's Name*.
5 x 5, 24 pp, Board, Full-color illus., ISBN 1-893361-10-1 **$7.95**

Children's Spirituality

God Said Amen
by *Sandy Eisenberg Sasso*
Full-color illus. by *Avi Katz*

For ages 4 & up

MULTICULTURAL, NONDENOMINATIONAL, NONSECTARIAN

A warm and inspiring tale of two kingdoms: Midnight Kingdom is overflowing with water but has no oil to light its lamps; Desert Kingdom is blessed with oil but has no water to grow its gardens. The kingdoms' rulers ask God for help but are too stubborn to ask each other. It takes a minstrel, a pair of royal riding-birds and their young keepers, and a simple act of kindness to show that they need only reach out to each other to find God's answer to their prayers.

9 x 12, 32 pp, HC, Full-color illus., ISBN 1-58023-080-6 **$16.95**

For Heaven's Sake
by *Sandy Eisenberg Sasso*; Full-color illus. by *Kathryn Kunz Finney*

For ages 4 & up

MULTICULTURAL, NONDENOMINATIONAL, NONSECTARIAN

Everyone talked about heaven: "Thank heavens." "Heaven forbid." "For heaven's sake, Isaiah." But no one would say what heaven was or how to find it. So Isaiah decides to find out, by seeking answers from many different people. "This book is a reminder of how well Sandy Sasso knows the minds of children. But it may surprise—and delight—readers to find how well she knows us grown-ups too." —*Maria Harris*, National Consultant in Religious Education, and author of *Teaching and Religious Imagination* 9 x 12, 32 pp, HC, Full-color illus., ISBN 1-58023-054-7 **$16.95**

But God Remembered: Stories of Women from Creation to the Promised Land
by *Sandy Eisenberg Sasso*; Full-color illus. by *Bethanne Andersen*

For ages 8 & up

NONDENOMINATIONAL, NONSECTARIAN

A fascinating collection of four different stories of women only briefly mentioned in biblical tradition and religious texts. Award-winning author Sasso vibrantly brings to life courageous and strong women from ancient tradition; all teach important values through their actions and faith. "Exquisite. . . . A book of beauty, strength and spirituality." —*Association of Bible Teachers* 9 x 12, 32 pp, HC, Full-color illus., ISBN 1-879045-43-5 **$16.95**

God in Between
by *Sandy Eisenberg Sasso*; Full-color illus. by *Sally Sweetland*

For ages 4 & up

MULTICULTURAL, NONDENOMINATIONAL, NONSECTARIAN

If you wanted to find God, where would you look? A magical, mythical tale that teaches that God can be found where we are: within all of us and the relationships between us. "This happy and wondrous book takes our children on a sweet and holy journey into God's presence." —*Rabbi Wayne Dosick, Ph.D.*, author of *Golden Rules* and *Soul Judaism*
9 x 12, 32 pp, HC, Full-color illus., ISBN 1-879045-86-9 **$16.95**

Healing/Wellness/Recovery

Jewish Pastoral Care
A Practical Handbook from Traditional and Contemporary Sources
Ed. by *Rabbi Dayle A. Friedman*

This innovative resource builds on the classic foundations of pastoral care, enriching it with uniquely Jewish traditions and wisdom. Gives today's Jewish pastoral counselors practical guidelines based in the Jewish tradition. 6 x 9, 352 pp, HC, ISBN 1-58023-078-4 **$34.95** (Avail. Nov. 2000)

Healing of Soul, Healing of Body
Spiritual Leaders Unfold the Strength & Solace in Psalms
Ed. by *Rabbi Simkha Y. Weintraub, CSW*, for The National Center for Jewish Healing

A source of solace for those who are facing illness, as well as those who care for them. Provides a wellspring of strength with inspiring introductions and commentaries by eminent spiritual leaders reflecting all Jewish movements. 6 x 9, 128 pp, Quality PB, Illus., 2-color text, ISBN 1-879045-31-1 **$14.95**

Self, Struggle & Change: *Family Conflict Stories in Genesis and Their Healing Insights for Our Lives*
by *Dr. Norman J. Cohen*

How do I find wholeness in my life and in my family's life? Here a modern master of biblical interpretation brings us greater understanding of the ancient text and of ourselves in this intriguing re-telling of conflict between husband and wife, father and son, brothers and sisters. 6 x 9, 224 pp, Quality PB, ISBN 1-879045-66-4 **$16.95**; HC, ISBN 1-879045-19-2 **$21.95**

  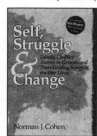  

Twelve Jewish Steps to Recovery: *A Personal Guide to Turning from Alcoholism & Other Addictions . . . Drugs, Food, Gambling, Sex . . .* by Rabbi Kerry M. Olitzky & Stuart A. Copans, M.D. Preface by Abraham J. Twerski, M.D.; Intro. by Rabbi Sheldon Zimmerman; "Getting Help"by JACS Foundation 6 x 9, 144 pp, Quality PB, ISBN 1-879045-09-5 **$13.95**

One Hundred Blessings Every Day: *Daily Twelve Step Recovery Affirmations, Exercises for Personal Growth & Renewal Reflecting Seasons of the Jewish Year* by Rabbi Kerry M. Olitzky, with selected meditations prepared by Rabbi James Stone Goodman, Danny Siegel, and Gordon Tucker. Foreword by Rabbi Neil Gillman, The Jewish Theological Seminary of America; Afterword by Dr. Jay Holder, Director, Exodus Treatment Center 4½ x 6½, 432 pp, Quality PB, ISBN 1-879045-30-3 **$14.95**

Recovery from Codependence: *A Jewish Twelve Steps Guide to Healing Your Soul* by Rabbi Kerry M. Olitzky; Foreword by Marc Galanter, M.D., Director, Division of Alcoholism & Drug Abuse, NYU Medical Center; Afterword by Harriet Rossetto, Director, Gateways Beit T'shuvah 6 x 9, 160 pp, Quality PB, ISBN 1-879045-32-X **$13.95**; HC, ISBN 1-879045-27-3 **$21.95**

Renewed Each Day: *Daily Twelve Step Recovery Meditations Based on the Bible* by Rabbi Kerry M. Olitzky & Aaron Z. *Vol. I: Genesis & Exodus*; Intro. by Rabbi Michael A. Signer; Afterword by JACS Foundation. *Vol. II: Leviticus, Numbers and Deuteronomy*; Intro. by Sharon M. Strassfeld; Afterword by Rabbi Harold M. Schulweis
Vol. I: 6 x 9, 224 pp, Quality PB, ISBN 1-879045-12-5 **$14.95**
Vol. II: 6 x 9, 280 pp, Quality PB, ISBN 1-879045-13-3 **$14.95**

Jewish Meditation

Discovering Jewish Meditation
Instruction & Guidance for Learning an Ancient Spiritual Practice

by *Nan Fink Gefen*

Gives readers of any level of understanding the tools to learn the practice of Jewish meditation on your own, starting you on the path to a deep spiritual and personal connection to God and to greater insight about your life. 6 x 9, 208 pp, Quality PB, ISBN 1-58023-067-9 **$16.95**

Meditation from the Heart of Judaism: *Today's Teachers Share Their Practices, Techniques, and Faith*

Ed. by *Avram Davis*

A "how-to" guide for both beginning and experienced meditators, drawing on the wisdom of 22 masters of meditation who explain why and how they meditate. A detailed compendium of the experts' "best practices" offers advice and starting points. 6 x 9, 256 pp, Quality PB, ISBN 1-58023-049-0 **$16.95**; HC, ISBN 1-879045-77-X **$21.95**

The Way of Flame
A Guide to the Forgotten Mystical Tradition of Jewish Meditation

by *Avram Davis* 4½ x 8, 176 pp, Quality PB, ISBN 1-58023-060-1 **$15.95**

  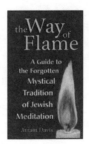  

Entering the Temple of Dreams: *Jewish Prayers, Movements, and Meditations for the End of the Day* by *Tamar Frankiel* and *Judy Greenfeld*

Nighttime spirituality is much more than bedtime prayers! Here, you'll uncover deeper meaning to familiar nighttime prayers—and learn to combine the prayers with movements and meditations to enhance your physical and psychological well-being.
7 x 10, 192 pp, Illus., Quality PB, ISBN 1-58023-079-2 **$16.95**

Minding the Temple of the Soul: *Balancing Body, Mind, and Spirit through Traditional Jewish Prayer, Movement, and Meditation*

by *Tamar Frankiel* and *Judy Greenfeld*

This new spiritual approach to physical health introduces readers to a spiritual tradition that affirms the body and enables them to reconceive their bodies in a more positive light. Focuses on traditional Jewish prayers, with exercises, movements, and meditations. 7 x 10, 184 pp, Quality PB, Illus., ISBN 1-879045-64-8 **$16.95**; Audiotape of the Blessings, Movements and Meditations (60-min. cassette), JN01 **$9.95**; Videotape of the Movements and Meditations (46-min. VHS), S507 **$20.00**

Life Cycle & Holidays

How to Be a Perfect Stranger, In 2 Volumes
A Guide to Etiquette in Other People's Religious Ceremonies
Ed. by *Stuart M. Matlins* & *Arthur J. Magida* **AWARD WINNER!**

What will happen? What do I do? What do I wear? What do I say? What should I avoid *doing, wearing, saying? What are their basic beliefs? Should I bring a gift?* In question-and-answer format, *How to Be a Perfect Stranger* explains the rituals and celebrations of America's major religions/denominations, helping an interested guest to feel comfortable, participate to the fullest extent possible, and avoid violating anyone's religious principles. It is not a guide to theology, nor is it presented from the perspective of any particular faith.

Vol. 1: *America's Largest Faiths,* 6 x 9, 432 pp, HC, ISBN 1-879045-39-7 **$24.95**
Vol. 2: *Other Faiths in America,* 6 x 9, 416 pp, HC, ISBN 1-879045-63-X **$24.95**

Putting God on the Guest List, 2nd Ed.
How to Reclaim the Spiritual Meaning of Your Child's Bar or Bat Mitzvah
by *Rabbi Jeffrey K. Salkin* **AWARD WINNER!**

The expanded, updated, revised edition of today's most influential book (over 60,000 copies in print) about finding core spiritual values in American Jewry's most misunderstood ceremony.
6 x 9, 224 pp, Quality PB, ISBN 1-879045-59-1 **$16.95**; HC, ISBN 1-879045-58-3 **$24.95**

For Kids—Putting God on Your Guest List
How to Claim the Spiritual Meaning of Your Bar or Bat Mitzvah
by Rabbi Jeffrey K. Salkin 6 x 9, 144 pp, Quality PB, ISBN 1-58023-015-6 **$14.95**

Bar/Bat Mitzvah Basics
A Practical Family Guide to Coming of Age Together
Ed. by Cantor Helen Leneman 6 x 9, 240 pp, Quality PB, ISBN 1-879045-54-0 **$16.95**;
HC, ISBN 1-879045-51-6 **$24.95**

The New Jewish Baby Book AWARD WINNER!
Names, Ceremonies, & Customs—A Guide for Today's Families
by Anita Diamant 6 x 9, 336 pp, Quality PB, ISBN 1-879045-28-1 **$16.95**

Hanukkah: The Art of Jewish Living
by Dr. Ron Wolfson 7 x 9, 192 pp, Quality PB, Illus., ISBN 1-879045-97-4 **$16.95**

The Shabbat Seder: The Art of Jewish Living
by Dr. Ron Wolfson 7 x 9, 272 pp, Quality PB, Illus., ISBN 1-879045-90-7 **$16.95**
Also available are these helpful companions to *The Shabbat Seder*: Booklet of the Blessings and Songs, ISBN 1-879045-91-5 **$5.00**; Audiocassette of the Blessings, DN03 **$6.00**; Teacher's Guide, ISBN 1-879045-92-3 **$4.95**

The Passover Seder: The Art of Jewish Living
by Dr. Ron Wolfson 7 x 9, 352 pp, Quality PB, Illus., ISBN 1-879045-93-1 **$16.95**
Also available are these helpful companions to *The Passover Seder*: Passover Workbook, ISBN 1-879045-94-X **$6.95**; Audiocassette of the Blessings, DN04 **$6.00**; Teacher's Guide, ISBN 1-879045-95-8 **$4.95**

Life Cycle

Jewish Paths toward Healing and Wholeness
A Personal Guide to Dealing with Suffering
by *Rabbi Kerry M. Olitzky*; Foreword by *Debbie Friedman*

"Why me?" Why do we suffer? How can we heal? Grounded in the spiritual traditions of Judaism, this book provides healing rituals, psalms and prayers that help readers initiate a dialogue with God, to guide them along the complicated path of healing and wholeness.
6 x 9, 192 pp, Quality PB, ISBN 1-58023-068-7 **$15.95**

Mourning & Mitzvah: *A Guided Journal for Walking the Mourner's Path through Grief to Healing*
by *Anne Brener, L.C.S.W.*; Foreword by *Rabbi Jack Riemer*; Intro. by *Rabbi William Cutter*

For those who mourn a death, for those who would help them, for those who face a loss of any kind, Brener teaches us the power and strength available to us in the fully experienced mourning process. 7½ x 9, 288 pp, Quality PB, ISBN 1-879045-23-0 **$19.95**

Tears of Sorrow, Seeds of Hope
A Jewish Spiritual Companion for Infertility and Pregnancy Loss
by *Rabbi Nina Beth Cardin*

A spiritual companion that enables us to mourn infertility, a lost pregnancy, or a stillbirth within the prayers, rituals, and meditations of Judaism. By drawing on the texts of tradition, it creates readings and rites of mourning, and through them provides a wellspring of compassion, solace—and hope. 6 x 9, 192 pp, HC, ISBN 1-58023-017-2 **$19.95**

Lifecycles
V. 1: *Jewish Women on Life Passages & Personal Milestones* AWARD WINNER!
Ed. and with Intros. by Rabbi Debra Orenstein
V. 2: *Jewish Women on Biblical Themes in Contemporary Life* AWARD WINNER!
Ed. and with Intros. by Rabbi Debra Orenstein and Rabbi Jane Rachel Litman
V. 1: 6 x 9, 480 pp, Quality PB, ISBN 1-58023-018-0 **$19.95**; HC, ISBN 1-879045-14-1 **$24.95**
V. 2: 6 x 9, 464 pp, Quality PB, ISBN 1-58023-019-9 **$19.95**; HC, ISBN 1-879045-15-X **$24.95**

Grief in Our Seasons: *A Mourner's Kaddish Companion*
by Rabbi Kerry M. Olitzky 4½ x 6½, 448 pp, Quality PB, ISBN 1-879045-55-9 **$15.95**

A Time to Mourn, A Time to Comfort: *A Guide to Jewish Bereavement and Comfort*
by Dr. Ron Wolfson 7 x 9, 336 pp, Quality PB, ISBN 1-879045-96-6 **$16.95**

When a Grandparent Dies
A Kid's Own Remembering Workbook for Dealing with Shiva and the Year Beyond
by Nechama Liss-Levinson, Ph.D.
8 x 10, 48 pp, HC, Illus., 2-color text, ISBN 1-879045-44-3 **$15.95**

So That Your Values Live On: *Ethical Wills & How to Prepare Them*
Ed. by Rabbi Jack Riemer & Professor Nathaniel Stampfer
6 x 9, 272 pp, Quality PB, ISBN 1-879045-34-6 **$17.95**

Theology/Philosophy

Torah of the Earth: *Exploring 4,000 Years of Ecology in Jewish Thought*
In 2 Volumes Ed. by *Rabbi Arthur Waskow*

Major new resource offering us an invaluable key to understanding the intersection of ecology and Judaism. Leading scholars provide us with a guided tour of ecological thought from four major Jewish viewpoints. Vol. 1: *Biblical Israel & Rabbinic Judaism*, 6 x 9, 272 pp, Quality PB, ISBN 1-58023-086-5 **$19.95**; Vol. 2: *Zionism & Eco-Judaism*, 6 x 9, 336 pp, Quality PB, ISBN 1-58023-087-3 **$19.95**

Broken Tablets: *Restoring the Ten Commandments and Ourselves*
Ed. by *Rabbi Rachel S. Mikva*; Intro. by *Rabbi Lawrence Kushner*;
Afterword by *Rabbi Arnold Jacob Wolf* **AWARD WINNER!**

Twelve outstanding spiritual leaders each share profound and personal thoughts about these biblical commands and why they have such a special hold on us.
6 x 9, 192 pp, HC, ISBN 1-58023-066-0 **$21.95**

Evolving Halakhah: *A Progressive Approach to Traditional Jewish Law*
by *Rabbi Dr. Moshe Zemer*

Innovative and provocative, this book affirms the system of traditional Jewish law, *halakhah*, as flexible enough to accommodate the changing realities of each generation. It shows that the traditional framework for understanding the Torah's commandments can be the living heart of Jewish life for all Jews. 6 x 9, 480 pp, HC, ISBN 1-58023-002-4 **$40.00**

  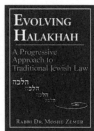  

God & the Big Bang
Discovering Harmony Between Science & Spirituality **AWARD WINNER!**
by Daniel C. Matt
6 x 9, 216 pp, Quality PB, ISBN 1-879045-89-3 **$16.95**; HC, ISBN 1-879045-48-6 **$21.95**

Israel—A Spiritual Travel Guide AWARD WINNER!
A Companion for the Modern Jewish Pilgrim
by Rabbi Lawrence A. Hoffman 4¾ x 10, 256 pp, Quality PB, ISBN 1-879045-56-7 **$18.95**

Godwrestling—Round 2: *Ancient Wisdom, Future Paths* **AWARD WINNER!**
by Rabbi Arthur Waskow
6 x 9, 352 pp, Quality PB, ISBN 1-879045-72-9 **$18.95**; HC, ISBN 1-879045-45-1 **$23.95**

Ecology & the Jewish Spirit: *Where Nature & the Sacred Meet* Ed. and with Intros. by Ellen Bernstein 6 x 9, 288 pp, Quality PB, ISBN 1-58023-082-2 **$16.95**;
HC, ISBN 1-879045-88-5 **$23.95**

Israel: *An Echo of Eternity* by Abraham Joshua Heschel; New Intro. by
Dr. Susannah Heschel 5½ x 8, 272 pp, Quality PB, ISBN 1-879045-70-2 **$18.95**

The Earth Is the Lord's: *The Inner World of the Jew in Eastern Europe*
by Abraham Joshua Heschel 5½ x 8, 112 pp, Quality PB, ISBN 1-879045-42-7 **$13.95**

A Passion for Truth: *Despair and Hope in Hasidism* by Abraham Joshua Heschel
5½ x 8, 352 pp, Quality PB, ISBN 1-879045-41-9 **$18.95**

Theology/Philosophy

A Heart of Many Rooms
Celebrating the Many Voices within Judaism
by *Dr. David Hartman*   **AWARD WINNER!**

Named a *Publishers Weekly* "Best Book of the Year." Addresses the spiritual and theological questions that face all Jews and all people today. From the perspective of traditional Judaism, Hartman shows that commitment to both Jewish tradition and to pluralism can create understanding between people of different religious convictions.
6 x 9, 352 pp, HC, ISBN 1-58023-048-2 **$24.95**

A Living Covenant: *The Innovative Spirit in Traditional Judaism*
by *Dr. David Hartman*   **AWARD WINNER!**

Winner, National Jewish Book Award. Hartman reveals a Judaism grounded in covenant—a relational framework—informed by the metaphor of marital love rather than that of parent-child dependency. 6 x 9, 368 pp, Quality PB, ISBN 1-58023-011-3 **$18.95**

The Death of Death: *Resurrection and Immortality in Jewish Thought*
by *Dr. Neil Gillman*   **AWARD WINNER!**

Does death end life, or is it the passage from one stage of life to another? This National Jewish Book Award Finalist explores the original and compelling argument that Judaism, a religion often thought to pay little attention to the afterlife, not only offers us rich ideas on the subject—but delivers a deathblow to death itself. 6 x 9, 336 pp, Quality PB, ISBN 1-58023-081-4 **$18.95**; HC, ISBN 1-879045-61-3 **$23.95**

   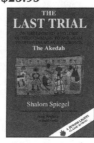 

Aspects of Rabbinic Theology by Solomon Schechter; New Intro. by Dr. Neil Gillman
6 x 9, 448 pp, Quality PB, ISBN 1-879045-24-9 **$19.95**

The Last Trial: *On the Legends and Lore of the Command to Abraham to Offer Isaac as a Sacrifice* by Shalom Spiegel; New Intro. by Judah Goldin
6 x 9, 208 pp, Quality PB, ISBN 1-879045-29-X **$17.95**

Judaism and Modern Man: *An Interpretation of Jewish Religion* by Will Herberg;
New Intro. by Dr. Neil Gillman 5½ x 8½, 336 pp, Quality PB, ISBN 1-879045-87-7 **$18.95**

Seeking the Path to Life **AWARD WINNER!**
Theological Meditations on God and the Nature of People, Love, Life and Death
by Rabbi Ira F. Stone
6 x 9, 160 pp, Quality PB, ISBN 1-879045-47-8 **$14.95**; HC, ISBN 1-879045-17-6 **$19.95**

The Spirit of Renewal: *Finding Faith after the Holocaust* **AWARD WINNER!**
by Rabbi Edward Feld
6 x 9, 224 pp, Quality PB, ISBN 1-879045-40-0 **$16.95**

Tormented Master: *The Life and Spiritual Quest of Rabbi Nahman of Bratslav*
by Dr. Arthur Green
6 x 9, 416 pp, Quality PB, ISBN 1-879045-11-7 **$18.95**

Your Word Is Fire: *The Hasidic Masters on Contemplative Prayer*
Ed. and Trans. with a New Introduction by Dr. Arthur Green and Dr. Barry W. Holtz
6 x 9, 160 pp, Quality PB, ISBN 1-879045-25-7 **$14.95**

  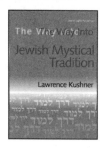 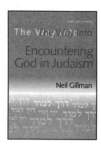